T0215038

Advanced Platform Development with Kubernetes

Enabling Data Management, the Internet of Things, Blockchain, and Machine Learning

Craig Johnston

Apress®

Advanced Platform Development with Kubernetes: Enabling Data Management, the Internet of Things, Blockchain, and Machine Learning

Craig Johnston
Los Angeles, CA, USA

ISBN-13 (pbk): 978-1-4842-5610-7   ISBN-13 (electronic): 978-1-4842-5611-4
https://doi.org/10.1007/978-1-4842-5611-4

Managing Director, Apress Media LLC: Welmoed Spahr
Acquisitions Editor: Natalie Pao
Development Editor: James Markham
Coordinating Editor: Jessica Vakili

Distributed to the book trade worldwide by Springer Science+Business Media New York, 1 NY Plaza, New York, NY 10004. Phone 1-800-SPRINGER, fax (201) 348-4505, e-mail orders-ny@springer-sbm.com, or visit www.springeronline.com. Apress Media, LLC is a California LLC and the sole member (owner) is Springer Science + Business Media Finance Inc (SSBM Finance Inc). SSBM Finance Inc is a **Delaware** corporation.

For information on translations, please e-mail booktranslations@springernature.com; for reprint, paperback, or audio rights, please e-mail bookpermissions@springernature.com.

Apress titles may be purchased in bulk for academic, corporate, or promotional use. eBook versions and licenses are also available for most titles. For more information, reference our Print and eBook Bulk Sales web page at http://www.apress.com/bulk-sales.

Any source code or other supplementary material referenced by the author in this book is available to readers on GitHub via the book's product page, located at www.apress.com/978-1-4842-5610-7. For more detailed information, please visit http://www.apress.com/source-code.

Printed on acid-free paper

Table of Contents

About the Author

Craig Johnston currently holds the position of Chief Architect at Deasil Works, Inc. and has been developing software for over 25 years. Craig's expertise revolves around microservices, artificial intelligence, algorithms, machine learning, and blockchain technologies.

Craig has helped lead his team to significantly improved productivity and return on investment across many client projects, leveraging Kubernetes, Docker, Golang, Cassandra, Kafka, and Elastic, to name a few. The team and he are developing more productive, stable, clean, and faster applications than ever in the past, and the results are beautiful and innovative IoT management systems, IoT implementations, mobile applications, business intelligence, data management, and machine learning platforms.

As the former Director of R&D at Napster and later a handful of Universal and Sony subsidiaries, Craig has been fortunate to spend many of his early days on the bleeding edge, in the open green fields of new media and disruptive technology.

Craig is successfully operating multiple commercial Kubernetes platforms utilizing all the technology and concepts proposed in *Advanced Platform Development with Kubernetes*.

About the Technical Reviewer

David Gonzalez is a DevOps engineer who has written three books about DevOps and microservices. He works as a consultant, helping large companies to advance their systems development, by tweaking related software processes and tools. David is also a Google Developer Expert (`https://developers.google.com/experts/people/davidgonzalez-gonzalez`) in Kubernetes (Google Container Engine) and a member of the Node.js Foundation, working on security in third-party npm packages. In his free time, he enjoys cycling and walking with his dogs in the green fields of Ireland.

Acknowledgments

I want to start by thanking Kelsey Hightower, who inspired me and so many others with his passion and excitement for technologies that advance a developer's productivity. Kelsey's live demonstrations, talks, and tutorials convinced me that Kubernetes is a platform for developing platforms. Kelsey is also responsible for the popularity of my Kubernetes development utility kubefwd.

A big thank you to my friend, co-worker, author, and software developer, David Elsensohn. David poured over every draft to ensure my English syntax would compile in the readers' minds. Thanks to everyone at Deasil Works, especially Jeff Masud, for helping me carve out time to write a book in one of our busiest years (and for fixing the clusters I broke along the way).

Thanks to Apress editors Natalie Pao and Jessica Vakili for their patience and encouragement. Thanks again to Natalie Pao for having a vision for this book and encouraging me to write it. Thanks to my technical reviewer David González for correcting my mistakes, unintentional obfuscations, and providing valuable guidance for technical clarity.

Lastly, thanks to my family and friends (most of them having no idea what a "Kubernetes" is) who encouraged me to stay focused and motivated. Thank you!

CHAPTER 1

Software Platform and the API

On October 28, 2018, IBM announced a $34 billion deal to buy Red Hat,[1] the company behind Red Hat Enterprise Linux (RHEL), and more recently Red Hat OpenShift, an enterprise Docker/Kubernetes application platform. What we see is $34 billion of evidence that Cloud-native and open source technologies, centered on the Linux ecosystem and empowered by Kubernetes, are leading disruption in enterprise software application platforms.

Any exposure to enterprise software marketing presents a steady stream of platform services released almost daily by major cloud providers, including products like Google Cloud Machine Learning Engine, Microsoft's Azure Machine Learning service, Amazon Managed Blockchain, and IBM Watson IoT Platform, to name a few. Big providers like Amazon, Microsoft, IBM, and Google are not only responding to market demand for these technologies but creating a greater awareness of their accessibility for solving problems across a variety of industries. Large software vendors are rapidly responding to the demand for these capabilities and perpetuate their demand by refining and marketing products that demonstrate their value. These vendors are often merely

---

[1]IBM to Buy Red Hat, the Top Linux Distributor, for $34 Billion." The New York Times, October 28, 2018, sec. Business. https://www.nytimes.com/2018/10/28/business/ibm-red-hat-cloudcomputing.html

© Craig Johnston 2020
C. Johnston, *Advanced Platform Development with Kubernetes*,
https://doi.org/10.1007/978-1-4842-5611-4_1

service-wrapping the latest in open source software, adding polished user interfaces and proprietary middleware. Peek under the hood of these hyper-cloud services and you often find a mesh of cloud-native and even vendor-neutral technologies for machine learning (ML), like TensorFlow, Keras, and PyTorch, or Blockchain capabilities powered by Ethereum and Hyperledger, and high-performance IoT data collectors like Prometheus and Kafka. These vendors are not stealing this technology from the open source community; some of the most significant contributions in this ecosystem are the vendors themselves.

Developing an enterprise-grade platform from the ground up, with capabilities as diverse as Blockchain and Machine Learning, would have required an enormous effort only a few years ago. Your other option would have been a significant investment and long-term commitment to a commercial platform. Google disrupted the entire commercial platform business with Kubernetes, a free, open source, cloud-native, and vendor-neutral system for the rapid development of new platforms that can easily support almost any technology with enterprise-grade security, stability, and scale. Expect to see another significant wave of platform innovation, as Kubernetes matures and allows software and platform developers to focus more time on features, with less custom work needed on infrastructure, networking, scaling, monitoring, and even security.

This book aims to build a simple demonstration platform in a vendor-neutral approach using Kubernetes. With only minimal modifications, this new platform should run on any primary cloud provider able to run Kubernetes and offer a small number of widely available dependencies such as storage, memory, and CPU. Each existing, open source technology implemented in this platform has a specialized focus on a particular solution. Offering Machine Learning, Blockchain, or IoT-based services will not in themselves be a core differentiator for a platform. However, operating these technologies together within Kubernetes provides a foundation in which to build and offer novel solutions through their combined efforts, along with providing a template for future additions.

In the early 1990s, databases were often operated and accessed as independent applications. The combination of a database and a web server revolutionized the Internet with dynamic database-driven websites.

2

These combinations seem obvious now, and Kubernetes together with service mesh technologies like Istio and Linkerd is making connections between diverse applications, even with conflicting dependencies, not only possible but adding security and telemetry to the platform.

Software Applications vs. Software Platforms

You may be a software developer and have a solution to a problem in a specific industry vertical. With a specific mix of closed and open source software, you wish to combine these capabilities under an API and expose them in support of a specific application. Alternatively, you may be a value-added reseller and want to offer customers an application development platform that comes with a suite of prepackaged features such as Machine Learning, Blockchain, or IoT data ingestion. Software platforms like Kubernetes are the ideal environment for developing a singular focused application or a platform as a service (PaaS) offering customers an environment in which they can develop and extend their applications (Figure 1-1).

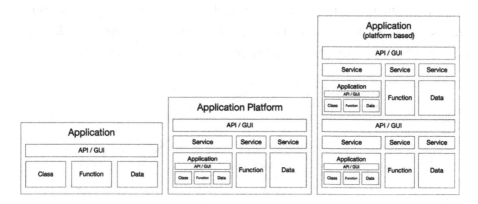

Figure 1-1. *A software application, a platform as a collection of applications, and a platform-based application*

Dependency Management and Encapsulation

Containerization has made running software applications more portable than ever by creating a single dependency, a container runtime. However, applications often need access to a sophisticated mix of resources, including external databases, GPUs (graphics processing units for machine learning), or persistent storage, and likely need to communicate with other applications for authentication, database access, and configuration services. Even a single containerized application typically needs some form of management over it and its access to external resources. The problem of managing connected containers is where Kubernetes comes in; Kubernetes orchestrates the containers of applications and manages their relationship to resources.

Network of Applications

Not all software applications need sophisticated platform architecture. Most software applications can be developed and merely run on a computer that meets their operational dependencies. Platforms come into play when you wish to operate multiple applications together and form an interconnected network of services, or when multiple applications can benefit from shared functionality, configuration, or resource management (Figure 1-2).

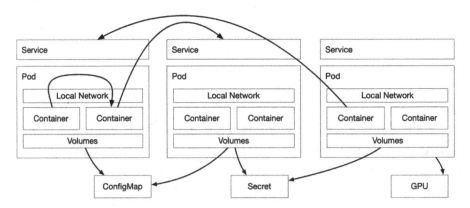

Figure 1-2. *Network of containerized applications*

Application Platform

Even if your goal is to develop a single-purpose online application, there are several reasons to embark on developing a software platform in Kubernetes. Large and small, complex and straightforward, enterprise and small-scale applications benefit when implemented in the context of a software platform. Software platforms provide an architecture to solve common problems and reduce the need for custom development in several areas, including communication, storage, scaling, security, and availability.

Architecting an application as a platform means that from the ground up the software is intended to be extended beyond its fundamental requirements, with the ability to upgrade and deploy new components independently. A proper platform welcomes the addition of the latest trends in open source, and when innovations arise, and open source products are released, it is successful software platforms that wrap and leverage their functionality to stay current. A proper software platform should never assume the label legacy; it should remain in a constant, iterative cycle of improvement.

The next section goes more in-depth into how this is accomplished with Kubernetes as the central component. Kubernetes solves the problems that traditional enterprise solutions like the service-oriented architecture (SOA) have attempted to solve for decades, only Kubernetes does this with protocols and methodologies that power the global Internet, like DNS, TCP, and HTTP, and wraps them in an elegant and robust API, accessible through those very same protocols. The platform is architected around Kubernetes's concept of a Service and its relationship to containerized applications (Figure 1-3).

5

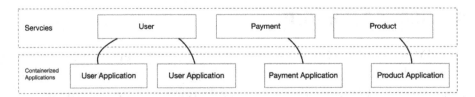

Figure 1-3. *The relationship between services and application*

Platform Requirements

This book focuses on implementing a foundational data-driven, Data Science, and Machine Learning platform, primarily but not limited to IoT data, and providing opportunities for interconnection with Blockchain technology. If this sounds like a lot of hype, it is, and as the hype fades, it's time to get to work. As these technologies leave the lab, they begin to fade into the background, and over the next decade, they will begin to silently provide their solutions behind new and innovative products.

If you are familiar with the "Gartner Hype Cycle for Emerging Technologies" (Figure 1-4) in 2018,[2] you would have seen deep neural networks (deep learning), IoT platforms, and Blockchain still on the "peak of inflated expectations" and rolling toward the "trough of disillusionment." Disillusionment sounds dire, but Gartner marks the following phase for these technologies as the "slope of enlightenment" and a later plateau in the next 5–10 years. Much innovation happens before these technologies plateau, and a flexible architecture built from a collection of connected containers, managed by Kubernetes, should easily keep you relevant for the next decade or more.

---

[2]Walker, Mike. "Hype Cycle for Emerging Technologies, 2018." Gartner. https://www.gartner.com/en/documents/3885468/hype-cycle-for-emerging-technologies-2018.

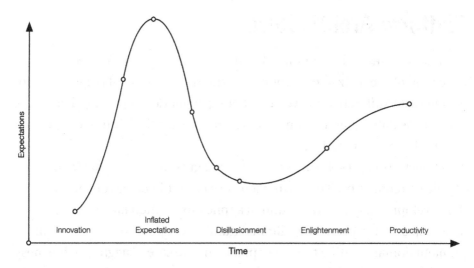

Figure 1-4. *Gartner's Hype Cycle for Emerging Technologies, 2018*[3]

While individual components may come and go as trends peak and plateau, data is here to stay; the platform needs to store it, transform it, and provide access to it by the latest innovations that produce value from it. If there is a central requirement for Advanced Platform Development with Kubernetes, it would be accessing the value of data, continuously, through the latest innovative technologies in IoT, Machine Learning, Blockchain, and whatever comes next.

A final requirement of Advanced Platform Development with Kubernetes is to stay open source, Cloud native, and vendor neutral. A platform with these principles can leverage open source to harness the global community of contributing software developers looking to solve the same problems we are. Remaining Cloud native and vendor neutral means not being tied to or constrained by a specific vendor and is just as functional in a private data center, as it can on AWS, GKE, Azure, or all of them combined as the concept of "hybrid cloud" grows in popularity.

---

[3]Walker, Mike. "Hype Cycle for Emerging Technologies, 2018." Gartner. https://www.gartner.com/en/documents/3885468/hype-cycle-for-emerging-technologies-2018.

Platform Architecture

With Kubernetes it is common to build software platforms from a collection of specialized components, written in a variety of languages and having vastly different and even conflicting dependencies. A good platform can encapsulate different components and abstract their interfaces into a standard API or set of APIs.

Object-oriented software concepts are a great reference tool for overall platform architecture. Trends in microservice architectures encourage the development of several, minimal applications, often taking the form of an object Class, providing a limited number of operations in a specific problem domain, letting the larger platform take care of aggregate business logic. To implement this approach, take the concept of an Object and apply it to the Kubernetes implementation of a Service (Figure 1-5). Like software interfaces, Kubernetes services represent one or more entry points to an application. The object-oriented software principles of abstraction, encapsulation, inheritance, and polymorphism can express every layer of the platform architecture.

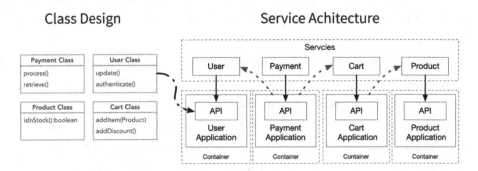

Figure 1-5. *Class design and service architecture*

Kubernetes is well suited for platform development and may be overkill for any lesser task. I believe, as I hope you discover in this book, that there is not much to debate on Kubernetes fitness for platform development. Containers solved many of the problems with dependency management by isolating and encapsulating components; Kubernetes manages these containers and in doing so forms the framework for a software platform.

Platform Capabilities

The purpose of the platform outlined in this book is to demonstrate how Kubernetes gives developers the ability to assemble a diverse range of technologies, wire them together, and manage them with the Kubernetes API. Developing platforms with Kubernetes reduces the risk and expense of adopting the latest trends. Kubernetes not only enables rapid development but can easily support parallel efforts. We develop a software platform with as little programming as necessary. We use declarative configurations to tell Kubernetes what we want. We use open source applications to build a base software platform, providing IoT data collection, Machine Learning capabilities, and the ability to interact with a private managed Blockchain.

Starting with the ingestion, storage, and retrieval of data, a core capability of the platform is a robust data layer (Figure 1-6). The platform must be able to ingest large amounts of data from IoT devices and other external sources including a private managed Blockchain. Applications such as Elasticsearch, Kafka, and Prometheus manage data indexing, message queueing, and metrics aggregation. Specific services capture Blockchain transactions from applications such as Ethereum Geth nodes and send them to Apache Kafka for queueing and Elasticsearch for indexing.

Above the data layer sits an application layer (Figure 1-6), providing capabilities utilizing this data, such as Machine Learning automation. Platform services wire together and expose data sources that export and serve persistent and streaming data usable for Machine Learning experiments, production AI inference, and business analytics.

The Platform naturally supports the expansion of features through the management of containers by Kubernetes. Serverless technologies including OpenFaaS provide higher-level expansion of features. Serverless support allows the rapid development and deployment of real-time data processors, operations that run at specific intervals, and new API endpoints, allowing specialized access to data, performing AI operations, or modifying the state of the platform itself.

The platform envisioned in this book forms a data-driven foundation for working with trending technologies, specializing in Machine Learning, Blockchain, and IoT. Components for the ingestion, storage, indexing, and queueing of data are brought together and allow efficient access to data between the specialized technologies. The platform provides data scientists the access to data and tools needed to perform Machine Learning experimentation and the development of production-ready neural network models for deployment by way of Serverless functions able to make predictions, perform classification, and detect anomalies from existing and inbound data. Blockchain technology is used to demonstrate how third-party ledger transactions and smart contract executions can seamlessly inner-connect to the data processing pipeline.

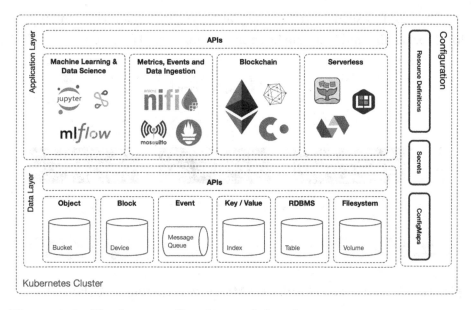

Figure 1-6. *Platform application and data layers*

The platform, developed iteratively, eventually consists of a large number of services, ranging in size and complexity, mixing giant monoliths mixed with small serverless functions. Some services consist of a cluster of Java applications, while some services only execute a few lines of Python. If this sounds like a nightmare, it is not. Fortunately, containerization has helped us isolate an application's operation and dependencies, exposing what is needed to configure, control, and communicate with the application. However, containerization only gives us limited options for visibility and control over our collection of services. Kubernetes gives us great configuration access controls over infrastructure resources, security, and networking, but leaves platform application–level concerns like encrypted communication between services, telemetry, observability, and tracing, to the applications themselves or higher-level specialized systems like Istio or Linkerd. The platform developed in this book is a collection of services that can operate with or without Istio or Linkerd. Istio and Linkerd are still young, and best practices for implementing them are still maturing.

11

The next few sections define the platform's three main requirements: IoT, Blockchain, and Machine Learning in more detail (Figure 1-7).

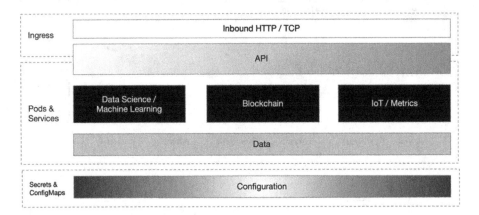

Figure 1-7. *IoT, Blockchain, and Machine Learning in Kubernetes*

IoT

The Internet of Things (IoT) and the newer Industrial Internet of Things (IIoT) are technologies that have matured past the hype phase. The physical devices of an industry are not only expected to be connected and controlled over the Internet but have a closer relationship to their larger data platforms. Kubernetes is capable of managing both the data and control plane in every aspect of IoT. This book focuses on three main uses for Kubernetes in the IoT domain, including the ingestion of data, as an edge gateway, and even an operating system (Figure 1-8).

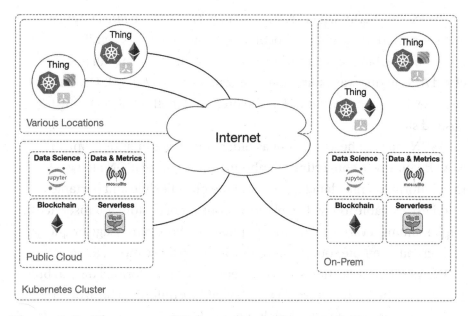

Figure 1-8. *Three uses of Kubernetes platforms in IoT*

Ingestion of Data

The first and most obvious use of Kubernetes is to orchestrate a data
ingestion platform. IoT devices have the potential of producing a large
volume of metrics. Gathering metrics is only one part of the problem.
Gathering, transforming, and processing metrics into valuable data and
performing actions on that data requires a sophisticated data pipeline.
IoT devices utilize a wide range of communication protocols, with
varying quality of support from various software products built to specific
devices and protocols. To effectively support data from a range of IoT
and IIoT devices, the platform needs to speak in protocols like AMQP
(Advanced Message Queuing Protocol), MQTT (Message Queue Telemetry
Transport), CoAP (Constrained Application Protocol), raw TCP, and HTTP,
to name a few.

JSON (JavaScript Object Notation) over HTTP is the most popular and supported messaging protocol on the Internet. Every significant programming language supports JSON. JSON drives nearly all public cloud APIs in one way or another. Kubernetes's own API is JSON-based, and YAML, a superset of JSON, is the preferred method of declaring the desired state.

JSON may not be as efficient as binary messages or as descriptive as XML; however, converting all inbound messages to JSON allows the platform to unify data ingestion on the most flexible and portable standard available today. The platform consists of custom microservices implementing a variety of protocols, parsing inbound message or querying and scraping remote sources, and transforming these messages to JSON. An HTTP collection service accepts JSON transformed data to buffer and batch. This architecture (Figure 1-9) allows unlimited horizontal scaling, accommodating large volumes of data.

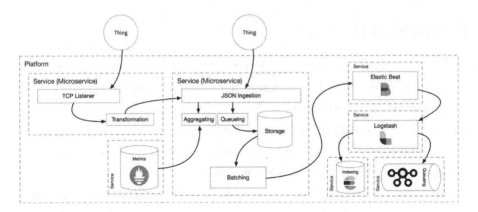

Figure 1-9. IoT data ingestion

The chapter *"Pipeline"* covers the implementation of the ingestion and transformation services: Apache NiFi, Prometheus, Logstash, Elasticsearch, and Kafka.

Edge Gateway

Kubernetes in the IoT space is beginning to include on-premises, edge deployments. These are mini-clusters that often include as little as a single node. On-premises clusters often operate a scaled-down version of the larger platform and are typically responsible for communicating with IoT devices on the local area network, or the nodes themselves are attached to proprietary hardware and protocols, legacy control systems, or lower-level, serial communication interfaces. Industrial use cases for the collection of data can often include sub-second sampling of device sensors or merely a volume of data only useful for classification, anomaly detection, or aggregation.

An on-premises platform (Figure 1-10) can handle the initial gathering and processing of metrics and communicate results back to a larger data processing platform. New Kubernetes distributions such as Minikube, Microk8s, k3s, and KubeEdge specialize in small or single-node implementations on commodity hardware.

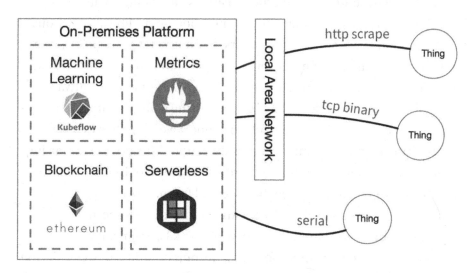

Figure 1-10. *On-premises Kubernetes platform*

Running a scaled-down platform on-premises solves many security and compliance issues with data handling. In scenarios where data must remain on-premises by strict compliance rules, on-premises clusters can process data, whose resulting metadata, inference, and metrics aggregation can transmit to a remote platform for further processing, analysis, or action.

IoT OS

The third use of Kubernetes for IoT addressed in this book is just starting to take root, that is, Kubernetes as an IoT operating system (Figure 1-11). ARM processors are cheap and energy efficient. Products like the Raspberry Pi have made them incredibly popular for hobbyists, education, and commercial prototyping. Container support for ARM-based systems has been around for a few years now, and running containerized applications on IoT devices has nearly all the advantages as does running them on more powerful and sophisticated hardware. IoT devices running containers orchestrated by Kubernetes can take advantage of features like rolling updates to eliminate downtime when upgrading applications. Running a small collection of containers in Kubernetes on an IoT device lets you take advantage of microservices application architecture, resource allocation, monitoring, and self-healing. The development of software for small, low-power devices once required using a proprietary operating system and writing much of the code to support activities like firmware updates, crash reporting, and resource allocation. IoT devices supporting scaled-down versions of Kubernetes are still new and poised for growth as more developers begin to see the potential for many of the common challenges with IoT software solved with platforms like Kubernetes.

Slimmed down distributions, like the 40mb k3s, are making Kubernetes an excellent choice for small, resource-limited devices like the Raspberry Pi and the large family of SOC boards on the market today.

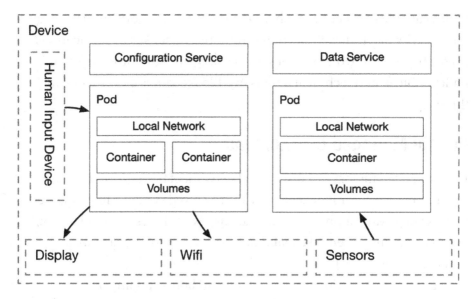

Figure 1-11. *Kubernetes platform on an IoT device*

Blockchain

With the maturity of Smart Contracts,[4] Blockchain technology is now a type of platform[5] itself. Smart contracts allow the storage and execution of code within the distributed, immutable ledger of the Blockchain (see Chapters 9 and 10). The inclusion of Blockchain technology provides the platform a capability for transactional communication with untrusted participants. Untrusted in this context means no personal or legal contractional trust is needed to transmit value expressed as data. Blockchain provides a permanent record of a transaction, verified in a shared ledger. The external parties only need to operate Blockchain

---

[4]https://en.wikipedia.org/wiki/Smart_contract

[5]Blockgeeks. "Smart Contract Platforms [A Deep Dive Investigation]," May 11, 2018. https://blockgeeks.com/guides/different-smart-contract-platforms/.

nodes capable of executing a shared mathematical algorithm. Trusting the integrity of a transaction comes from the consensus of verifications from a broader network of nodes. Describing the in-depth conceptual, philosophical, and technical details of a Blockchain is out of scope for this book.

Private Managed Blockchains

Blockchain technology is a distributed network of nodes, and there are very few use cases for Blockchains within a closed system. However, the concept of private or protected Blockchains is the focus of this platform, which represents essential capabilities for participation in a managed network.

The platform provides the allocation and bootstrapping of third-party participants within its selected network of nodes (Figure 1-12). Private Blockchains do not imply a level of trust beyond the allowance of participation. In closed systems, this trust is one way. Traditional platforms can allow a third party to create an account and utilize the system. However, that third party must also trust the platform operator. We trust that Google does not edit and modify emails we receive; we trust that Twitter does not tweet on our behalf. Blockchain participants rely on a majority of participants to verify a transaction rather than a central authority. With Blockchain technology, the platform is only responsible for equal participation and management of participants. Incorporating Blockchain technology directly into the platform brings it under a unified communication network with other services and facilitates the management and configuration of this technology as its concepts and capabilities rapidly mature. The chapter "Platforming Blockchain" describes the technical details for implementation.

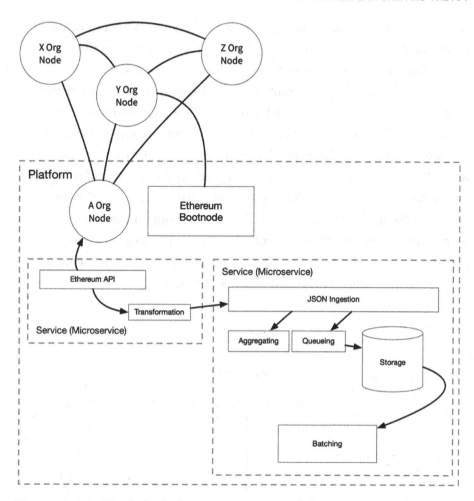

Figure 1-12. *Blockchain bootstrapping, and the ingestion of Blockchain transactions*

Use Cases

Industry verticals including finance, supply chain, logistics, manufacturing, process compliance, and many more are all looking for solutions provided by Blockchain capabilities, especially around the execution of Smart Contracts. Smart Contracts are blocks of immutable code that sit in the

Blockchain and are executable by anyone in the network of connected Blockchain nodes able to meet the criteria of the contract's interface. Streaming transactional events related to Smart Contracts and the execution of Smart Contracts provides a wealth of opportunities beyond recording the active intentions of third parties; they can communicate the state of IoT devices, or the automated results of artificial intelligence derived from Machine Learning. X Corp can verify that Z Corp sent data while Z Corp can verify that the platform processed the data and provided X Corp the results, while additional entities can execute Smart Contracts related to this activity (Figure 1-13). The platform not only facilitates access to this trustless network but interacts with it through streaming, real-time data queues. The platform can index the transactions and provide in-depth analysis of transaction types, frequency, and values.

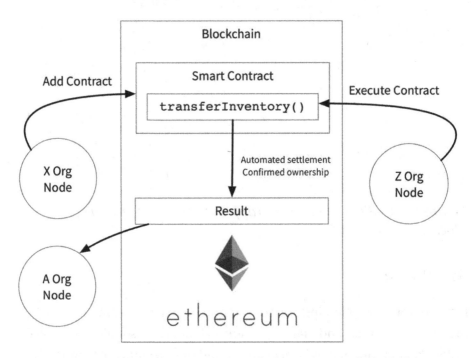

Figure 1-13. *Addition, execution, and observation of Blockchain Smart Contracts*

Ethereum and Hyperledger are popular choices for private/ permissioned Blockchains supporting smart contracts. Hyperledger was designed explicitly for private enterprise blockchains and does not contain currency features. Although it's unlikely the platform's enterprise use cases require a Blockchain currency, neither is it a deterrent. The platform in this book uses Ethereum, making its capabilities compatible with public or private blockchains, with or without the need for currency. The platform is not limited to Ethereum and can easily be extended to support Hyperledger or the newest trends in Blockchain.

The chapter "Blockchain" covers the implementation of Ethereum nodes into the platform and provides examples for interconnecting with the platform's data layer.

Machine Learning

Machine Learning and specifically deep learning is another field of technology nearing, or at peak hype according to Gartner. All the major hyper-cloud providers including Google, IBM, AWS, and Azure either offer platforms with service-wrapped versions of TensorFlow, PyTorch, Keras, or their in-house developed Machine Learning development and production automation tools. The major cloud providers respond quickly to the hype, but this response is also an indication that the technology has matured to the point of a commodity. Commodity technology might have lost a bit of its novelty and excitement, but if it survives past that initial phase, then it's ready for business. We may be at the tip of the expectation iceberg for Machine Learning, but it can and does solve industry problems today, and so its capabilities belong in the platform and exposed to its connected data.

Providing a simple service-wrapping of Kubeflow with some limited custom configurations would be powerful enough to call this a data science platform. Kubeflow as a service would alone be a decent competitor to the hyper-clouds. Wrapping Kubeflow would take less than a chapter to describe and, more importantly, miss out on the combinatorial power of the adjacent capabilities of Blockchain and IoT data, all sitting atop the core components, covered in the next section.

Industry wants real-time answers from real-time data. Data science needs static data and the ability to perform reproducible experiments and learn from a known quantity. Machine Learning is an application of data science, and machines learn best on fixed sets of data. The platform provides both by providing access to persistent data and the ability to label and snapshot subsets of data to form trained neural network models that can then be immediately deployed and tried against streams of real-time data (Figure 1-14). The cost of iterative experimentation is high when the technological ecosystem of the data science lab is alien to production concerns of the enterprise. Kubeflow and other cloud-native technologies help bring these environments closer together, reducing the cost and risk associated with experimentation. The reduction of risk leads to new opportunities for experimentation and the testing of novel theories or approaches to machine learning and artificial intelligence.

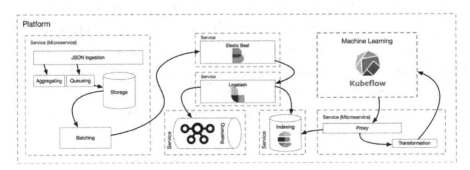

Figure 1-14. *High-velocity data pipelines to Machine Learning*

Automation and Management

With software frameworks like Keras or PyTorch, you can now easily configure a simple yet trainable neural network in a few dozen lines of code. The entire machine learning life cycle (Figure 1-15) requires more than a few moving parts, from data access, transformation, and experimentation to the deployment of trained models. Kubernetes-compatible solutions like Apache Airflow and Kubeflow are making great strides in the areas of automation. This book focuses on a few components of Kubeflow as a sub-platform for data science. Kubeflow came from Google's internal solution for automating the use of TensorFlow, a popular Machine Learning framework also developed by Google and open sourced. The chapters "In-Platform CI/CD," "Indexing and Analytics," and "Platforming AIML" explore some of the technology that powers Kuberflow, including JupyterLab, JupyterHub, MLflow and Seldon Core.

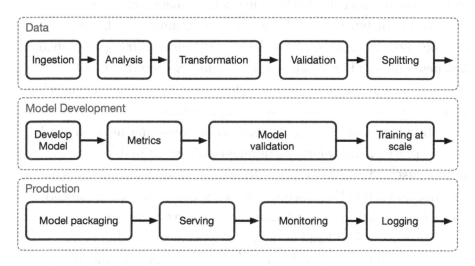

Figure 1-15. *Kubeflow process*

Core Components

The following section covers platform components you will likely never see on Gartner's hype charts. However, these core components form the essential glue that holds the platform together. These components include configuration, ingress, data management, metrics, APIs, and protocols.

Containers, configuration, ingress, data management, and metrics collection are the core components that make up the platform's core infrastructure, discussed later. The following briefly reviews their purpose, the problems they solve, and their role in tying together specialized applications. Realizing the potential of trends in the Internet of Things, Machine Learning, Blockchain, and future innovations is only amplified when incorporated into a platform that can combine their focused expertise. Solve problems across new domains, harnessing the combinatorial effect of their specific solutions—for example, utilizing Artificial Intelligence driven from models developed through deep learning on metrics collected from IoT devices that execute a Smart Contract on the Blockchain whose results communicate a change in the operational state of other IoT devices. Machine Learning developed independent from Blockchain and IoT technology is certainly not dependent on any of them. A wide variety of languages is used to develop these technologies, each with diverse dependencies. However, with little effort, they can all run in containers and communicate in protocols that are proven in reliability and limitless scale, because they scale the Internet itself. TCP/IP, HTTP, and DNS are the underlying protocols of the Internet, and within Kubernetes they are the methods of communication and service discovery. This relationship between Containers comes from the Container API and its orchestrator, Kubernetes. Kubernetes makes containers easy and elegant to configure, scale, and maintain. Therefore, Kubernetes itself, along with containers, forms the primary core component of the platform. If you are reading a book on advanced platform development, you probably have a firm grasp on the advantages of containers as well as the many supporting objects Kubernetes provides, including the powerful ConfigMap and Secret.

Configuration

Two forms of configuration make up the platform: the configuration of the platform itself, a set of Kubernetes objects expressed in YAML files, and the configuration of various applications within the platform. This book uses the kubectl utility for configuring Kubernetes. The kubectl utility provides three kinds of object management: imperative commands, imperative object configuration, and declarative object configuration. This book relies primarily on declarative object configuration by describing a desired state in a series of YAML files and using kubectl to apply them. The chapter "Development Environment" presents a method of organizing and maintaining the Kubernetes configuration manifests, an essential aspect of keeping your platform configuration organized and documented.

The configuration of individual applications within the platform is the concern here and why configuration is considered a core component. Kubernetes provides the object types ConfigMap and Secret to provide a rich set of options for application configuration.

Application Parameters

A container can wrap nearly any application, and the three most common ways to configure an application include command-line parameters, configuration files, environment variables, and combinations of the three. If you have spent any time with Docker or Kubernetes, it is not uncommon to specify a long list of parameters required to configure an application for execution, or to populate a series of environment variables, or to mount a configuration directory. With these three methods of configuration, nearly any application can be configured and have a standard method to manage the configuration for all components of the platform. This is an essential component of the platform's core infrastructure.

ConfigMaps and Secrets are configuration object types provided by Kubernetes; they are persistent and available throughout the cluster. The key/value pairs of ConfigMaps and Secrets can be mounted as filesystems within a Pod, the keys being file names and value as data whose mount points are shared by one or more containers in the Pod. ConfigMaps and Secrets can populate environment variables within containers or populate command-line arguments used in the execution of the container's application.

The chapter "Development Environment" on infrastructure covers the management and organization of ConfigMaps and Secrets in further detail, and if you come from any experience with Kubernetes, you may be well versed in their use. The intention here is to more clearly define their value as core infrastructure components to the platform.

Ingress

Ingress is defined as "the act of entering" and is the basic concept of accepting inbound data to the platform. However, ingress is one of the most critical components of the framework. Ingress is responsible for providing a means of securing inbound communication over protocols like Transport Layer Security (TLS), routing HTTP traffic to various services based on a variety of configured rules. Although majority interaction with the platform is over the HTTP protocol, consisting of REST-style API calls from external systems or web and native applications, the platform also provides listeners for custom inbound TCP traffic for specific IoT devices and protocols. In some software platforms, infrastructure-level ingress is an afterthought; large monolithic and stateful applications often assume a direct interaction with inbound requests and expect the ingress layers above to be thin. Unfortunately, these more traditional ways of utilizing popular and influential proxies like Nginx and Envoy often fail to take advantage of their power in this specialization or do so as a means to work around implementation requirements.

The platform described in this book only scrapes the surface of utilizing Nginx to manage ingress. However, it is a core component and essential to the network and architectural layout of the platform. Envoy is another new and popular choice for reverse-proxy support and one of the core components of Istio. The platform described in this book will use Nginx for public HTTP ingress.

Data Management

Data management is the fundamental core component of the enterprise platform. The platform must manage data after it's accepted through ingress and retrieved through APIs. The data management layer of the platform is also the necessary means of communicating the results of various processors. Raw data comes into the platform in the form of metrics from IoT devices, results of Blockchain transaction, and communication through HTTP APIs and TCP ports. This data is retrieved and processed to form new Blockchain transactions, send commands to IoT devices, and form predictions derived from machine learning models; the results of which become new data, traveling and continuously refined through this recursive ecosystem.

The platform can harness the best in class technologies for message queues, indexing, and metrics aggregation by incorporating modern and proven open source technologies, including Apache Kafka, Elasticsearch, and Prometheus. Implementing each of these technologies is addressed in the chapters "Pipeline," and "Indexing and Analytics." From the perspective of the software platform, the core components are the underlying infrastructure that wrap all specialized functionality. The purpose of the platform is not merely to service-wrap technologies like Apache Kafka or Elasticsearch for external platform capabilities. Integrating these technologies into the platform infrastructure gives the advantages of standardized management capabilities through Kubernetes, but simplifies communication and observability through their deep integration.

These technologies form a higher-level infrastructure of the stack and provide their capabilities through custom intermediaries, connecting the specialized applications of IoT data, Machine Learning, and Blockchain by normalizing access to their resulting data.

Metrics

There is no shortage of hosted PaaS offerings willing to collect your metrics, and they offer APIs and beautiful dashboards for developing reports, business analytics, and intelligence. Aggregating, sorting, and organizing metrics is big business, and thanks to open source community and SoundCloud, we have Prometheus as a free and open source solution. SoundCloud developed and open sourced Prometheus in 2015, after which it became the second Cloud Native Computing Foundation incubated project in 2016 following Kubernetes. Prometheus is now a graduate project of the Cloud Native Computing Foundation and actively developed.

SoundCloud developed Prometheus when they determined that solutions like StatsD and Graphite could not handle their needs. Prometheus is a high-performance metrics aggregator and records real-time metrics into a time series database. Prometheus can not only scale to our future needs but has a robust and flexible query language. The platform in this book utilizes Grafana to build visually stunning dashboards that query our metrics scraped by Prometheus.

Prometheus scrapes metrics from applications and offers official and mature client libraries in Go, Java, and Python on Ruby with unofficial third-party client libraries in Bash, C++, Common Lisp, Elixir, Erlang, Haskell, Lua, .Net, C#, Node.js, Perl, PHP, and Rust. This collection of SDKs means you can add deep instrumentation to nearly any modern application. The client libraries are well written and easy to implement. Prometheus forms an essential fork in the platform's data pipeline, for use in rich analytics dashboards and also allowing Blockchain and Machine Learning capabilities to not only feed into this data stream but react to it.

APIs and Protocols

The application programming interface (or the platform API) provides external access for interacting with the platform. An API is a broad term and can be used to describe how one portion of software communicates with another, how an enterprise accesses its data, or how to invoke programmatically driven business logic, either internally or externally. The latter, external access, being the concern of the platform API. This external interface to the platform is concerned with the storage and retrieval of data, the recording of events, the configuration of the desired platform state, the invocation of business logic, and the extension of platform functionality. The platform API empowers the construction of web-based and native applications customized to a specific vertical, or allows existing IT systems to interact with its capabilities or report data and events. The platform uses its API to perform multiple actions necessary in the provisioning of accounts and users, supply data to business analytics and intelligence solutions, and provide front-end user interfaces for extending and augmenting data pipelines for data science and machine learning.

The Platform presented in this book is reflective of many real-world data platform implementations, being a collection of monolithic applications, microservices, and (Serverless) functions. Each component of the platform may have different methods of interaction. Elasticsearch uses a RESTful API for processing user requests as well as an asynchronous transport protocol for internal communication with its nodes. Communication with Kafka is performed over a TCP-based binary protocol and additionally offers a REST proxy. This book covers Elasticsearch and Kafka implementation in the "Pipeline," and "Indexing and Analytics" chapters. In the world of API development, there is no shortage of solutions; new and innovative protocols like gRPC and GraphQL are maturing and gaining traction, as older ideas such as SOAP are less likely to be considered in new development.

The Platform in this book takes the middle road when it comes to the fundamental interactions involving configuration. REST, or representational state transfer, is by far the most popular API implementation due to its simplicity and ubiquity across the Internet and the range of tools and clients for working with it. REST may not be as fast and compact as gRPC or as flexible as GraphQL, but REST has no requirements for its clients beyond HTTP and its verbs POST, GET, PUT, PATCH, and DELETE. The platform uses JSON (JavaScript Object Notation) for communication over REST. REST is widely accessible mostly because HTTP is the only requirement, a universally established, mature, and stable protocol.

Although the platform's core API is an implementation of REST, established through HTTP endpoints exposed by Ingress, there is the opportunity to develop custom, low-level TCP listeners as well as offer specialized services over gRPC and GraphQL. The Platform is not limited or constrained by implementing any particular API protocol; constructing platforms in Kubernetes makes adding additional interfaces easier than ever. Traditionally businesses often have a hard time seeing APIs beyond their endpoints, often evidenced by monolithic applications evolving into large and unwieldy collections of highly coupled dependencies between the API and underlying data. While it is possible to develop a traditional monolithic system in Kubernetes, you would be working out an anti-pattern and failing to take full advantage of one of Kubernetes's best features, Services. Kubernetes Services may be backed by a collection of both monolithic and micro application architectures.

In regard to the platform API architecture, Kubernetes services compare to the concept of a Class in object-oriented design (OOD), although a strained analogy. There has been a lot of thought and theory put into the description and organization of services in the world of microservice architectures, and that is well beyond the scope of this book, but thinking of services as nouns providing access to corresponding verbs is a good starting point for platform design. Kubernetes services are the persistent gateways for all API calls, JSON-REST, gRPC, GraphQL, binary- or text-based TCP, and UDP; virtually anything that can listen on a port assigned to an IP address can be an endpoint of a Service, internal or external to the platform. The Platform centers design around Kubernetes services.

Summary

The goal of this book is to give you examples and inspiration to develop productive and compelling software platforms and distributed applications leveraging Kubernetes, with examples that tie together capabilities from a range of technologies. This chapter defined a type of data-driven software platform, set to combine the capabilities of IoT technology, Machine Learning, and Blockchain. While demand for specific capabilities comes and goes, the platform's core components center on configuration, Ingress, data management, and metrics. These core capabilities form a framework of essential services, supporting limitless combinations of new technology and their relationship to its data.

Infrastructure has often been the sole domain of operations. As the gap between development and operations has narrowed in recent years, the term DevOps has gained popularity. While some organizations see DevOps as a role, a more accurate expression may be a range of responsibilities and tasks performed by many different roles. DevOps encompasses the provisioning of hardware, installation and management of server clusters, configuration management, continuous integration and continuous deployment, to name a few. The following chapter on infrastructure covers the DevOps needed for essential core components as well as configuration management, integration, operations, monitoring, and maintenance of the platform.

CHAPTER 2

DevOps Infrastructure

Kubernetes abstracts the physical infrastructure of its underlying servers and network. This chapter covers how to leverage Kubernetes in the management of the entire development life cycle. This chapter and the next take a break from the specific concerns of the Platform functionality and center the focus on development operations (DevOps), including the vital tools for rapid and efficient integration, testing, and deployment for teams building platforms on Kubernetes by setting up a GitLab instance.

Kubernetes is a vendor-neutral, Cloud-native technology, making it highly portable across the major Cloud vendors, bare-metal data centers, and local workstations. In keeping with this principle, the following chapter constructs a portable DevOps toolchain that leverages Kubernetes, standardizing the configuration and management for all aspects of development and production.

Cloud Computing

Writing portable software has always been a leading driver of innovations and productivity. The earliest computers of the 1940s required programmers to write in assembly language, specifically tailored to a particular machine. In the late 1950s, FORTRAN became the first successful, commercially available, high-level, general-purpose programming language. Utilizing a compiler, FORTRAN could be written generically to solve specific problems, and by the early 1960s, over 40

© Craig Johnston 2020
C. Johnston, *Advanced Platform Development with Kubernetes*,
https://doi.org/10.1007/978-1-4842-5611-4_2

FORTRAN compilers were available. FORTRAN still exists today, outliving nearly all of the physical infrastructure available when it was first released. Even at the cost of some performance, it has always been wise for software developers to keep a layer of abstraction between the concepts embedded in the code and the implementations achieved in the circuitry.

Virtualization and Cloud computing are the latest players in the race for abstraction, not to mention containerization adding a new form of portable encapsulation to the mix. However, in the race to abstract physical infrastructure, Cloud computing itself can take the form of the specialized systems of the 1940s. Cloud vendors have become a type of specialized infrastructure. Specialization might be acceptable for many organizations looking to harness turnkey solutions or leverage performance realized from a vendor's custom solution. Trends in Cloud computing are now moving toward a goal of providing Cloud-native solutions with a vendor-neutral approach, not only to abstract the physical infrastructure but abstracting the vendors themselves. If FORTRAN was the first answer to portable applications, Kubernetes might be the new answer to portable platforms.

Data centers were once the exclusive domain of large enterprises. In 1991 the National Science Foundation lifted commercial restrictions on what is now the Web and along came a crowd of web hosting providers, allowing anyone with a few dollars a month to participate in its global network, along with a handful of static HTML files on a server in some remote data center. Racks of servers soon filled data centers, and new data centers sprang up in every major city. The Internet generated a boom of cheap, commodity servers running the free and open source Linux operating system. Your bank needed proprietary communication protocols over point-to-point telecom connections to transmit data globally; all you needed was someone to visit your URL, and for a few dollars a month, you could do what your bank spent a fortune to achieve.

Back in the early 1990s, computers attached to the Internet, delivered data nearly the same as they do today, primarily over HTTP. Back then,

HTTP served HTML documents, images, and a variety of files. Web servers grew in power and the ability to execute code, standardized in 1993 with the common gateway interface (CGI). CGI provided the opportunity to develop web-based applications under a simple and clear standard. Applications written to receive and respond to HTTP messages could run on nearly any provider supporting CGI, aside from unique dependencies. If this sounds like a Cloud-native and vendor-neutral solution, it was and still is. The need for and the ideas behind the Cloud-native and vendor-neutral movement is a type of correction in the self-healing nature of the Internet and covered in the next section.

Sophisticated web applications need much more than simple CGI execution from a web server; they often need a specified amount of CPU or GPU resource, memory, and storage, along with the ability to run on multiple compute instances and in multiple regions. Renting and maintaining servers in data centers is a complex and specialized task, with a large amount of up-front planning and long-term commitment. Setting up new platforms once required a significant amount of manual labor. Companies like Google and Amazon built robust internal platforms for the allocation of compute resource, accommodating their massive workloads and constant release cycles. It made sense for new Internet-based enterprises to further capitalize on their infrastructure investments by offering them as products. These companies differentiated themselves from web hosting and colocation services by marketing a Cloud platform. Enterprises could now grasp these offerings as another option for their enterprise applications. The Cloud was not simple web hosting and servers. It was now another option for enterprises to deploy and operate all of their business applications. The Cloud was, in concept, a platform as a service (PaaS).

The traditional Cloud is not a standard like HTTP or CGI, the traditional Cloud is not an operating system, and applications cannot compile and execute on it natively. To master the Cloud, you needed to pick one and might pursue a certificate in Amazon AWS, Microsoft Azure, or Google Cloud. However, there is little distinction in the features offered by these major providers, only their proprietary implementations. When one vendor releases a particular feature, the others quickly follow. This competition has been excellent for innovation, and the major providers are some of the leading innovators in bringing cutting-edge technology to market. Along with the innovation has come proprietary APIs, and if you leverage these at the core of your architecture, your system is considered vendor-locked. Additionally, there has become a growing trend of enterprises looking for hybrid-Cloud solutions, attempting to leverage the strengths of multiple Cloud providers; this can mean better diversification or unfortunately multiple vendor lock-ins.

This book is about building platforms in Kubernetes and implemented in a way that can run on instances by Amazon, Google, IBM, Microsoft, or custom servers in a private data center, or all of them combined. Kubernetes can operate on any Cloud that supports generic compute instances, which is all of them. However, even this is no longer necessary, as the major Cloud providers are now offering Kubernetes as a service, a fully Cloud-native and vendor-neutral option.

Cloud Native and Vendor Neutral

The early days of the Internet moved quickly, primarily due to open source technology and open standards. Cloud computing has solved the problem of efficiently managing compute resource by abstracting the physical infrastructure into a set of API calls. The first major Cloud offering was a type of on-demand utility computing called the Elastic Compute Cloud (EC2). Amazon was the first to make the term Cloud computing popular in 2006 with the release of their EC2 Platform. Google released Google App Engine in 2008, and in 2010, Microsoft launched Azure. These major Cloud providers now offer far more than virtualized compute instances; they are full-featured PaaS and SaaS solutions that continue to proliferate with features and capabilities released daily. The major Cloud providers solved the problem of startups and new development efforts needing a fast and cost-effective way to spin up and manage compute resource and attach their business needs to on-demand solutions. Architecting solutions that leverage these offerings may bring many up-front advantages by taming development costs and reducing time to market; however, they also bring the concerns of vendor lock-in.

Vendor lock-in occurs when your application or business process would require significant effort to port to a new platform or vendor. If your application or Platform is essential to the operation of your business, being deeply tied to the future stability and strategic decisions of another organization can pose a significant risk, or impose arbitrary technological limitations at best. Long-term contracts and service-level agreements (SLAs) only contractually guarantee stability, but technology managed by a third party is always prone to unexpected failures and depreciation. In some cases, it's easier for a business to move buildings or relocate to another state than it would be to refactor a decade or more of business logic that has become deeply entrenched in the specialized platforms offered by IBM, Microsoft, Amazon, or Google. Vendor lock-in is not necessarily a problem for some organizations, especially value-added resellers (VARs) in the business of supporting or extending traditional Cloud services. However, if your business only wishes to leverage Cloud services, then you are best served with a Cloud-native vendor-neutral approach to your architecture, and Kubernetes provides this.

Redundancy

In September of 2015, Amazon Web Services (AWS) suffered a five-hour outage in their US-EAST-1 region. Websites and applications from high-profile organizations such as IMDb, Tinder, Airbnb, Nest, and many others suffered up to eight hours of limited or full outages of their systems. However, Netflix is another significant user of AWS and only suffered a temporary disruption. Netflix had correctly architected against the risk of running critical business operations tied to infrastructure they don't fully control. Redundancy is a sound principle that should be part of the design for any critical system's architecture; unfortunately, many systems rely on the traditional Cloud to abstract this from them.

It is not a stretch to assume there are a high number of redundant components to Amazon's AWS offerings; Amazon's 99.95% uptime service-level agreements necessitate this. However, genuine redundancy should be something you have control over, not a faith-based reliance on a third party. In 2015, Netflix did not have to wait patiently for Amazon to restore its US-EAST-1 region; Netflix had failure contingencies planned[1] through their internally redundant architecture. However, what if the issues that caused AWS to go down had cascaded to other regions?

The ability to stand up and operate a Kubernetes-based platform on nearly any Cloud provider could offer redundancy at massive cross-cloud scale and provide an ultimate contingency plan. A Kubernetes-based platform leverages the most fundamental value of the Cloud, on-demand compute instances, and with the proper consideration, it can remain vendor neutral.

Portable Platforms

Many organizations are not interested or able to purchase and maintain a vast array of physical infrastructure across national and even global regions. Cloud computing has become an essential aspect of operating sophisticated workloads flexibly and cost-effectively. The concept of Cloud-native means leveraging this world of ephemeral compute instances, storage, and networks, where efforts shift from the implementation of processes involved in forming the desired state to merely describing it.

---

[1]Heath, "AWS Outage."

In 2017 Amazon announced its intentions to buy grocery retailer Whole Foods.[2] With Amazon's expansion into brick-and-mortar retail, there arose concern from other retailers that Amazon would now be considered a direct competitor. In an email to CNBC, Walmart spokesman Dan Toporek is quoted "Our vendors have the choice of using any cloud provider that meets their needs and their customers' needs. It shouldn't be a big surprise that there are cases in which we'd prefer our most sensitive data isn't sitting on a competitor's Platform."[3] Walmart was not worried about the cost or stability of its vendors using AWS; they preferred not to, for strategic business reasons. Solutions deeply tied to AWS may have lost opportunities to engage with Walmart or may have been passed up by competitors using Microsoft or IBM Cloud services. The idea of vendor-neutral means not needing to miss out on doing business with companies like Walmart if all it entails is a standing-up Kubernetes Cluster on an alternate Cloud.

Kubernetes, along with a growing ecosystem of applications, frameworks, and concepts, is solving problems by developing applications that are both cloud native and vendor neutral. If an application can run on a generic install of Kubernetes, it can likely run anywhere, with only minimal changes typically needed in the configuration of custom network and storage interfaces. So, are the Cloud vendors worried about this new technology so quickly enabling a vendor-neutral approach? Not only is Kubernetes able to be installed and operated on every major Cloud, surprisingly all the traditional Cloud providers now offer Kubernetes as a service.

Choosing the location for operating your Platform is out of the scope for this book. If you have experience with AWS, you might be interested in Amazon Elastic Container Service for Kubernetes (Amazon EKS). If you

---

[2]Wingfield and Merced, "Amazon to Buy Whole Foods for $13.4 Billion."

[3]Thomas, "Wal-Mart Is Reportedly Telling Its Tech Vendors to Leave Amazon's Cloud."

are comfortable with Azure, you should explore Azure Kubernetes Service (AKS). IBM offers the IBM Cloud Kubernetes Service, and Google provides Google Kubernetes Engine (GKE).

Getting Started Vendor Neutral

While Kubernetes itself is vendor neutral, managed Kubernetes services from vendors such as Google, Microsoft, and Amazon often include vendor-specific requirements, often around identity and access management. If constructing a portable, vendor-neutral platform is a goal or business requirement, it may be beneficial to install a custom/vanilla Kubernetes cluster using only generic compute instances from the major cloud providers. Otherwise, explicitly documenting nonstandard configurations used for a specific vendor provides a vendor-neutral road map, should portability or multi-cloud support be a future concern.

Developing a platform with Kubernetes means it should be able to operate on a local workstation, on a private Cloud, on a public cloud with generic compute instances, or on public cloud Kubernetes service. There is a wealth of books and online tutorials for setting up and configuring Kubernetes for every environment and vendor, from a few simple clicks on AWS or Google to "Kubernetes The Hard Way" by Kelsey Hightower.[4] This book assumes you have some experience with Kubernetes and development operations and only covers basic setups for review.

Development toolchains and environments can and often should have the same level of portability as the platforms they support. The following section, "DevOps Toolchain," assembles a working development operations pipeline and workflow using open source technology compatible with a pure vendor-neutral, Cloud-native approach. While traditional cloud providers offer some integrated development solutions,

---

[4]Hightower, Bootstrap Kubernetes the Hard Way on Google Cloud Platform. No Scripts.

the goal of this book is not only to build a vendor-neutral platform supporting Blockchain, Machine Learning, and IoT data management solutions but additionally keep the entire development toolchain as portable and flexible as possible.

DevOps Toolchain

Application platforms exist to increase the productivity of the development process. They often go beyond abstracting access to complex subsystems. Mature application platforms establish conventions, provide methods for observability, and promote specific architectural design patterns. Developers building applications for iOS or Windows or extending the functionality of CMS systems like SharePoint or Salesforce have well-established ecosystems, consisting of tools and methods for developing on those platforms. However, Kubernetes, at its core, is just a robust container orchestration system, making it an excellent environment for developing large enterprise platforms. Kubernetes is a higher level of concern than Linux or Windows development, and a much lower level than extending popular content management systems. Kubernetes leaves developers only one concern, applying the configuration. There have been several tools developed to ease the management of complex configurations, yet these can obfuscate the simplicity of Kubernetes core tenant—declarative configuration. The central tool used in this book for configuring, managing, and developing Kubernetes is kubectl, establishing a single standard on which to introduce more complex tooling when required.

Later on, a small Kubernetes Cluster is set up in the section "Development Environment." Repositories, registries, and CI/CD are essential components for organizing, configuring, and maintaining the manifests, code, and container images supporting platform development in this new development Cluster. Each of these concepts is covered briefly, and this section concludes with the installation of GitLab[5] on a single-Node k3s[6] Cluster (see Figure 2-1).

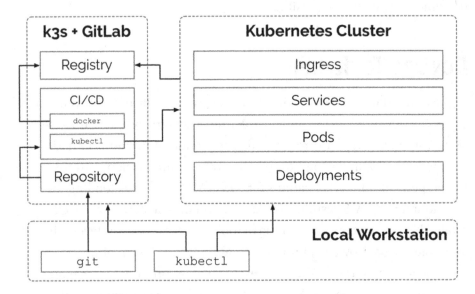

Figure 2-1. Toolchain

Repositories

Repositories are used to store, distribute, and manage source code, specifically YAML files in the case of the Platform developed in this book. Kubernetes has no dependency on developers managing configurations in repositories; however, as any platform develops, a growing tome of YAML manifests necessitates a well-organized system for managing them. Git has become the industry standard for source code management and version control. Git repositories are distributed and portable and meet the vendor-neutral standards strived for in this book. Git is ubiquitous thanks in large

---

[5]https://about.gitlab.com/
[6]https://k3s.io/

part to the popularity of GitHub. GitHub hosts nearly every major open source project, yet GitHub is only a value-add atop Git's standard features.

Although this book focuses on the development of YAML configurations related to running applications within Kubernetes, source code repositories play a central role at every level of development operations. Infrastructure-as-code[7] (IaC) technologies, such as Terraform, Ansible, Puppet, Chef, and the new Cluster API, abstract the construction and maintenance of underlying infrastructure through code and benefit[8] greatly from well-managed source code repositories and management systems such as GitHub and GitLab.

This book not only promotes Kubernetes's vendor-neutral and Cloud-native approach to platform development but to the entire toolchain supporting it.

Registries

Kubernetes runs and manages Containers. An image is a file that contains executable code and configuration needed to create a run a Container. Docker is by far the most popular option for building Container images, and so this book focuses on Docker and its accompanying ecosystem of applications and utilities. Container image registries are a critical component for developing and maintaining platforms in Kubernetes. The registry is responsible for maintaining the versioning and distribution of container images. The Platform in this book pulls containers from several registries including the public Docker Hub. Docker Hub is free for hosting public containers; however, many organizations, such as Elastic, chose to self-host their public container registries. Public containers created in this book use Docker Hub, and private containers use GitLab's built-in Docker

---

[7]https://techbeacon.com/enterprise-it/infrastructure-code-engine-heart-devops
[8]https://devops.com/version-your-infrastructure/

registry. It may also be wise to mirror all containers used for the platform into the private registry, adding an additional layer of control and security (see Figure 2-2).

Building and hosting containers in private registries may ensure greater trust in the providence of an image. However, it is common to construct new images from base images, including distributions such as Ubuntu, Alpine, or CentOS. Nearly all software eventually contains common vulnerabilities and exposures (CVEs). Solutions for detecting CVEs and other security risks, such as Clair by CoreOS,[9] may be integrated directly into the build pipeline.

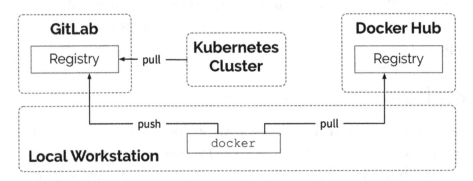

Figure 2-2. *Container image registries*

CI/CD

Continuous integration and deployment to Kubernetes is essential for productive and efficient platform development and stable production releases. There are a large number of commercial CI/CD offerings, and most of them work well with Kubernetes. The open source application GitLab has a stable and mature CI/CD component, able to perform build operations and testing directly in a Kubernetes Cluster. The ability to test code against existing services running in the Cluster is a tremendous

---

[9]https://coreos.com/clair/docs/latest/

advantage over many other services. The process of developing sophisticated platforms necessitates the operation and communication of many different services, and developing custom components that communicate with more than one of them can be challenging in isolated integration and test environments. The following illustrates a GitLab Runner building and testing code from within a development Kubernetes Cluster (see Figure 2-3).

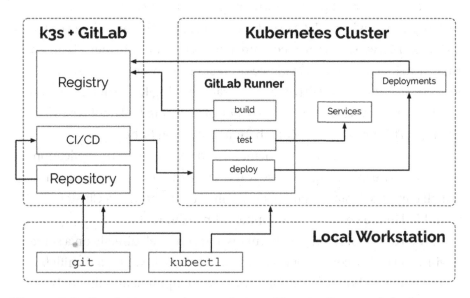

Figure 2-3. *In-cluster continuous integration, testing, and deployment*

GitLab for DevOps

Git is only a version control system, and additional tooling is needed to support the larger development operations (DevOps) concern. GitHub is by far the most popular hosted repository for open source projects, and although extremely popular and well trusted in the open source community, GitHub itself is not open source, and if you wish to avoid vendor lock-in, it's best not to rely on GitHub's value-add features for critical components in your development toolchain. This book utilizes GitHub as a mirror for public access to open source components. However, this book uses GitLab for continuous integration and continuous deployment. Like GitHub, GitLab.com offers hosted plans ranging from free to enterprise. Unlike GitHub.com, GitLab is open source and can be installed and run entirely on infrastructure you control.

"GitLab Community Edition (CE) is an open source end-to-end software development platform with built-in version control, issue tracking, code review, CI/CD, and more. Self-host GitLab CE on your bare-metal servers, VMs, in a container, or on a cloud provider."[10] GitLab can be run on stand-alone instances or inside a Kubernetes Cluster; however, in either case, GitLab can leverage existing Kubernetes Clusters by setting up remote Runners able to perform testing and deployment activities. This book utilizes GitLab for maintaining Kubernetes configurations, continuous deployment, and serving private application containers. The following exercise walks through setting up GitLab on a small compute instance and able to utilize the Kubernetes Cluster assembled in the chapter "Development Environment."

GitLab does not require Kubernetes and runs well directly on a server or within a Docker container on a server. Yet, there is value to a unified control plane for both the platform under development and the tools that support it. While a full production-ready Kubernetes Cluster may be overkill for many small isolated applications, there is a growing list of Kubernetes-compliant solutions focused on low-resource single-Node Clusters. The next section covers installing GitLab into a single-Node k3s[11] Cluster.

---

[10]"GitLab.Org / GitLab Community Edition."
[11]https://k3s.io

k3s + GitLab

k3s is 40MB binary that runs "a fully compliant production-grade Kubernetes distribution" and requires only 512MB of RAM.

k3s is a great way to wrap applications that you may not want to run in a full production Cluster but would like to achieve greater uniformity in systems deployment, monitoring, and management across all development operations. GitLab plays a central role in the development operations of the platform in this book, and k3s will be used along with other single-Node solutions for IoT devices and on-site appliances. Using k3s to host GitLab is great way to become familiar with single-Node Clusters and with the added benefit of a management plane unified under the Kubernetes API.

The following outlines a process for setting up a GitLab application running in a single-Node custom Kubernetes (k3s) Cluster on Vultr.[12] Vultr is chosen as an alternative to the major cloud providers, such as Amazon, Google, or Microsoft. Vultr, along with providers like Digital Ocean,[13] Linode,[14] OVH,[15] Hetzner,[16] or Scaleway,[17] provide a great way to quickly stand up cheap, generic compute (virtual machine) instances without needing to dive deep into specialized workflows and account management system of the major providers. However, once a generic virtual machine is set up on any provider, there is little difference in implementation.

---

[12]https://vultr.com

[13]www.digitalocean.com/

[14]www.linode.com/

[15]https://us.ovhcloud.com/public-cloud/

[16]https://www.hetzner.com/

[17]www.scaleway.com

Server Setup

Vultr, Scaleway, and Hetzner are excellent choices for development of experimental clusters, and typically offering virtual servers at a fraction of the cost of the major public clouds. They often include SSD storage and a sufficient amount of network transfer included in the price. This chapter demonstrates setting up a Kubernetes development cluster on Vultr; however, the following instructions are easily translatable to other providers.

Sign up for an account on Vultr or choose an equivalent alternative. This exercise requires an Ubuntu 18.04 server with at least two CPU cores and 4096MB of memory.

First, choose a server location (see Figure 2-4). Choose a server location geographically close to the majority of your team. While GitLab will be able to communicate with Kubernetes Clusters anywhere in the world, choosing an instance in a city closest to the majority of your team will reduce network latency for development operations.

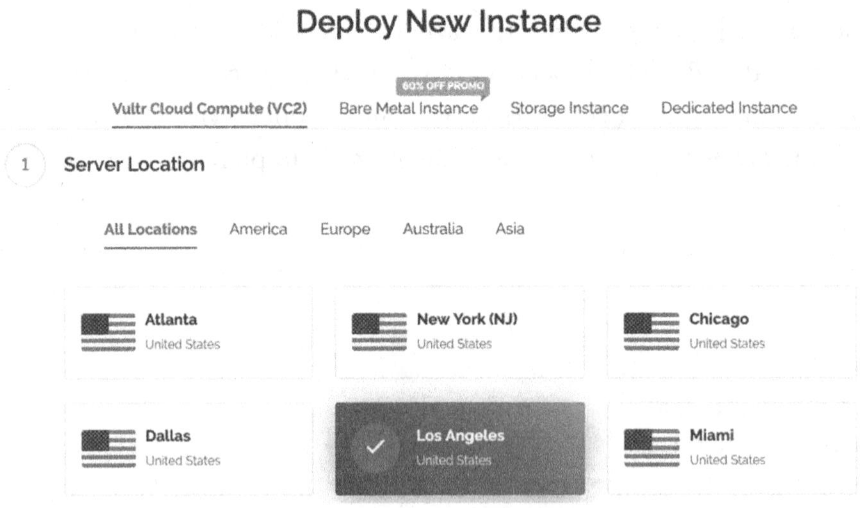

Figure 2-4. *Server locations*

Next, choose a server type of Ubuntu 18.04 (see Figure 2-5). "Ubuntu is a free and open-source Linux distribution based on Debian" and well supported by Canonical Ltd. Ubuntu 18.04 a long-term support release and will be supported until 2028.

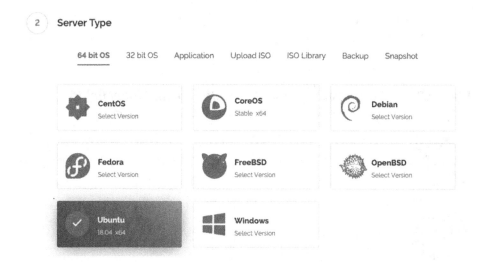

Figure 2-5. *Server types*

Next, select a server size (see Figure 2-6). GitLab on k3s will need at least two CPU cores and 4086MB of memory to run efficiently, supporting a small team.

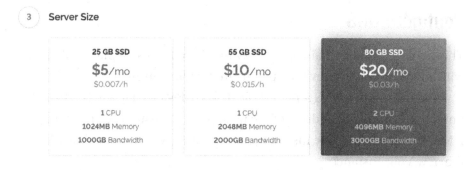

Figure 2-6. *Server sizes*

Finally, give the new instance a hostname with a domain you own. Vultr, like many providers, provisions the server with the hostname preconfigured if you supply it in the provisioning configuration (see Figure 2-7 and Figure 2-8.)

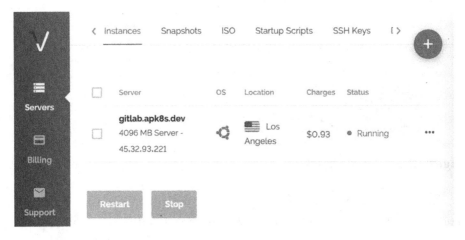

7 **Server Hostname & Label**

Enter server hostname
gitlab.apk8s.dev

Enter server label
gitlab.apk8s.dev

Figure 2-7. *Vultr dashbaord server hostname and label fields*

Figure 2-8. *Vultr dashboard*

Configure DNS

This book uses the domain apk8s.dev for all examples. Replace apk8s.dev with your domain wherever it appears in the following text.

Add at least two DNS A records for apk8s.dev (see Figure 2-9) that point to the public IP address of the new server. Consult your Domain/DNS provider for specific instructions. Figure 2-9 shows the public IP of the new Vultr instance.

A	*.gitlab	45.32.93.221
A	gitlab	45.32.93.221

Figure 2-9. *DNS entries*

Install k3s

Open the Server Information page (see Figure 2-10) on Vultr and locate the root password.

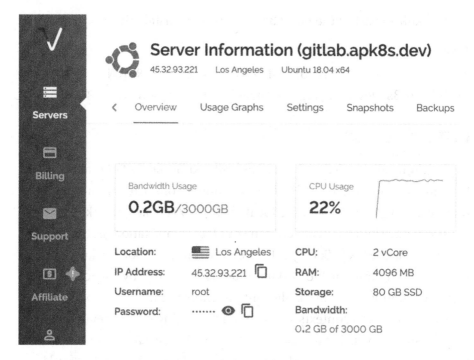

Figure 2-10. *Server Information*

Log in to the new server and upgrade any outdated packages. Upgrading packages ensures the new server is equipped with the latest security, bug fixes, and performance improvements.

```
$ ssh root@PUBLIC.IP.ADDRESS
```

```
$ apt update && apt upgrade -y
```

Download the k3s installer with `curl` and pipe it to the shell for execution:

```
$ curl -sfL https://get.k3s.io | sh -
```

Use kubectl to test the new k3s (Kubernetes) installation:

```
$ kubectl get Nodes
NAME              STATUS   ROLES    AGE    VERSION
gitlab.apk8s.dev  Ready    <none>   5m     v1.14.1-k3s.4
```

Remote Access

k3s is now installed on the new server, and a Kubernetes API that is listening on port 6443 is ready to accept connections. Credentials for remote access to the Cluster are located at /etc/rancher/k3s/k3s.yaml.

If you have kubectl installed[18] on your local workstation, notice that the /etc/rancher/k3s/k3s.yaml file on the new k3s node is a kubectl config file similar to the file ~/.kube/config generated by kubectl on your local workstation. The config file contains three main sections of interest: Clusters, users, and contexts, each containing a single entry related to the new Cluster. Add each entry from the k3s.yml on the k3s server to the ~/.kube/config file on your local workstation, replacing the word default with a sensible alternative, such as gitlab (see Figure 2-11), and replace localhost in the Cluster section with the public IP address of the server.

---

[18]https://kubernetes.io/docs/tasks/tools/install-kubectl/

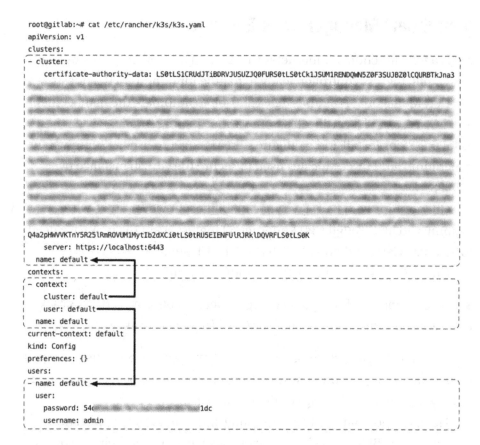

Figure 2-11. kubectl configuration

Adding a new Cluster, user, and context to the existing ~/.kube/config file on your local workstation is one simple method of configuring kubectl. kubectl supports the use of multiple config files and other alternative configuration methods; see the documentation on kubectl for more on this. kubectl is the central application used throughout this book; a well-organized configuration is essential when working with multiple Clusters.

Install Cert Manager/Let's Encrypt

k3s is a fully functional Kubernetes Cluster and comes preconfigured with the Traefik Ingress controller, ready to handle inbound HTTP requests.

Cert Manager[19] "is a Kubernetes add-on to automate the management and issuance of TLS certificates from various issuing sources." The following steps install and configure Cert Manager to use Let's Encrypt for generating free TLS certificates used to secure the GitLab instance over HTTPS.

GitLab ships with Let's Encrypt capabilities; however, since we are running GitLab through k3s (Kubernetes) Ingress (using Traefik), we need to generate Certs and provide TLS from the Cluster.

Create Cert Manager's custom resource definitions:

```
$ kubectl apply -f https://raw.githubusercontent.com/jetstack/
cert-manager/release-0.8/deploy/manifests/00-crds.yaml
```

Next, create a directory called `00-cluster` used to store Cluster scoped configuration; within the new directory, create the file `00-cert-manager-helm.yml` with the following configuration (see Listing 2-1).

Helm is a popular utility for installing and maintaining applications in Kubernetes. Billing itself as a type of package manager, Helm abstracts away the often-numerous configurations required to operate an application in Kubernetes. This abstraction is a collection of templatized YAML files representing Kubernetes objects. Helm renders and applies these templates, populated with user-supplied values. It is typical to use Helm as a command-line utility; however, k3s contains the custom resource definition (CRD) `HelmChart` and, when applied, installs or updates Helm deployments internally.

---

[19]https://github.com/jetstack/cert-manager

Note   The numbers prefixing configuration files in this book are intended to represent an order in which to apply them or express a chain of dependencies. Other methods of organization involve placing multiple configurations in the same file, which can make large configurations challenging to navigate. The majority of Kubernetes objects expressed in this book are written as individual files, organized by directories.

Listing 2-1. Cert Manager

```
apiVersion: k3s.cattle.io/v1
kind: HelmChart
metadata:
  namespace: kube-system
  name: cert-manager
spec:
  chart: cert-manager
  repo: https://charts.jetstack.io
  targetNamespace: cert-manager
```

Apply the configuration:

```
$ kubectl apply -f 00-cert-manager-helm.yml
```

Ensure that Cert Manager is now running in the cert-manager Namespace:

```
$ kubectl get all -n cert-manager
```

```
NAME                                         READY   STATUS    RESTARTS   AGE
pod/cert-manager-5d669ffbd8-2s6pm            1/1     Running   0          5m11s
pod/cert-manager-cainjector-79b7fc64f-n9qdt  1/1     Running   0          5m11s
pod/cert-manager-webhook-6484955794-j6cpr    1/1     Running   0          5m11s

NAME                          TYPE        CLUSTER-IP     EXTERNAL-IP   PORT(S)    AGE
service/cert-manager-webhook  ClusterIP   10.43.103.18   <none>        443/TCP    5m11s

NAME                                       READY   UP-TO-DATE   AVAILABLE   AGE
deployment.apps/cert-manager               1/1     1            1           5m11s
deployment.apps/cert-manager-cainjector    1/1     1            1           5m11s
deployment.apps/cert-manager-webhook       1/1     1            1           5m11s

NAME                                              DESIRED   CURRENT   READY   AGE
replicaset.apps/cert-manager-5d669ffbd8           1         1         1       5m11s
replicaset.apps/cert-manager-cainjector-79b7fc64f 1         1         1       5m11s
replicaset.apps/cert-manager-webhook-6484955794   1         1         1       5m11s
```

Figure 2-12. *Cert Manager resources*

Next, a ClusterIssuer that is configured to retrieve TLS certificates from Let's Encrypt is needed. Later on, a Certificate configuration is added that utilizes this ClusterIssuer named letsencrypt-production.

Create the file 05-cluster-issuer.yml with the configuration in Listing 2-2. Replace YOUR_EMAIL_ADDRESS with a valid email address.

Listing 2-2. 05-cluster-issuer.yml

```
apiVersion: certmanager.k8s.io/v1alpha1
kind: ClusterIssuer
metadata:
  name: letsencrypt-production
spec:
  acme:
    server: https://acme-v02.api.letsencrypt.org/directory
    # Email address used for ACME registration
    email: YOUR_EMAIL_ADDRESS
    privateKeySecretRef:
      name: letsencrypt-production
    # Enable the HTTP-01 challenge provider
    http01: {}
```

Apply the configuration:

```
$ kubectl apply -f 05-cluster-issuer.yml
```

Install GitLab

The Namespace gitlab is used to contain the GitLab application. Create another directory on the same level as 00-cluster named 01-gitlab. The new directory 01-gitlab is used to store the remaining configuration files, named after the Namespace it represents.

Namespace

Create the file 00-namespace.yml with the configuration in Listing 2-3.

Note   Imperative commands for some configurations in this book would save time and require less up-front effort; for example, kubectl create namespace gitlab is one step—however, declarative configuration has the added benefits of explicit documentation and versioning of the desired state. This Namespace configuration is simple, yet more involved configurations are likely when needing to add labels and resource limitations.

Listing 2-3. GitLab Namespace

```
apiVersion: v1
kind: Namespace
metadata:
  name: gitlab
```

Apply the configuration:

```
$ kubectl apply -f 00-namespace.yml
```

TLS Certificate

Ensure two DNS A records for your domain name point to the public IP of the new Cluster. In this example `gitlab.apk8s.dev` and `*.gitlab.apk8s.dev` both resolve to the new Cluster. The following Certificate configuration produces a valid certificate for these domains using the ClusterIssuer `letsencrypt-production` created earlier.

The following exercise creates a Certificate resource describing multiple domains; cert-manager uses this Certificate resource to generate a single TLS key pair and populate a Secret with it. Any Ingress with the domains listed in this Certificate may use the generated Secret as a valid TLS certificate. Additionally, cert-manager offers an alternative method of requesting Certificates directly within an Ingress resource through an annotation.[20]

Create the file `05-certs.yml` with the configuration in Listing 2-4.

Listing 2-4. GitLab TLS Certificate

```
apiVersion: certmanager.k8s.io/v1alpha1
kind: Certificate
metadata:
  name: gitlab-apk8s
  namespace: gitlab
spec:
  secretName: gitlab-apk8s-tls
  issuerRef:
    name: letsencrypt-production
    kind: ClusterIssuer
```

---

[20]https://cert-manager.netlify.com/docs/usage/ingress/

```
commonName: gitlab.apk8s.dev
dnsNames:
  - gitlab.apk8s.dev
  - reg.gitlab.apk8s.dev
acme:
  config:
    - http01:
        ingressClass: traefik
      domains:
        - gitlab.apk8s.dev
        - reg.gitlab.apk8s.dev
```

Apply the configuration:

```
$ kubectl apply -f 05-certs.yml
```

Check the status of the Certificate:

```
$ kubectl describe certificate -n gitlab
```

If the "Certificate issued successfully," there is now the Secret gitlab-apk8s-tls in the gitlab Namespace containing the keys tls.crt and tls.key making up the TLS certificate. The Secret is a type of kubernetes.io/tls used by Ingress to secure HTTPS traffic.

Services

Defined in this configuration are the services gitlab and gitlab-ssh. The gitlab service provides a backend service for Ingress by exposing port 80 (gitlab:80) for the GitLab website and port 5050 (gitlab:5050) for the container registry, connecting to pods matching the label app: gitlab and the ports 80 and 5050, later defined in a Deployment. The service gitlab-ssh exposes the **NodePort** 32222 used by the git ssh protocol for operations such as git clone, push, and pull.

Note   NodePorts are exposed across the cluster.

Create the file `10-services.yml` with the configuration in Listing 2-5. Apply the configuration:

```
$ kubectl apply -f 10-services.yml
```

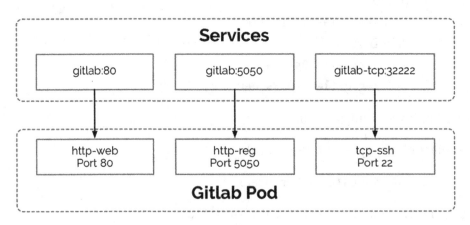

Figure 2-13. *GitLab Services*

Listing 2-5. GitLab Services Configuration

```
apiVersion: v1
kind: Service
metadata:
  name: gitlab
  namespace: gitlab
  labels:
    app: gitlab
spec:
  selector:
    app: gitlab
```

```
    ports:
      - name: http-web
        protocol: "TCP"
        port: 80
        targetPort: 80
      - name: http-reg
        protocol: "TCP"
        port: 5050
        targetPort: 5050
    type: ClusterIP
---
apiVersion: v1
kind: Service
metadata:
  name: gitlab-ssh
  namespace: gitlab
  labels:
    app: gitlab-ssh
spec:
  selector:
    app: gitlab
  ports:
    - name: tcp-git
      protocol: "TCP"
      targetPort: 22
      port: 32222
      NodePort: 32222
  type: NodePort
```

ConfigMap

A Kubernetes ConfigMap is used to manage the main GitLab configuration file `gitlab.rb`. This example configuration only defines the settings needed to get a minimal operating instance of GitLab up and running along with a built-in container registry. An extensive list of configuration options is available and well documented on docs.gitlab.com.[21] Make sure to set the `initial_root_password` to a strong password; GitLab uses this setting during the original setup to provide an initial admin user named root with the configured password.

Create the file `20-configmap.yml` with the configuration in Listing 2-6. Apply the configuration:

```
$ kubectl apply -f 20-configmap.yml
```

Listing 2-6. GitLab configuration

```
apiVersion: v1
kind: ConfigMap
metadata:
  name: gitlab-config
  namespace: gitlab
data:
  gitlab.rb: |-
    gitlab_rails['gitlab_shell_ssh_port'] = 32222
    prometheus['monitor_kubernetes'] = false

    gitlab_rails['initial_root_password'] = "password"

    external_url 'https://gitlab.apk8s.dev'
```

---

[21]https://docs.gitlab.com/omnibus/settings/configuration.html

```
nginx['listen_port'] = 80
nginx['listen_https'] = false
nginx['proxy_set_headers'] = {
  'X-Forwarded-Proto' => 'https',
  'X-Forwarded-Ssl' => 'on'
}

registry_external_url 'https://reg.gitlab.apk8s.dev'

gitlab_rails['registry_enabled'] = true

registry_nginx['listen_port'] = 5050
registry_nginx['listen_https'] = false
registry_nginx['proxy_set_headers'] = {
  'X-Forwarded-Proto' => 'https',
  'X-Forwarded-Ssl' => 'on'
}
```

Deployment

A Deployment defines the GitLab application as a single Pod, and because this runs on a single-Node Cluster, we can use hostPath to mount directories on the server, providing persistent storage for the Pod. The directory /srv/gitlab/ is created automatically on the server. All configuration and data persist as files on the server, while gitlab-configmap-volume mounts the ConfigMap created earlier with the contents of gitlab.rb.

Create the file 40-deployment.yml with the configuration in Listing 2-7. Apply the configuration:

```
$ kubectl apply -f 40-deployment.yml
```

Listing 2-7. GitLab Deployment

```
apiVersion: apps/v1
kind: Deployment
metadata:
  namespace: gitlab
  name: gitlab
  labels:
    app: gitlab
spec:
  replicas: 1
  revisionHistoryLimit: 1
  selector:
    matchLabels:
      app: gitlab
  template:
    metadata:
      labels:
        app: gitlab
    spec:
      containers:
        - name: gitlab
          image: gitlab/gitlab-ce:11.10.4-ce.0
          imagePullPolicy: IfNotPresent
          volumeMounts:
            - name: config-volume
              mountPath: /etc/gitlab
            - name: logs-volume
              mountPath: /var/log/gitlab
            - name: data-volume
              mountPath: /var/opt/gitlab
```

```
            - name: reg-volume
              mountPath: /var/opt/gitlab/gitlab-rails/shared/
              registry
            - name: uploads-volume
              mountPath: /var/opt/gitlab/gitlab-rails/uploads
            - name: gitlab-configmap-volume
              mountPath: /etc/gitlab/gitlab.rb
              subPath: gitlab.rb
          ports:
            - name: http-web
              containerPort: 80
            - name: tcp-ssh
              containerPort: 22
            - name: http-reg
              containerPort: 5050
      volumes:
        - name: gitlab-configmap-volume
          configMap:
            name: gitlab-config
        - name: config-volume
          hostPath:
            path: /srv/gitlab/config
        - name: logs-volume
          hostPath:
            path: /srv/gitlab/logs
        - name: data-volume
          hostPath:
            path: /srv/gitlab/data
```

```
   - name: reg-volume
     hostPath:
       path: /srv/gitlab/reg
   - name: uploads-volume
     hostPath:
       path: /srv/gitlab/uploads
```

Ingress

k3s is preconfigured with a Traefik Ingress controller managing requests to HTTP port 80 and HTTPS port 443. Listing 2-8 is a basic Kubernetes Ingress configuration along with an added annotation requesting that Traefik route any HTTP requests to HTTPS.

Create the file 50-ingress.yml with the configuration in Listing 2-8. Apply the configuration:

```
$ kubectl apply -f 50-ingress.yml
```

Listing 2-8. GitLab Ingress

```
apiVersion: extensions/v1beta1
kind: Ingress
metadata:
  name: gitlab
  namespace: gitlab
  labels:
    app: gitlab
  annotations:
```

```
    traefik.ingress.kubernetes.io/redirect-entry-point: https
spec:
  rules:
    - host: gitlab.apk8s.dev
      http:
        paths:
          - backend:
              serviceName: gitlab
              servicePort: 80
            path: /
    - host: reg.gitlab.apk8s.dev
      http:
        paths:
          - backend:
              serviceName: gitlab
              servicePort: 5050
            path: /
  tls:
    - hosts:
        - reg.gitlab.apk8s.dev
        - gitlab.apk8s.dev
      secretName: gitlab-apk8s-tls
```

Disable Sign-up

GitLab, by default, allows new users to sign up for an account. However, the instance installed here is for internal use by a development team working on the software platform defined later in this book. Disabling the sign-up option requires the admin (root) user to configure this feature in the administration section of the user interface. See Figure 2-14.

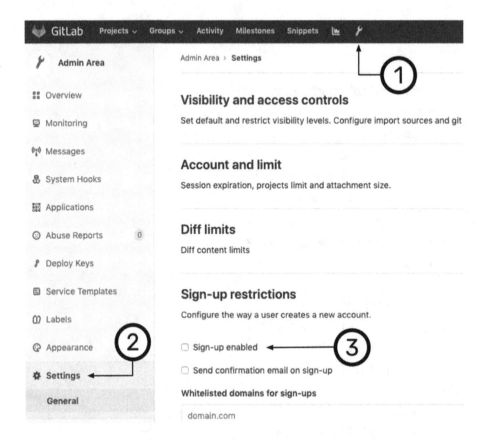

Figure 2-14. *Disable GitLab sign-up*

Summary

Setting up GitLab on a single-Node Kubernetes Cluster with k3s provides several benefits. k3s and a growing ecosystem of mini-Kubernetes distributions are extending the opportunities to utilize Kubernetes at any scale. Wrapping GitLab in Kubernetes provides the ability to extend it in the same manner as other Kubernetes-based platforms, by merely adding additional container-backed services able to interact within a mesh of services. GitLab not only interacts with external Clusters though its ability to install and operate CI/CD containers within them, GitLab itself is now under the same control plane as the platforms developed within it.

Next Steps

Now that GitLab is up and running in a single-Node Kubernetes Cluster, the next chapter sets up a development Kubernetes Cluster representing a scaled-back version of its eventual production equivalent. GitLab utilizes this Cluster for software integration, build, testing, and deployment operations.

CHAPTER 3

Development Environment

Developing a platform supporting components such as Blockchain, Machine Learning, and IoT data management requires at least three areas of essential functionality provided by the Kubernetes Cluster: Ingress, TLS, and persistent data storage. This chapter stands up a small-scale development cluster that meets these minimal requirements for platform development. The following cluster can easily be scaled both in the number of nodes and the size of each node as requirements demand additional resources.

Many Kubernetes tutorials walk you through examples using a local copy of Minikube. Minikube costs nothing more than a bit of CPU and memory on your local workstation. However, a healthy development environment should reflect a scaled-down version of production, and while Minikube is great for experimentation and some local development, it is limited in its ability to reflect the challenges of a production environment. A development Cluster may need to be shared between remote developers or be available to external resources for collecting data, metrics, and events; this all becomes a challenge with a local workstation-based Kubernetes install. If you are serious about testing the Cloud-native and vendor-neutral aspects of your Platform on Kubernetes, it might be beneficial to have a development environment on one vendor, with a

© Craig Johnston 2020
C. Johnston, *Advanced Platform Development with Kubernetes*,
https://doi.org/10.1007/978-1-4842-5611-4_3

staging test and production on another. Developing your application to run on a generic virtual machine (VM)-based Cluster and later publishing to a test environment reflective of your production Cluster can ensure your portability between vendors, with only minimal differences in configuration and no significant architectural changes.

Custom Development Kubernetes Cluster

Today there are several production-ready, turnkey Kubernetes offerings, such as Google Kubernetes Engine (GKE), Amazon Elastic Container Service for Kubernetes (Amazon EKS), Azure Kubernetes Service (AKS), and IBM Cloud Kubernetes Service. These options may be a safe choice for the production deployment of a commercial platform, and these providers offer opportunities for deep integration into their more extensive suite of services. In keeping the Platform portable and vendor neutral, a custom, self-managed Kubernetes Cluster can provide a cost-effective neutral environment for development. Segregating development into a custom Kubernetes Cluster has many benefits for Platform developers, forcing a deeper understanding of the underlying infrastructure without losing the benefits of abstraction. Platform development on a custom Kubernetes Cluster ensures portability and provides an opportunity for redundancy, leveraged by compatibility with multiple vendors.

GitLab was set up in the previous chapter on a single Vultr instance running k3s. While Kubernetes was developed to schedule and manage container workloads on hundreds or even thousands of Nodes, k3s utilized its features on just a single Node. Setting up a custom development Kubernetes Cluster involves multiple servers, one (or more) for the master Node, and one or more worker Nodes.

The following section takes a more in-depth look at Kubernetes Nodes and walks through the process of setting up a custom Kubernetes Cluster on Digital Ocean. Like Vultr, Digital Ocean offers affordable compute instances they call Droplets. Instructions for setting up Custom Kubernetes are easily translatable to any alternative service offering generic compute instances or virtual or bare-metal machines. There is an ongoing debate on the manageability and cost-effectiveness of operating custom Kubernetes Clusters for critical, high-profile production platforms. However, there is great benefit from the knowledge and skills gained through installing, configuring, and maintaining a custom Cluster when at the end you have a working development environment, and quite possibly a backup or a redundant version ready for production.

Nodes

A Kubernetes Cluster is made up of Nodes. One or more master Nodes, and as of Kubernetes 1.14 no more than 5000 Nodes in total. If you ran all 5000 Nodes on 1U servers, you would fill over 100 racks in a typical data center, not including routers, power management, and all the other infrastructure needed. Kubernetes not only abstracts individual servers from the Platform, but a few federated Kubernetes Clusters may also very well abstract away a small data center.

The initial size of a Kubernetes Cluster is a production concern, best calculated by the performance of a test or development Cluster operating a developed application platform along with projected utilization. Scaling Kubernetes is as easy as adding compute resource and joining it as a Node. It's important to note that the size of any Master Node may need to be scaled as the Cluster grows. However, for the small development Cluster setup in this book, a small, single master Node is sufficient.

> **Note**   A single master node in a Kubernetes cluster is not
> necessarily a single point of failure for the entire Cluster. The failure
> of the Kubernetes master node is an urgent concern; however,
> networking and container workloads (not reliant on the Kubernetes
> API) continue to operate without the Kubernetes control plane.[1]

The examples in this book utilize a small development Cluster set up in this section, starting with one Master Node and two Worker Nodes (see Figure 3-1). The previous chapter used k3s to operate a scaled-down Master Node to run workloads. However, in a multi-node Cluster, Master Nodes should only be concerned with managing the Cluster.

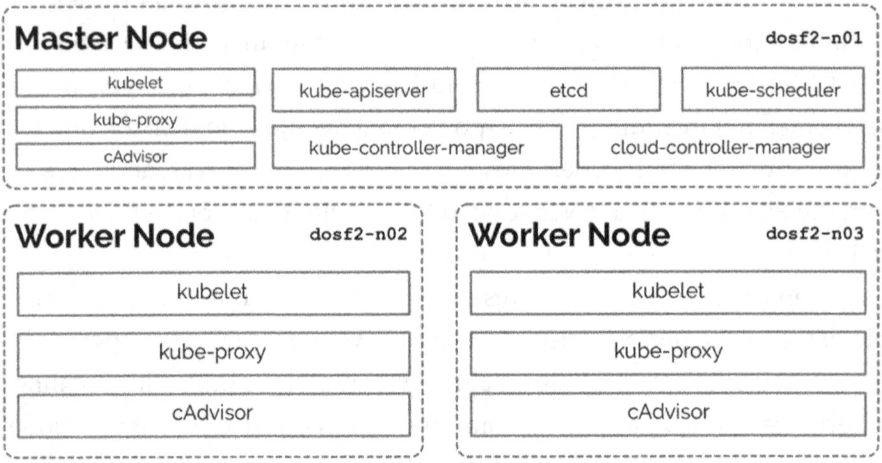

Figure 3-1. *Kubernetes Nodes*

---

[1]https://kubernetes.io/docs/concepts/#kubernetes-control-plane

Server Setup

This section sets up three Ubuntu 18.04 x64 servers (Droplets) on Digital Ocean at the minimal required hardware specification of 2 CPUs and 2 GB RAM.

Note   Digital Ocean allows Droplets to be scaled up when future demand may require more CPU or RAM for the Master or Worker Nodes.

After setting up an account and logging in to Digital Ocean, click the *Create* button and choose *Droplets* from the resulting menu. Choose an image for the Droplets by selecting *Ubuntu 18.04 x64* under *Distributions* (see Figure 3-2).

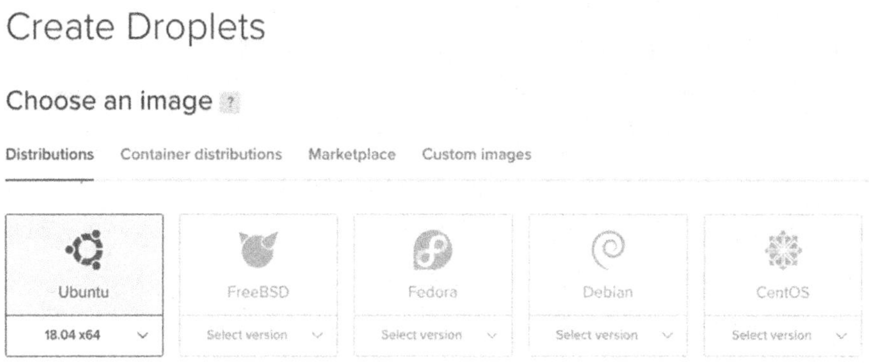

Figure 3-2. *Create Droplets*

Next, under Standard starter plans, find and select the option with 2 GB/2 CPUs, as shown in Figure 3-3. At the time of this writing, the cost for a Droplet with these options is $15 per month ($0.022 hour). At this price point, the development Cluster assembled here costs $45 per month ($0.066 per hour).

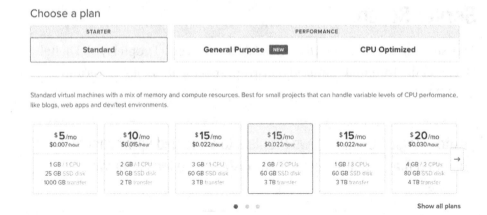

Figure 3-3. *Choose a plan*

Next, choose a data center region closest to you or your development team. Digital Ocean offers one or more choices with a region. Figure 3-4 shows San Francisco/2 selected.

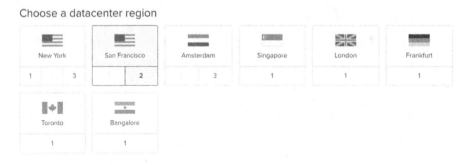

Figure 3-4. *Choose a region*

Next, select the additional options Private Networking and Monitoring (see Figure 3-5). Private Networking is later used by the Kubernetes API to communicate privately between Nodes. Additionally, with Digital Ocean and most providers, data transfer over Private Networking does not count against data transfer limitations.

Select additional options ?

☑ Private networking   ☐ IPv6   ☐ User data   ☑ Monitoring

Figure 3-5. *Private networking and monitoring*

Finally, select a quantity of three Droplets for this development Cluster and provide descriptive hostnames, as shown in Figure 3-6. This book uses hostnames dosf2-n01.apk8s.dev, hostnames dosf2-n02.apk8s.dev, and hostnames dosf2-n03.apk8s.dev.

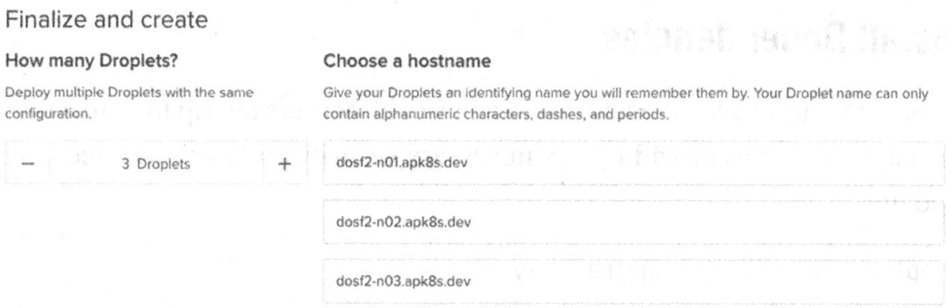

Finalize and create

How many Droplets?

Deploy multiple Droplets with the same configuration.

Choose a hostname

Give your Droplets an identifying name you will remember them by. Your Droplet name can only contain alphanumeric characters, dashes, and periods.

—	3 Droplets	+	dosf2-n01.apk8s.dev
			dosf2-n02.apk8s.dev
			dosf2-n03.apk8s.dev

Figure 3-6. *Droplet quantity and hostnames*

Once the new Droplets (Servers) are up and running, note the public and private IP address assigned to each Droplet. Figure 3-7 shows the assigned public IP address for dosf2-n01.apk8s.dev as 138.68.18.212 and the private IP address as 10.138.28.155.

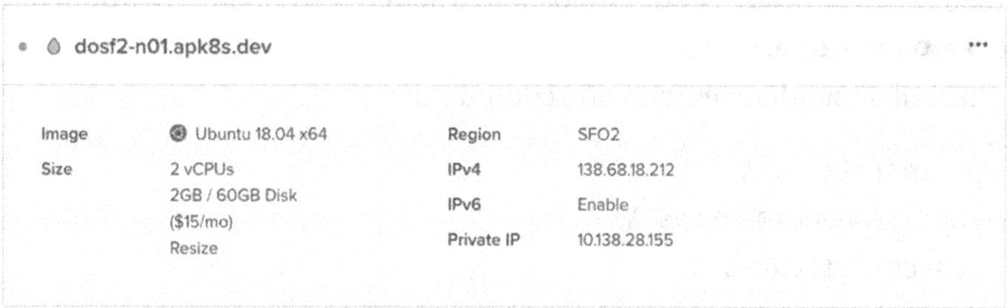

● ◊ dosf2-n01.apk8s.dev   •••

Image	⊕ Ubuntu 18.04 x64	Region	SFO2
Size	2 vCPUs	IPv4	138.68.18.212
	2GB / 60GB Disk	IPv6	Enable
	($15/mo)	Private IP	10.138.28.155
	Resize		

Figure 3-7. *Droplet details*

Prepare Nodes

Using a terminal, ssh as the user root into each new Droplet (server). Digital Ocean would email you a generated, one-time use root password if you did not add an SSH key when setting up the Droplet. Update packages and install Docker and Kubernetes utilities on each server, with the following instructions:

```
$ ssh root@PUBLIC_IP
```

Install Dependencies

Update and upgrade all packages to ensure the servers are up to date with the latest packages providing any necessary security and performance updates:

```
$ apt update && apt upgrade -y
```

Install the following packages: `apt-transport-https` allows the apt package manager to pull packages from HTTPS endpoints. `ca-certificates` installs SSL/TLS certificates from the Certificate Authorities along with an updater. `curl` is a command-line HTTP client essential for interacting with HTTP-based endpoints from the command line. `gnupg-agent` provides a system daemon for GPG signing and the management of keys. `software-properties-common` supports the management of independent software vendor repositories added later on for **WireGuard**, **Docker**, and **Kubernetes**.

Install dependencies with one command:

```
$ apt install -y \
    apt-transport-https \
    ca-certificates \
    curl \
    gnupg-agent \
    software-properties-common
```

Install WireGuard VPN

All cloud providers offer private networking, the ability to assign IP address only accessible within the provider's internal network, and often only within the same region. Although these private IP addresses are not accessible by public Internet, depending on the provider, other customers may access them if running instances in the same region. Encrypting all traffic between nodes in the Cluster is always a good practice.

This exercise is optional. Using a VPN to encrypt traffic over a private network is not necessary for most situations. In the past, some cloud providers shared private networks with multiple clients, and while not exposed to the public,[2] network traffic was potentially visible to other clients on the same network. Although most providers have abandoned shared private networking,[3] nevertheless this exercise demonstrates the use of a VPN to secure all network traffic in high-security environments on untrusted networks.

Operating a Kubernetes cluster over a VPN encrypts network traffic between nodes; however, within the cluster, network traffic is not encrypted by default. Service meshes such as Istio[4] and Linkerd[5] offer options for mutual TLS communication between Pods.

WireGuard[6] is a fast, secure VPN, easy to install, configure, and route all internal Cluster traffic through. The next steps walk through the process of generating public and private keys for each server, adding a WireGuard configuration file, starting the service, and creating an overlay network to tunnel Kubernetes traffic through.

---

[2]https://blog.digitalocean.com/introducing-private-networking/
[3]www.digitalocean.com/docs/platform/release-notes/2018/
 private-networking/
[4]https://istio.io/docs/tasks/security/authentication/mutual-tls/
[5]https://linkerd.io/2/features/automatic-mtls/
[6]www.wireguard.com/

Add the WireGuard repository:

```
$ add-apt-repository -y ppa:wireguard/wireguard
```

Update the package list now that the WireGuard repository has been added:

```
$ apt update
```

Install WireGuard:

```
$ apt install -y wireguard
```

Generate private and public keys for each server. The following is a small shell command for generating three key pairs. Once the keys are generated, store them securely for use in configuring WireGuard on each server. The private keys (priv) are used for the VPN interface on each server and public (pub) keys are used to communicate with peers.

```
$ for i in {1..3}; do prvk=$(wg genkey); \
echo "$i - priv: $prvk pub: $(echo $prvk | wg pubkey)"; done
```

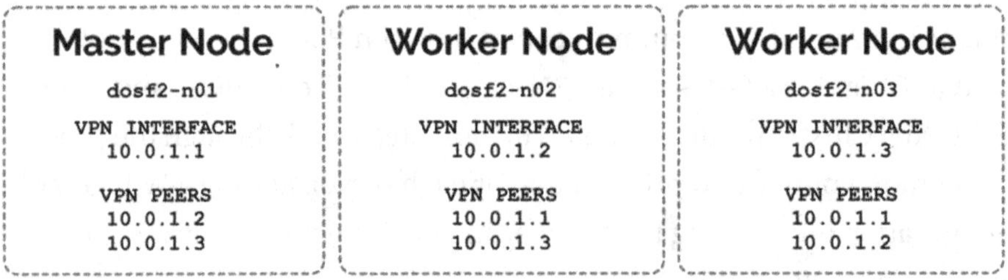

Master Node	Worker Node	Worker Node
dosf2-n01	dosf2-n02	dosf2-n03
VPN INTERFACE	VPN INTERFACE	VPN INTERFACE
10.0.1.1	10.0.1.2	10.0.1.3
VPN PEERS	VPN PEERS	VPN PEERS
10.0.1.2	10.0.1.1	10.0.1.1
10.0.1.3	10.0.1.3	10.0.1.2

Figure 3-8. *VPN interfaces and peers*

Next, configure WireGuard for each server. The following example configuration for the first server will set up a new network interface named **wg0** with the IP address **10.0.1.1**. Adjust the configuration according to each server; the second server's interface IP should be **10.0.1.2** and **10.0.1.3** for the third (see Figure 3-8). Use the public or private keys generated previously.

```
$ cat <<EOF >/etc/wireguard/wg0.conf
[Interface]
Address = 10.0.1.1
PrivateKey = SERVER_1_PRIVATE_KEY
ListenPort = 51820

[Peer]
PublicKey = SERVER_2_PUBLIC_KEY
AllowedIps = 10.0.1.2/32
Endpoint = SERVER_2_PRIVATE_IP:51820

[Peer]
PublicKey = SERVER_3_PUBLIC_KEY
AllowedIps = 10.0.1.3/32
Endpoint = SERVER_3_PRIVATE_IP:51820
EOF
```

Next, ensure that IP forwarding is enabled. If running `sysctl`
`net.ipv4.ip_forward` returns 0, then you need to run the following
commands:

```
$ echo "net.ipv4.ip_forward=1" >> /etc/sysctl.conf
$ sysctl -p
```

After adding the configuration file, start the WireGuard VPN on each
server:

```
$ systemctl start wg-quick@wg0
$ systemctl enable wg-quick@wg0
```

Install Docker

Kubernetes supports several Container Runtime Interface[7] (CRI)–based runtimes including rkt,[8] frakti,[9] cri-o,[10] and cri-containerd.[11] Docker is the default CRI and a well-established industry standard, although each alternative has benefits worth exploring. The following commands walk through the process of installing Docker.

Add the Docker repository GPG key:

```
$ curl -fsSL https://download.docker.com/linux/ubuntu/gpg |
sudo apt-key add -
```

Add the Docker repository:

```
$ add-apt-repository -y \
    "deb [arch=amd64] https://download.docker.com/linux/ubuntu \
    $(lsb_release -cs) stable"
```

Update the package list now that the Docker repository has been added:

```
$ apt update
```

Install the latest versions of the Docker CE (Community Edition) daemon, the Docker command-line interface, and containerd:[12]

```
$ apt install -y docker-ce docker-ce-cli containerd.io
```

---

[7]https://kubernetes.io/docs/setup/cri/
[8]https://github.com/rkt/rkt
[9]https://github.com/kubernetes/frakti
[10]https://cri-o.io/
[11]https://github.com/containerd/cri
[12]https://containerd.io/

The Ubuntu operating system uses Systemd[13] to track processes using Linux cgroups,[14] and by default Docker uses cgroupfs. Having separate cgroup managers can cause instability when managing resources under load. Configure Docker to use Systemd by supplying a configuration file.[15]

```
$ cat > /etc/docker/daemon.json <<EOF
{
  "exec-opts": ["native.cgroupdriver=systemd"],
  "log-driver": "json-file",
  "log-opts": {
    "max-size": "100m"
  },
  "storage-driver": "overlay2"
}
EOF
```

Create a Systemd drop-in directory for Docker:

```
$ mkdir -p /etc/systemd/system/docker.service.d
```

Enable the Docker service:

```
$ systemctl enable docker.service
```

Restart Docker:

```
$ systemctl daemon-reload && systemctl restart docker
```

---

[13]www.freedesktop.org/wiki/Software/systemd/

[14]www.kernel.org/doc/Documentation/cgroup-v2.txt

[15]https://github.com/kubernetes/kubeadm/issues/1394#issuecomment-462878219

Install Kubernetes Utilities

In addition to Docker, each Node will also need kubelet[16] and kubeadm.[17] kubectl[18] is optional but helpful to have when needing to debug directly from a Node.

Add Google GPG key for apt:

```
$ curl -s https://packages.cloud.google.com/apt/doc/apt-key.gpg \
| apt-key add -
```

Add Kubernetes apt repository:

```
$ cat <<EOF >/etc/apt/sources.list.d/kubernetes.list
deb https://apt.kubernetes.io/ kubernetes-xenial main
EOF
```

Update the package list now that the Kubernetes repository has been added:

```
$ apt update
```

Install Kubernetes packages:

```
$ apt install -y kubelet kubeadm kubectl
```

Lock the installed packages to their current version:

```
$ apt-mark hold kubelet kubeadm kubectl
```

---

[16]https://kubernetes.io/docs/reference/command-line-tools-reference/kubelet/

[17]https://kubernetes.io/docs/reference/setup-tools/kubeadm/kubeadm/

[18]https://kubernetes.io/docs/reference/kubectl/overview/

Install Master Node

kubeadm is the official Kubernetes install utility and does all the work of configuring the master Node. If you wish to dive deeper and learn how to install and configure each component, study "Kubernetes The Hard Way"[19] by Kelsey Hightower. Otherwise, run the kubeadm installer on node 1, configured with the private VPN IP address (`--apiserver-advertise-address`) of the master Node to advertise on, and add a public address (`--apiserver-cert-extra-sans`) as an extra for inclusion into the generated TLS certificate, allowing external access to the API on the public interface. The domain `api.cluster.dev1.apk8s.dev` is assigned a DNS A record with the public IP address of the master Node later in the section DNS.

```
$ kubeadm init \
--apiserver-advertise-address=10.0.1.1 \
--apiserver-cert-extra-sans=api.cluster.dev1.apk8s.dev
```

After a successful installation, the message "Your Kubernetes control-plane has initialized successfully!" will present along with instructions for configuring kubectl.

```
$ mkdir -p $HOME/.kube
$ cp /etc/kubernetes/admin.conf $HOME/.kube/config
```

Additional instruction for joining worker Nodes is provided after the install process, similar to the following command (keys redacted). Copy and save the provided command for use in the next section, "Join Worker Nodes."

```
kubeadm join 10.0.1.1:6443 --token REDACTED --discovery-token-
ca-cert-hash REDACTED
```

---

[19]https://github.com/kelseyhightower/kubernetes-the-hard-way

Next, a pod network is necessary for communication between Pods on the Cluster. At this time there are over a dozen choices, each with a wide range of features worth exploring when setting up a network-intensive production Cluster. Weave Net[20] is an excellent choice for development or production Clusters needing only simple networking and network policies. Weave can be installed in one command and does not require an external database or other dependencies.

Install Weave with the kubectl utility previously installed on the master Node (node 1):

```
$ kubectl apply -f "https://cloud.weave.works/k8s/net?k8s-
version=$(kubectl version | base64 | tr -d '\n')&env.IPALLOC_
RANGE=10.32.0.0/16"
```

Optional—Install Weave Scope[21] for network visualization and monitoring:

```
$ kubectl apply -f https://cloud.weave.works/k8s/scope.
yaml?k8s-version=$(kubectl version | base64 | tr -d '\n')
```

Route all Pod network (Weave) 10.96.0.0/16 traffic over the WireGuard VPN. Do this on each server in the Cluster 10.0.1.1 on the first node, 10.0.1.2 on the second, and 10.0.1.3 on the third.

```
$ ip route add 10.96.0.0/16 dev wg0 src 10.0.1.1
```

Persist this route with the following file on each server, replacing 10.0.1.1 with the VPN interface corresponding to the server:

```
$ cat <<EOF >/etc/systemd/system/overlay-route.service
[Unit]
Description=Overlay network route for Wireguard
After=wg-quick@wg0.service
```

---

[20]www.weave.works/oss/net/

[21]www.weave.works/docs/scope/latest/introducing/

```
[Service]
Type=oneshot
User=root
ExecStart=/sbin/ip route add 10.96.0.0/16 dev wg0 src 10.0.1.1

[Install]
WantedBy=multi-user.target
EOF
```

Apply the new configuration on each server:

```
$ systemctl enable overlay-route.service
```

Join Worker Nodes

The second and third servers are Kubernetes worker Nodes. Log in to each server and run the join command provided after the master Node installation.

```
$ kubeadm join 10.0.1.1:6443 --token REDACTED --discovery-token-ca-cert-hash REDACTED
```

Adding additional nodes requires only that the server meets the minimum hardware specifications of 2 CPUs and 2 GB RAM, along with the WireGuard, Docker, and Kubernetes applications installed previously in this section. Additional Nodes must be added to the WireGuard VPN network along with routing the Pod network's IP subnet 10.96.0.0/16 over its interface.

DNS

This custom Kubernetes development Cluster does not sit behind a sophisticated (and often expensive) load balancer; instead, it uses a basic DNS round-robin technique to distribute requests across the Cluster.

Implement DNS round-robin by adding multiple DNS A records for the same hostname. The development Cluster has two A records, each pointing to the public IP address of a worker Node using the wildcard hostname *.dev1 (see Figure 3-9). Wild cards allow any number of *.dev1.apk8s.dev subdomains to resolve to nodes on the Cluster. Refer to your domain name/DNS provider for instructions on adding A records.

TYPE	HOST ↑	VALUE
A	*.dev1	142.93.90.55
A	*.dev1	142.93.93.13

Figure 3-9. Development Cluster DNS

Next, add an additional A record api.cluster.dev1.apk8s.dev for the Kubernetes API pointed to the public IP of the master node (node 1).

Remote Access

The "k3s + GitLab" section covered one method of configuring kubectl for remote access by copying and pasting the Cluster, user, and context sections of a generated config. The following instructions give an alternative method of configuring kubectl.

After installing the master Node, kubeadm provided instructions for copying a generated kubectl configuration to $HOME/.kube/config. Logged in as root on the master Node, this path will resolve to /root/.kube/config. Secure copy the kubeadm-generated configuration to a location workstation with the following command:

```
$ scp root@api.cluster.dev1.apk8s.dev:/root/.kube/config
~/.kube/apk8s-dev1
```

Open the file and replace the IP address 10.0.1.1 with **api.cluster. dev1.apk8s.dev**. Optionally, change the context kubernetes-admin@ kubernetes to something more descriptive. The following commands use the command sed to edit the file inline:

```
$ sed -i .bak \
 's/10.0.1.1/api.cluster.dev1.apk8s.dev/g' \
 ~/.kube/apk8s-dev1

$ sed -i .bak 's/kubernetes-admin@kubernetes/apk8s-dev1/g'
~/.kube/apk8s-dev1
```

In the same terminal, set the environment variable KUBECONFIG to ~/.kube/apk8s-dev1:

```
$ export KUBECONFIG=~/.kube/apk8s-dev1
```

Exporting an environment variable makes it available for the current terminal session only. Although this is not the most efficient method of switching kubectl contexts, it's a good option when working with a large number of Clusters and prevents the default ~/.kube/config from becoming overly cluttered. Test the new configuration and context:

```
$ kubectl get nodes
```

```
NAME        STATUS   ROLES     AGE    VERSION
dosf2-n01   Ready    master    15m    v1.15.0
dosf2-n02   Ready    <none>    11m    v1.15.0
dosf2-n03   Ready    <none>    11m    v1.15.0
```

The new development Cluster is ready for the configuration of additional components to satisfy the dependencies in the remainder of this book. TLS Certificates, persistent storage, and Ingress are essential requirements for the IoT, Machine Learning, and Blockchain capabilities added later on. The next section, "Configuration," covers the organization and application of YAML manifests used to satisfy these requirements and makes use of the new GitLab instance for keeping them versioned and documented.

Configuration

Kubernetes supports declarative configuration; this means we tell Kubernetes what we want it to be, as opposed to issuing a list of commands required to achieve a state. This book uses YAML to describe the desired state for Kubernetes; this state is a collection of Deployments, StatefulSets, ConfigMaps, Services, and others that make up the operational Platform. Keeping state configuration as a set of static YAML files in a Git repository will not only reflect the current state of the Platform but provide a valuable commit log of changes over time.

There is a growing ecosystem in configuration management techniques and utilities for enterprise software platforms. This book attempts to keep things simple by sticking with plain YAML as the standard means of configuration. This book demonstrates a straightforward method for organizing Kubernetes configuration manifests describing various applications added to the Platform. As the platform and configuration needs grow, more sophisticated configuration tools may be layered in, such as Jsonnet,[22] Kapitan,[23] or Kustomize.[24] New concepts like GitOps[25] aim to completely manage the active configuration state directly with Git. Kubernetes provides endless ways to manage configuration creatively. However, starting with a well-organized directory structure categorized by environment, namespace, component, and object type provides a sane foundation to build on.

---

[22]https://jsonnet.org/
[23]https://github.com/deepmind/kapitan
[24]https://github.com/kubernetes-sigs/kustomize
[25]www.weave.works/technologies/gitops/

Repository

Now that the development Cluster is operational and kubectl can access it from the local workstation, a series of YAML files containing additional configuration for Namespaces, Volumes, Ingress, and monitoring are applied to the Cluster. Developing the Cluster produces a growing number of YAML configuration files. These configuration files (or manifests) not only define the desired state for Kubernetes, they provide verbose and accurate documentation for developers and systems administrators, especially when accompanied by supplemental (README.md) markdown-style documentation.

The configuration manifests and documentation in this book is organized in the self-hosted GitLab repository installed in the previous chapter. A GitLab group named **apk8s** holds the project **k8s**. A common method for organizing multiple Kubernetes-based project is to nest them under GitLab groups, each project having a dedicated k8s repository. An example of two separate platform projects may include https://gitlab. apk8s.dev/apk8s/k8s, holding the Cluster configs for this platform, and https://gitlab.apk8s.dev/another-platform/k8s, holding the Kubernetes configs for "another-platform".

Note   GitHub provides the feature **Organizations**, with similar functionality to GitLab groups.

Once the group **apk8s** and project **k8s** are set up in GitLab, make a directory on the local workstation that matches the group (apk8s) and clone the new project into it.

```
$ mkdir -p ~/workspace/apk8s
$ cd ~/workspace/apk8s
$ git clone ssh://git@gitlab.apk8s.dev:32222/apk8s/k8s.git
$ cd k8s
```

> **Note**   If developing multiple projects on the same cluster, it is
> recommended to store cluster-wide configuration as a separate
> group such as **devops/k8s** and refer each project to it for cluster-
> wide requirements and documentation.

Create a directory to hold Cluster-wide configurations. These
configurations are specific to Cluster (cluster-apk8s-dev1).

```
$ mkdir -p cluster-apk8s-dev1/000-cluster
```

Ingress

In this platform the majority of Kubernetes Services[26] are assigned a
ClusterIP and are only accessible from within the cluster. Kubernetes
Ingress allows external HTTP and HTTPS connections to Services within
the Cluster. The Kubernetes Ingress Resource defines a configuration that
must be backed by an Ingress controller.

Kubernetes does not provide a default Ingress controller, leaving this
decision for administrators and systems architects to pick one that best
fits the needs of the platform. There are a large number of capable Ingress
controllers available. In the previous chapter, Traefik came packaged with
the k3s Kubernetes distribution and demonstrated its use by servicing a
GitLab installation. This chapter configures the new *dev1* cluster with an
Ingress Nginx[27] controller demonstrating variety for Ingress options.

---

[26]https://kubernetes.io/docs/concepts/services-networking/service/
[27]https://kubernetes.github.io/ingress-nginx/

This chapter builds configurations from the directory ~/workspace/ apk8s/k8s cloned from the k8s repository and GitLab group apk8s set up in the previous section. From this location create a directory to store the Ingress Nginx configuration manifests:

```
$ mkdir -p cluster-apk8s-dev1/000-cluster/00-ingress-nginx
$ cd cluster-apk8s-dev1/000-cluster/00-ingress-nginx
```

Create a configuration file for the Ingress Nginx namespace called 00-namespace.yml from Listing 3-1.

Listing 3-1. Ingress Nginx Namespace

```
apiVersion: v1
kind: Namespace
metadata:
  name: ingress-nginx
```

Apply the Ingress Nginx Namespace configuration:

```
$ kubectl apply -f 00-namespace.yml
```

Create a configuration file describing Role-Based Access Control (RBAC) Kubernetes Service Account for Ingress Nginx named 05-serviceaccount.yml from Listing 3-2.

Listing 3-2. Ingress Nginx RBAC Service Account

```
apiVersion: v1
kind: ServiceAccount
metadata:
  name: nginx-ingress-serviceaccount
  namespace: ingress-nginx
```

Apply the Ingress Nginx Service Account configuration:

```
$ kubectl apply -f 05-serviceaccount.yml
```

Create a configuration file describing an RBAC Cluster Role for Ingress Nginx named 06-clusterrole.yml from Listing 3-3.

Listing 3-3. RBAC Ingress Nginx Cluster Role

```
apiVersion: rbac.authorization.k8s.io/v1beta1
kind: ClusterRole
metadata:
  name: nginx-ingress-clusterrole
rules:
  - apiGroups: [""]
    resources: ["configmaps",
                "endpoints",
                "nodes",
                "pods",
                "secrets"]
    verbs: ["list", "watch"]
  - apiGroups: [""]
    resources: ["nodes"]
    verbs: ["get"]
  - apiGroups: [""]
    resources: ["services"]
    verbs: ["get", "list", "watch"]
  - apiGroups: ["extensions"]
    resources: ["ingresses"]
    verbs: ["get","list","watch"]
  - apiGroups: [""]
    resources: ["events"]
    verbs: ["create", "patch"]
  - apiGroups: ["extensions"]
    resources: ["ingresses/status"]
    verbs: ["update"]
```

Apply the Ingress Nginx Cluster Role configuration:

```
$ kubectl apply -f 06-clusterrole.yml
```

Create a configuration file describing an RBAC Role for Ingress Nginx named 07-role.yml from Listing 3-4.

Listing 3-4. RBAC Ingress Nginx Role

```
apiVersion: rbac.authorization.k8s.io/v1beta1
kind: Role
metadata:
  name: nginx-ingress-role
  namespace: ingress-nginx
rules:
  - apiGroups: [""]
    resources: ["configmaps",
                "pods",
                "secrets",
                "namespaces"]
    verbs: ["get"]
  - apiGroups: [""]
    resources: ["configmaps"]
    resourceNames:
      - "ingress-controller-leader-nginx"
    verbs: ["get", "update"]
  - apiGroups: [""]
    resources: ["configmaps"]
    verbs: ["create"]
  - apiGroups: [""]
    resources: ["endpoints"]
    verbs: ["get"]
```

Apply the Ingress Nginx Role configuration:

```
$ kubectl apply -f 07-role.yml
```

Create a configuration file describing an RBAC Role Binding for Ingress Nginx named 08-rolebinding.yml from Listing 3-5.

Listing 3-5. RBAC Ingress Nginx Role Binding

```
apiVersion: rbac.authorization.k8s.io/v1beta1
kind: RoleBinding
metadata:
  name: nginx-ingress-role-nisa-binding
  namespace: ingress-nginx
roleRef:
  apiGroup: rbac.authorization.k8s.io
  kind: Role
  name: nginx-ingress-role
subjects:
  - kind: ServiceAccount
    name: nginx-ingress-serviceaccount
    namespace: ingress-nginx
```

Apply the Ingress Nginx Role Binding configuration:

```
$ kubectl apply -f 08-rolebinding.yml
```

Create a configuration file describing an RBAC Cluster Role Binding for Ingress Nginx named 09-clusterrolebinding.yml from Listing 3-6.

Listing 3-6. RBAC Ingress Nginx Cluster Role Binding

```
apiVersion: rbac.authorization.k8s.io/v1beta1
kind: ClusterRoleBinding
metadata:
```

```
  name: nginx-ingress-clusterrole-nisa-binding
roleRef:
  apiGroup: rbac.authorization.k8s.io
  kind: ClusterRole
  name: nginx-ingress-clusterrole
subjects:
  - kind: ServiceAccount
    name: nginx-ingress-serviceaccount
    namespace: ingress-nginx
```

Apply the Ingress Nginx Cluster Role Binding configuration:

```
$ kubectl apply -f 09-clusterrolebinding.yml
```

Create a configuration file describing two Kubernetes Services for Ingress Nginx named 10-services.yml from Listing 3-7.

Listing 3-7. Ingress Nginx Services

```
apiVersion: v1
kind: Service
metadata:
  name: default-http-backend
  namespace: ingress-nginx
  labels:
    app: default-http-backend
spec:
  ports:
    - port: 80
      targetPort: 8080
  selector:
    app: default-http-backend
---
```

```
apiVersion: v1
kind: Service
metadata:
  name: ingress-nginx
  namespace: ingress-nginx
spec:
  type: NodePort
  ports:
    - name: http
      port: 80
      targetPort: 80
      protocol: TCP
    - name: https
      port: 443
      targetPort: 443
      protocol: TCP
  selector:
    app: ingress-nginx
```

Apply the Ingress Nginx Services configuration:

```
$ kubectl apply -f 10-services.yml
```

Create a configuration file describing three empty Kubernetes ConfigMaps for Ingress Nginx named 20-configmaps.yml from Listing 3-8.

Listing 3-8. Ingress Nginx Services ConfigMaps

```
kind: ConfigMap
apiVersion: v1
metadata:
  name: nginx-configuration
  namespace: ingress-nginx
  labels:
```

```
    app: ingress-nginx
---
kind: ConfigMap
apiVersion: v1
metadata:
  name: tcp-services
  namespace: ingress-nginx
---
kind: ConfigMap
apiVersion: v1
metadata:
  name: udp-services
  namespace: ingress-nginx
```

Apply the Ingress Nginx ConfigMaps configuration:

```
$ kubectl apply -f 20-configmaps.yml
```

Create a configuration file describing a Kubernetes Deployment for a default HTTP back-end server named 30-deployment.yml from Listing 3-9.

Listing 3-9. Ingress Nginx Deployment. Default back ends

```
apiVersion: apps/v1
kind: Deployment
metadata:
  name: default-http-backend
  labels:
    app: default-http-backend
  namespace: ingress-nginx
spec:
  replicas: 2
  revisionHistoryLimit: 1
  selector:
```

```
    matchLabels:
      app: default-http-backend
  template:
    metadata:
      labels:
        app: default-http-backend
    spec:
      affinity:
        podAntiAffinity:
          preferredDuringSchedulingIgnoredDuringExecution:
            - weight: 100
              podAffinityTerm:
                labelSelector:
                  matchExpressions:
                    - key: app
                      operator: In
                      values:
                        - default-http-backend
                topologyKey: kubernetes.io/hostname
      terminationGracePeriodSeconds: 60
      containers:
        - name: default-http-backend
          image: gcr.io/google_containers/defaultbackend:1.4
          livenessProbe:
            httpGet:
              path: /healthz
              port: 8080
              scheme: HTTP
            initialDelaySeconds: 30
            timeoutSeconds: 5
          ports:
```

```
    - containerPort: 8080
  resources:
    limits:
      cpu: 10m
      memory: 20Mi
    requests:
      cpu: 10m
      memory: 20Mi
```

Apply the Ingress Nginx default HTTP server back-end configuration Deployment:

```
$ kubectl apply -f 30-deployment.yml
```

Finally, create a configuration file describing a Kubernetes DaemonSet for the Ingress Nginx controller named 40-daemonset.yml from Listing 3-10. The DaemonSet instructs Kubernetes to ensure one Ingress Nginx controller is running on each node. Ingress Nginx controller listens on TCP ports 80 (HTTP) and 443 (HTTPS). Earlier in this chapter, the section DNS configured two A records for *.dev1.apk8s.dev, pointed to each worker node.

Note   The custom Kubernetes development cluster defined in this chapter does not use a LoadBalancer[28] and relies on DNS records to point to each worker node. Using a DaemonSet ensures that each worker node has an Nginx Ingress Pod listening on ports 80 (HTTP) and 443 (HTTPS).

---

[28]https://kubernetes.io/docs/tasks/access-application-cluster/
create-external-load-balancer/

Listing 3-10. Ingress Nginx DaemonSet

```
apiVersion: apps/v1
kind: DaemonSet
metadata:
  name: nginx-ingress-controller
  namespace: ingress-nginx
spec:
  revisionHistoryLimit: 1
  selector:
    matchLabels:
      app: ingress-nginx
  template:
    metadata:
      labels:
        app: ingress-nginx
      annotations:
        prometheus.io/port: '10254'
        prometheus.io/scrape: 'true'
    spec:
      serviceAccountName: nginx-ingress-serviceaccount
      hostNetwork: true
      containers:
        - name: nginx-ingress-controller
          image: quay.io/kubernetes-ingress-controller/nginx-
          ingress-controller:0.14.0
          args:
            - /nginx-ingress-controller
            - --default-backend-service=$(POD_NAMESPACE)/
            default-http-backend
            - --configmap=$(POD_NAMESPACE)/nginx-configuration
```

```
   - --tcp-services-configmap=$(POD_NAMESPACE)/tcp-
   services
   - --udp-services-configmap=$(POD_NAMESPACE)/udp-
   services
   - --annotations-prefix=nginx.ingress.kubernetes.io
env:
   - name: POD_NAME
     valueFrom:
       fieldRef:
         fieldPath: metadata.name
   - name: POD_NAMESPACE
     valueFrom:
       fieldRef:
         fieldPath: metadata.namespace
ports:
   - name: http
     containerPort: 80
     hostPort: 80
   - name: https
     containerPort: 443
     hostPort: 443
livenessProbe:
   failureThreshold: 3
   httpGet:
     path: /healthz
     port: 10254
     scheme: HTTP
   initialDelaySeconds: 10
   periodSeconds: 10
   successThreshold: 1
   timeoutSeconds: 1
```

```
readinessProbe:
  failureThreshold: 3
  httpGet:
    path: /healthz
    port: 10254
    scheme: HTTP
  periodSeconds: 10
  successThreshold: 1
  timeoutSeconds: 1
securityContext:
  runAsNonRoot: false
```

Apply the Ingress Nginx default HTTP server back-end configuration Deployment:

```
$ kubectl apply -f 40-daemonset.yml
```

Ingress Nginx is now configured and running on the new development cluster, ready to accept web traffic through ports 80 and 443 on each node. This exercise built each configuration manifest and stored it for the Cluster in the directory ~/workspace/apk8s/k8s/cluster-apk8s-dev1/000-cluster/00-ingress-nginx. This set of Ingress Nginx configuration manifests accurately represents the current or desired state of the Cluster, additionally providing documentation to others and the ability to reproduce this state at a later time, or on another cluster.

Finally, the Development Cluster needs the ability to generate TLS certificates that Ingress Nginx can use to service encrypted HTTPS (port 443) traffic. The next section, "TLS/HTTPS with Cert Manager," covers setting up the Cert Manager to generate free TLS certificates automatically with Let's Encrypt.

TLS/HTTPS with Cert Manager

Cert Manager is used "to automate the management and issuance of TLS certificates from various issuing sources."[29] This book utilizes Let's Encrypt[30] for secure, free TLS certificate issuance, later configured with a Cert Manager custom resource called a ClusterIssuer. Create the directory ~/workspace/apk8s/k8s/cluster-apk8s-dev1/000-cluster/10-cert-manager for the Cert Manager configuration manifests.

Create the file 00-namespace.yml with the contents of Listing 3-11.

Listing 3-11. Cert Manager Namespace

```
apiVersion: v1
kind: Namespace
metadata:
  name: cert-manager
  labels:
    certmanager.k8s.io/disable-validation: "true"
```

Apply the new namespace for Cert Manager:

```
$ kubectl apply -f 00-namespace.yml
```

Get Cert Manager's custom resource definitions (CRDs) and save them to the file 02-crd.yml:

```
$ curl -L https://github.com/jetstack/cert-manager/releases/
download/v0.8.0/cert-manager.yaml >02-crd.yml
```

Apply the Cert Manager CRDs:

```
$ kubectl apply -f 02-crd.yml
```

---

[29]Automatically Provision and Manage TLS Certificates in Kubernetes: Jetstack/ Cert-Manager. Jetstack, 2019. https://github.com/jetstack/cert-manager.
[30]https://letsencrypt.org/

Cert Manager is installed. Ensure all Pods supporting cert manager have achieved the Running status (kubectl get pods -n cert-manager).

Cert Manager defined new custom resources called ClusterIssuer and Certificate, among others. A Certificate describes the desired TLS certificate and the use of an Issuer to retrieve the TLS certificate from an authority such as Let's Encrypt. This book uses a ClusterIssuer for all Certificates, but you can read more about Issuers and ClusterIssuer in Cert Manager's official documentation.

Create the file 03-clusterissuer.yml with the contents of Listing 3-12.

Listing 3-12. Cert Manager Cluster Issuer

```
apiVersion: certmanager.k8s.io/v1alpha1
kind: ClusterIssuer
metadata:
  name: letsencrypt-production
spec:
  acme:
    server: https://acme-v02.api.letsencrypt.org/directory
    email: YOUR_EMAIL_ADDRESS
    privateKeySecretRef:
      name: letsencrypt-production
    http01: {}
```

Apply the Cert Manager ClusterIssuer:

```
$ kubectl apply -f 03-clusterissuer.yml
```

Any namespace in the Cluster can use the new ClusterIssuer. Get a list of ClusterIssuers with the command: kubectl get clusterissuers. Later sections use this new ClusterIssuer letsencrypt-production when defining Certificates (stored as Kubernetes Secrets) used for TLS communication by Ingress Nginx.

The new development Cluster is now able to accept inbound HTTP and HTTPS and perform automatic generation of TLS certificates. The final essential requirement for a suitable development environment is persistent storage, covered in the next section.

Persistent Volumes with Rook Ceph

Persistent storage is an essential and often tricky requirement for some Kubernetes deployments. Kubernetes Pods are considered transient and their file systems along with them. External databases are a great way to persist data obtained by an application container in a Pod. However, some Pods may represent databases or filesystems themselves, and therefore any connected data volumes must survive beyond the lifespan of the Pod itself.

This section enables Kubernetes Persistent Volumes[31] backed by Ceph[32] orchestrated by Rook.[33] Ceph is a distributed storage cluster, providing Kubernetes Persistent Volumes for object-, block-, and filesystem-based storage. The Rook operator is used to install and manage Ceph behind the scenes.

The following instructions install the Rook operator and create two storage classes (block and filesystem) for use by Kubernetes Persistent Volumes. The official Rook documentation for Ceph[34] suggests starting with their example configuration manifests and customizing them where desired. Keeping consistent with the previous examples, create the directory: ~/workspace/apk8s/k8s/cluster-apk8s-dev1/000-cluster/20-rook-ceph. Download the Rook custom resource definitions (CRDs), operator, cluster, and toolbox deployments from the following.

---

[31]https://kubernetes.io/docs/concepts/storage/persistent-volumes/
[32]https://ceph.com/
[33]https://rook.io/
[34]https://rook.io/docs/rook/v1.0/ceph-examples.html

Get the Rook Ceph Namespace CRDs and save them to the file
`00-namespace-crd.yml`:

```
$ curl -L \
https://github.com/rook/rook/raw/release-1.0/cluster/examples/
kubernetes/ceph/common.yaml >00-namespace-crd.yml
```

Apply the Rook Ceph Namespace and custom resource definitions:

```
$ kubectl apply -f 00-namespace-crd.yml
```

Get the Rook Ceph Operator Deployment configuration and save it to
the file `30-deployment-oper.yml`:

```
$ curl -L \
https://github.com/rook/rook/raw/release-1.0/cluster/examples/
kubernetes/ceph/operator.yaml >30-deployment-oper.yml
```

Apply the Rook Ceph Operator Deployment:

```
$ kubectl apply -f 30-deployment-oper.yml
```

Get the example Rook Ceph Cluster configuration and save it to the file
`60-cluster-rook-ceph.yml`:

```
$ curl -L \
https://github.com/rook/rook/raw/release-1.0/cluster/examples/
kubernetes/ceph/cluster-test.yaml >60-cluster-rook-ceph.yml
```

Apply the Rook Ceph Cluster Deployment configuration:

```
$ kubectl apply -f 60-cluster-rook-ceph.yml
```

Get the Rook Ceph toolbox Deployment configuration and save it to
the file `30-deployment-toolbox.yml`:

```
$ curl -L \
https://github.com/rook/rook/raw/release-1.0/cluster/examples/
kubernetes/ceph/toolbox.yaml >30-deployment-toolbox.yml
```

Apply the Rook Ceph Cluster toolbox Deployment configuration:

```
$ kubectl apply -f 30-deployment-toolbox.yml
```

The rook-ceph Namespace now contains Pods for managing the underlying Ceph cluster along with the ability to provision Persistent Volumes from Persistent Volume Claims.

View the list of Pods running in the rook-ceph Namespace (kubectl get pods -n rook-ceph); the Pod prefixed with rook-ceph-tools- contains the ceph command-line utility. Execute the bash shell on this Pod and then issue the command ceph status to view the status of the new storage cluster.

```
$ kubectl exec -it rook-ceph-tools-5f49756bf-m6dxv \
-n rook-ceph bash
$ ceph status
```

Example output:

```
cluster:
  id:     f67747e5-eb2a-4301-8045-c1e210488433
  health: HEALTH_OK

services:
  mon: 1 daemons, quorum a (age 22m)
  mgr: a(active, since 21m)
  osd: 2 osds: 2 up (since 21m), 2 in (since 21m)

data:
  pools:   0 pools, 0 pgs
  objects: 0 objects, 0 B
  usage:   9.1 GiB used, 107 GiB / 116 GiB avail
  pgs:
```

Block Storage

Pods requiring Persistent Volumes may do so through Kubernetes Persistent Volume Claims (PVCs). PVCs require a defined Storage Class used by Rook to provision a Persistent Volume.

Set up a new StorageClass called `rook-ceph-block` backed by a CephBlockPool able to provision Persistent Volumes from Persistent Volume Claim requests.

If continuing from the previous section, create the file `70-rook-ceph-block.yml` in the directory `~/workspace/apk8s/k8s/cluster-apk8s-dev1/000-cluster/20-rook-ceph` with the contents of Listing 3-13.

Listing 3-13. CephBlockPool and StorageClass

```
apiVersion: ceph.rook.io/v1
kind: CephBlockPool
metadata:
  name: replicapool
  namespace: rook-ceph
spec:
  failureDomain: host
  replicated:
    size: 1
---
apiVersion: storage.k8s.io/v1
kind: StorageClass
metadata:
  name: rook-ceph-block
provisioner: ceph.rook.io/block
parameters:
  blockPool: replicapool
  clusterNamespace: rook-ceph
  fstype: xfs
reclaimPolicy: Delete
```

110

Apply the CephBlockPool and StorageClass configuration:

```
$ kubectl apply -f 70-rook-ceph-block.yml
```

The development cluster now supports Persistent Volume Claims (PVCs) commonly used by (but not limited to) Kubernetes StatefulSets. Later on, this book uses PVCs for Stateful applications such as databases, data indexes, and event queues. The next section covers the implementation of a cluster-wide shared filesystem backed by Ceph.

Shared Filesystem

Shared filesystems provide opportunities to separate responsibility around the management of files. Shared filesystems allow scenarios where one set of Pods may enable users to upload files such as images, while another set of Pods retrieves and processes them. Although there are many other ways to share files across deployments, a shared filesystem backed by Ceph empowers flexible options in architecting a data-centric platform in the Cluster.

Create the file 75-rook-ceph-clusterfs.yml in the directory ~/workspace/apk8s/k8s/cluster-apk8s-dev1/000-cluster/20-rook-ceph with the contents of Listing 3-14.

Listing 3-14. CephFilesystem

```
apiVersion: ceph.rook.io/v1
kind: CephFilesystem
metadata:
  name: rook-ceph-clusterfs
  namespace: rook-ceph
spec:
  metadataPool:
    replicated:
      size: 1
```

```
dataPools:
  - failureDomain: host
    replicated:
      size: 2
metadataServer:
  activeCount: 1
  activeStandby: true
```

Apply the CephFilesystem configuration:

```
$ kubectl apply -f 75-rook-ceph-clusterfs.yml
```

The Development Cluster is now able to accept and route inbound web traffic with Ingress Nginx, create and use TLS certificates with Cert Manager and Let's Encrypt, provision Persistent Volume Claims, and offer a shared filesystem with Rook and Ceph. It may seem like a lot of effort to bring this custom Kubernetes Cluster up with these essential capabilities when the major cloud providers offer much of this stack in turnkey solutions. However, the development cluster configured in this chapter can run on nearly any provider, making it truly portable, cloud native, and vendor neutral.

The development cluster is complete in that it can support the majority of the required functionality for the Blockchain, Machine Learning, and IoT data processing components in this book.

The next section briefly covers monitoring. Monitoring is not an operational requirement but a crucial utility for the management of the Cluster, providing administrative metrics on performance and resource utilization.

Monitoring

The ecosystem of Kubernetes monitoring solutions is vast and matures daily. From commercial offerings to novel and niche open source projects, the realm of Cluster monitoring is well covered in books, blogs, and tutorials on Kubernetes administration.

This section sets up a minimal monitoring solution using the open source project kube-prometheus by CoreOS.[35] Production environments would likely have far more customized monitoring and alerting configurations. Therefore, the monitoring component of the development Cluster is not something that requires reproducibility in other environments. For this reason, it is only necessary to document the imperative commands used to create the development Cluster's monitoring solution.

In keeping with the organization of Cluster configuration from previous sections, create the directory ~/workspace/apk8s/k8s/cluster-apk8s-dev1/000-cluster/30-monitoring, adding the file README.md with the contents of Listing 3-15.

Listing 3-15. Monitoring README

```bash
# kube-prometheus
Installation guide for the **monitoring** namespace.

```bash
git clone git@github.com:coreos/kube-prometheus.git
cd kube-prometheus
git checkout v0.1.0

kubectl create -f manifests/

# Verify the resources are ready before proceeding.

until kubectl get customresourcedefinitions servicemonitors.
monitoring.coreos.com ; do date; sleep 1; echo ""; done

until kubectl get servicemonitors --all-namespaces ; do date;
sleep 1; echo ""; done
```

---

[35]https://github.com/coreos/kube-prometheus
```

```
# Apply the manifests.
# This command sometimes may need to be done twice
# (to work around a race condition).

kubectl apply -f manifests/
```
```

Execute each of the commands between the ```bash and ```. The instructions in the new README.md clone the kube-prometheus project, create new custom resource definitions for the CoreOS Prometheus, and apply several deployments representing the components needed to monitor the Cluster with Prometheus and Grafana.

There is no need to track the cloned kube-prometheus project with the rest of the development cluster configuration manifests. Exclude the kube-prometheus project with a Git ignore file (cd ../ && echo "kube-prometheus" >.gitignore).

---

**Note**    Documenting commands in markdown format provides instruction that is human readable as raw text or rendered as formatted HTML when browsing the repository in GitLab (or GitHub).

---

Visually monitor the new cluster by port-forwarding Grafana to a local workstation:

```
$ kubectl --namespace monitoring \
port-forward svc/grafana 3000
```

Open http://localhost:3000 on a local workstation, and log in to Grafana with the default administrator credentials, username: admin, password: admin. Explore the prebuilt dashboards for monitoring many aspects of the Kubernetes cluster, including Nodes, Namespaces, and Pods.
```

Note   The Prometheus Operator uses the custom resource definition (CRD) ServiceMonitor to configure targets for scraping metrics. To customize Prometheus monitoring this cluster, first review the preinstalled ServiceMonitors with `kubectl get ServiceMonitor -n monitoring` and review the official ServiceMonitor documentation.[36]

Summary

This chapter set up a small custom Kubernetes development Cluster with support for Ingress, automatic TLS certificate generation, block and filesystem storage, and essential monitoring. The configuration files developed in this chapter are intended to be committed to a Git repository (and optionally hosted on the GitLab instance set up in the previous chapter).

The process of developing a platform as a collection of domain-specific functionality such as Machine Learning, Blockchain, and IoT data management tied together with custom applications benefits from a well-integrated DevOps toolchain connected to this new development cluster. The next chapter covers CI/CD and combines the GitLab installation from Chapter 2 with this new development Cluster.

Note   Listing 3-16 displays the final list and organization of the configuration files developed through the course of this chapter. Starting from the directory ~/workspace/apk8s/k8s, Listing 3-16 represents the current state of the repository cloned from the GitLab group apk8s and the project k8s.

---

[36]https://github.com/coreos/prometheus-operator/blob/master/Documentation/api.md#servicemonitorspec

Listing 3-16. Development Cluster configuration layout

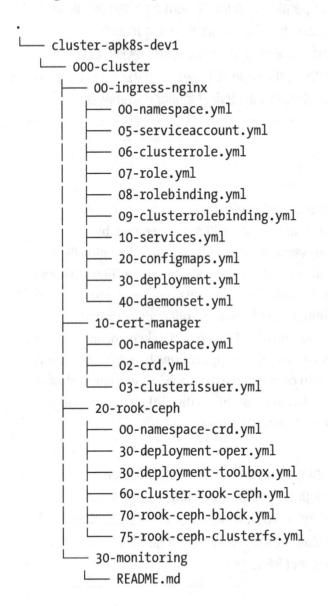

```
.
└── cluster-apk8s-dev1
    └── 000-cluster
        ├── 00-ingress-nginx
        │   ├── 00-namespace.yml
        │   ├── 05-serviceaccount.yml
        │   ├── 06-clusterrole.yml
        │   ├── 07-role.yml
        │   ├── 08-rolebinding.yml
        │   ├── 09-clusterrolebinding.yml
        │   ├── 10-services.yml
        │   ├── 20-configmaps.yml
        │   ├── 30-deployment.yml
        │   └── 40-daemonset.yml
        ├── 10-cert-manager
        │   ├── 00-namespace.yml
        │   ├── 02-crd.yml
        │   └── 03-clusterissuer.yml
        ├── 20-rook-ceph
        │   ├── 00-namespace-crd.yml
        │   ├── 30-deployment-oper.yml
        │   ├── 30-deployment-toolbox.yml
        │   ├── 60-cluster-rook-ceph.yml
        │   ├── 70-rook-ceph-block.yml
        │   └── 75-rook-ceph-clusterfs.yml
        └── 30-monitoring
            └── README.md
```

CHAPTER 4

In-Platform CI/CD

CI/CD stands for both continuous integration and delivery, and continuous integration and deployment. Continuous delivery consists of processes that compile, or otherwise prepare, code into a suitable release, while continuous deployment installs or updates existing applications (typically on servers) through automated processes. CI/CD continues to mature and widen its scope, from low-level development concerns to central platform operations. It has expanded beyond the limited focus of merging and compiling applications for stand-alone software packages. CI/CD is gaining new ground, deploying machine learning models, serverless functions, even so far as infrastructure provisioning. This chapter leverages CI/CD to develop and deliver containers used for enabling data science capabilities within the scope of an application platform. GitLab is used in this chapter to provide CI/CD capabilities for both platform development and production operations.

Development and Operations

CI/CD principles have expanded from the isolated build and delivery systems powering the development of traditional software applications. CI/CD concepts are expanding into the operational components of enterprise platforms. The fields of Data Science and specifically Machine Learning have a wide range of implementations and specialized processes just beginning to emerge from academic labs to cloud-based

© Craig Johnston 2020
C. Johnston, *Advanced Platform Development with Kubernetes*,
https://doi.org/10.1007/978-1-4842-5611-4_4

production deployments. Machine Learning automation has embraced containerization, and the automated building of containers to wrap complex logic and dependencies. CI/CD-style pipelines are well suited for the experimentation, testing, and production deployment of containerized artificial intelligence, lowering the cost and complexity of deployment and rollback capabilities.

Platform Integration

This chapter integrates GitLab with Kubernetes to form closer relationships between platform development and operations. Building containers from versioned source code from within the Kubernetes cluster opens new opportunities for access to platform functionality at all stages of integration, delivery, and deployment.

In Chapter 2, Figure 2-3 illustrates the relationship between a GitLab instance running on a single-node Kubernetes (k3s) cluster and a remote development cluster controlled externally through `git` and `kubectl` commands. Integrating the capabilities of `git` and `kubectl` from within the platform provides opportunities to bring development capabilities into the platform. Kubeflow is a popular machine learning automation platform that embraces much of this concept through custom JupyterLab[1] images containing `kubectl`. JupyterLab images are provisioned by JupyterHub[2] and mount a Kubernetes service account with RBAC defined permissions. The following exercise borrows some these concepts to demonstrate CI/CD integration with Data Science capabilities as a starting point for more in-depth customization (see Figure 4-1).

---

[1] https://jupyterlab.readthedocs.io
[2] https://jupyterhub.readthedocs.io

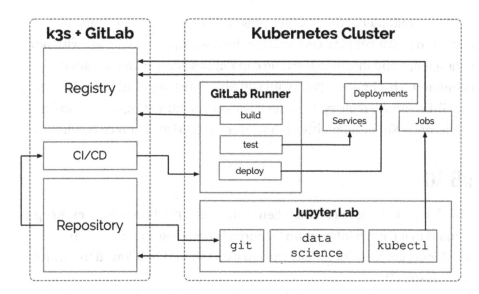

Figure 4-1. CI/CD integration with GitLab and JupyterLab

Yet Another Development Cluster

This chapter uses a four-node custom Kubernetes cluster setup at Scaleway[3] (a European discount cloud provider). Although many examples in this book use different providers, it is not necessary to spread services across providers, aside from demonstrating a vendor-neutral approach and portability of concepts and implementation. Scaleway is a cost-effective option for testing experimenting with various cluster configurations. The following cluster uses one **DEV1-M** (3 CPU/4G RAM/40G SSD) for the Kubernetes master node and three **DEV1-L** (4 CPU/8G RAM/80GB) for worker nodes. The total cost for this development cluster is just under 0.20 USD per hour at the time of this writing. Scaleway presents a user interface and options similar to Vultr and Digital Ocean. The instructions from the "Development Environment" chapter may be applied to Scaleway and many other vendors.

---

[3]`www.scaleway.com`

The remainder of this chapter uses GitLab to host a repository containing a Dockerfile customizing the base JupyterLab image with new data science and machine learning capabilities along with the kubectl command. This image is built with GitLab's CI features and hosted in the GitLab image registry. Chapter 2 walks through setting up GitLab on single-node Kubernetes cluster; however, any GitLab instance is suitable.

RBAC

GitLab uses a service account token with cluster-admin privileges. Keep in mind that GitLab integration "security is based on a model where developers are trusted, so only trusted users should be allowed to control your clusters."[4]

In keeping with the organization of manifests from Chapters 2 and 3, create the directory cluster-apk8s-dev2/000-cluster/40-gitlab-integration within the k8s git project.

Create a ServiceAccount and ClusterRoleBinding in a file named 05-rbac.yml from Listing 4-1.

Listing 4-1. ServiceAccount and ClusterRoleBinding for GitLab

```
    apiVersion: rbac.authorization.k8s.io/v1beta1
kind: RoleBinding
metadata:
  name: data-lab
  namespace: data-lab
roleRef:
  apiGroup: rbac.authorization.k8s.io
  kind: Role
  name: data-lab
```

---

[4]https://gitlab.apk8s.dev/help/user/project/clusters/index#security-implications

```
subjects:
  - kind: ServiceAccount
    name: data-lab
    namespace: data-lab
---
apiVersion: rbac.authorization.k8s.io/v1beta1
kind: RoleBinding
metadata:
  name: hub
  namespace: data-lab
roleRef:
  apiGroup: rbac.authorization.k8s.io
  kind: Role
  name: hub
subjects:
  - kind: ServiceAccount
    name: hub
    namespace: data
```

Apply the GitLab RBAC configuration:

```
$ kubectl apply -f 05-rbac.yml
```

GitLab Group Kubernetes Access

Although GitLab's Kubernetes integration is based on trusting developers, not all projects/repositories, or developers, need access to Kubernetes. GitLab allows individual projects or groups to each have individually integrated Kubernetes clusters. This chapter creates a new group called Data Science (ds) and integrates it with the new dev2 cluster set up on Scaleway. Figure 4-2 demonstrates setting up a new GitLab group.

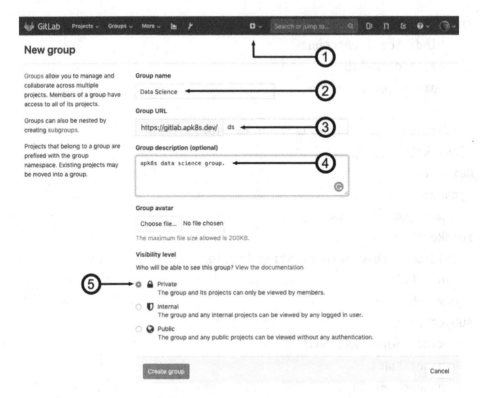

Figure 4-2. *Create GitLab group*

Configure Kubernetes Cluster Integration

Configure the new Data Science GitLab group to control a Kubernetes cluster (see Figure 4-3):

1. Select **Kubernetes** on left-side menu of the group.

2. Choose the tab **Add Existing Cluster**.

3. Provide a name for the cluster, in this case **dev2**.

4. Provide the fully qualified URL to the Kubernetes API exposed on the master node (e.g., https://n1.dev2.apk8s.dev:6443).

5. Provide the cluster CA Certificate. The certificate
    is easily found in the default-token in the default
    Namespace. To retrieve the certificate in the
    required PEM format, first list the Secrets in the
    default Namespace: kubectl get secrets. If this is
    a new cluster, the default-token will likely be the
    only Secret. Use the following command, replacing
    the <secret name> with the default-token:

```
kubectl get secret \
  $(kubectl get secret | grep default-token | awk
'{print $1}') -o jsonpath="{['data']['ca\.crt']}" \
| base64 --decode
```

6. Provide the Service Token from the gitlab-admin
    service account set up in the previous section. Use
    the following command:

```
kubectl -n kube-system describe secret $(kubectl -n
kube-system get secret | grep gitlab-admin | awk
'{print $1}')
```

7. Ensure that RBAC is enabled.

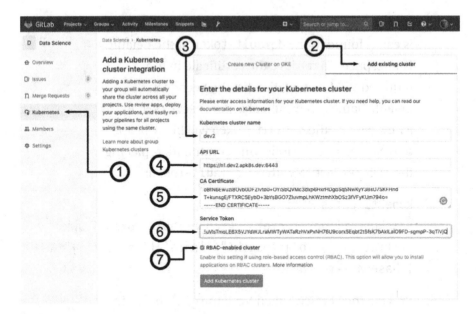

Figure 4-3. GitLab group Kubernetes configuration menu

Enable Dependencies

This chapter uses a GitLab Runner[5] installed on the **dev2** cluster for building custom containers with GitLab CI.[6] Complete the Kubernetes integration for the Data Science group (see Figure 4-4):

1. Provide a base domain. Although unused in this chapter, GitLab can use this base domain for Auto DevOps[7] and Knative[8] integration. The setup for **dev2** follows DNS instructions from Chapter 3 by assigning multiple A records for *.dev2 with

---

[5]https://docs.gitlab.com/runner/
[6]https://docs.gitlab.com/ce/ci/
[7]https://docs.gitlab.com/ee/topics/autodevops/
[8]https://knative.dev/

the public IP address of each worker node. Any subdomain of dev2.apk8s.dev will resolve to a worker node on the cluster.

2. Install Helm Tiller.[9] GitLab installs Helm into a new Namespace called gitlab-managed-apps on the cluster. GitLab manages its dependent applications behind the scenes with Helm charts. Helm Tiller may already be installed in the cluster and running in another namespace; however, GitLab requires its own Helm Tiller. Installation may take several minutes. The newly released Helm 3 does not require Helm Tiller, check GitLab documentation for the version installed.

3. Lastly, install the GitLab Runner. Installation may take several minutes.

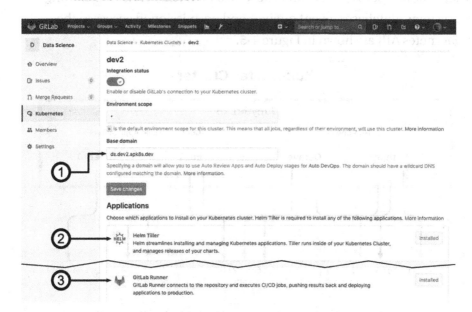

Figure 4-4. *Install applications on Kubernetes Cluster*

---

[9]https://helm.sh/docs/glossary/#tiller

Custom JupyterLab Image

Jupyter Notebooks[10] (Figure 4-8) are becoming a staple of Python-based data science. Jupyter Notebooks combine live runnable code with markdown-based text segments ideal for describing and demonstrating computational procedures and their corresponding results. JupyterLab is the next generation of Jupyter Notebooks, combining an updated user interface with an integrated file browser, and tabs for running multiple notebooks and terminals. JupyterLab (see Figure 4-6) provides a robust integrated development environment able to run within a container.

JupyterHub is an application designed to provision Jupyter Notebooks in a single or multiuser environment. The "Data Science" chapter explores the use of JupyterHub to provision custom JupyterLab images. Operating JupyterHub within the platform provides software developers, data scientists, and statisticians direct access to platform services, including filesystems, databases, event queues, and permissioned access to the Kubernetes API as shown in Figure 4-5.

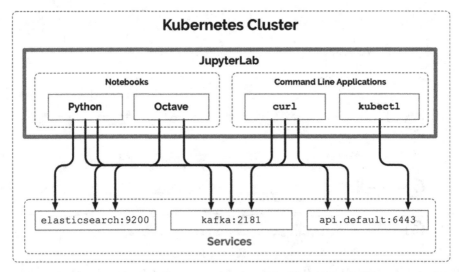

Figure 4-5. *JupyterLab within a Kubernetes cluster*

---

[10]https://jupyterlab.readthedocs.io/en/stable/user/notebook.html

This chapter demonstrates the use of GitLab CI for automating the process of building a custom JupyterLab container image and pushing it into GitLab's integrated container registry.

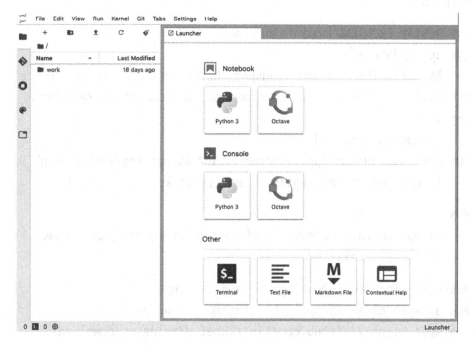

Figure 4-6. *Custom JupyterLab with Python and Octave kernels, and* `kubectl`

Repository and Container Source

Create a new project in the GitLab group Data Science (ds) called `notebook-apk8s`. The project begins with a single Dockerfile.

Create a file named `Dockerfile` with the contents of Listing 4-2.

Listing 4-2. Custom JupyterLab

```
FROM jupyter/minimal-notebook:7a3e968dd212

USER root

ENV DEBIAN_FRONTEND noninteractive
RUN apt update \
    && apt install -y apt-transport-https curl iputils-ping gnupg
RUN curl -s https://packages.cloud.google.com/apt/doc/apt-key.
gpg \
    | sudo apt-key add -
RUN echo "deb https://apt.kubernetes.io/ kubernetes-xenial main" \
    | sudo tee -a /etc/apt/sources.list.d/kubernetes.list

RUN apt update \
    && apt install -y kubectl git gcc mono-mcs musl-dev octave \
    && rm -rf /var/lib/apt/lists/*

# kubefwd for local development and testing
RUN apt-get clean && apt-get autoremove --purge
RUN wget https://github.com/txn2/kubefwd/releases/download/
v1.8.4/kubefwd_amd64.deb \
    && dpkg -i kubefwd_amd64.deb \
    && rm kubefwd_amd64.deb

USER $NB_UID

# Installs data science and machine learning Python packages
RUN pip install --no-cache \
    rubix \
    python-gitlab \
    scipy \
    numpy \
    pandas \
```

```
scikit-learn \
matplotlib \
tensorflow \
torch \
torchvision \
fastai \
octave_kernel \
jupyterlab-git

# JupyterLab and server extensions
RUN jupyter labextension install @jupyterlab/git
RUN jupyter labextension install @jupyterlab/plotly-extension
RUN jupyter serverextension enable --py jupyterlab_git
```

The new Dockerfile extends the official minimal Jupyter Notebook container,[11] adding the Kubernetes configuration utility kubectl along with several popular Python-based Machine Learning libraries. Jupyter Notebooks support a large number of languages aside from Python, including the Octave,[12] an open source alternative to MATLAB[13] by MathWorks.

Test the new Dockerfile by building a local Docker image. From the directory containing the Dockerfile, run:

```
docker build -t jupyterlab-apk8s
```

Building the custom Jupyter Notebook may take several minutes. The base jupyter/minimal-notebook comes in around nearly 3GB, and after adding more than a dozen Machine Learning and Data Science packages and their dependencies, the new jupyterlab-apk8s image is nearly 7GB.

---

[11]https://github.com/jupyter/docker-stacks/tree/master/minimal-notebook
[12]www.gnu.org/software/octave/
[13]www.mathworks.com/products/matlab.html

Local Testing

Run and test the new container with Docker on the same local workstation used to build it. Although the new jupyterlab-apk8s image is intended to run from within the cluster, a utility called kubefwd is installed to accommodate port-forwards from a remote Kubernetes cluster to local service names. Use the following command to start jupyterlab-apk8s:

```
docker run --rm --name jl -p 8888:8888 \
  -v "$(pwd)":"/home/jovyan/work" \
  -v "$HOME/.kube/apk8s-dev2":"/home/jovyan/.kube/config" \
  --user root \
  -e GRANT_SUDO=yes \
  -e JUPYTER_ENABLE_LAB=yes -e RESTARTABLE=yes \
  jupyterlab-apk8s:latest
```

The docker run command mounts the current working directory to /home/jovyan/work, the container runs as the user jovyan, and the initial working directory from within the container is /home/jovyan/. The next volume mount (-v) exposes the config apk8s-dev2 for the new **dev2** cluster. The argument --user root starts the container with the root user and is required for sudo access needed for the kubefwd utility and enabled with -e GRANT_SUDO=yes. See the official documentation[14] for a list of features exposed by the Jupyter Notebook base container.

Note   The user jovyan is convention from the Jupyter community and used in all official Jupyter Notebook images. The noun Jovian is a fictional inhabitant of the planet Jupiter.

---

[14]https://jupyter-docker-stacks.readthedocs.io/en/latest/using/common.html

Upon starting the new Jupyter Notebook container, review the initial log output for connection instructions containing a token. After retrieving the token from the container output, visit the URL: `http://localhost:8888?token=<token>`

Figure 4-6 represents a running instance of the new `jupyterlab-apk8s` container.

Port-Forwarding

The new `jupyterlab-apk8s` container is intended to run inside the **dev2** cluster, provisioned by JupyterHub. However, testing on a local workstations can mimic an in-cluster environment with the help of kubefwd[15] (developed by the author), previously installed in `jupyterlab-apk8s` for local testing support.

Within the Docker container (at `localhost:8888`), under the section titled **Other** within the running Jupyter Notebook, chose **Terminal**. Once the terminal launches, provide the following command to port-forward all services running in the `monitoring` Namespace on the **dev2** cluster (see Figure 4-7):

```
sudo kubefwd svc -n monitoring
```

---

[15]`https://github.com/txn2/kubefwd`

Figure 4-7. *Port-forwarding a remote Kubernetes cluster*

The utility kubefwd connects and port-forwards Pods backing Services on a remote Kubernetes cluster to a matching set of DNS names and ports on the local workstation (in this case a Jupyter Notebook). Once kubefwd is running, connections to services such as http://prometheus-k8s. monitoring:9200 are possible just as they are from within the remote cluster.

Test Notebook

Create a new Notebook for testing the custom Jupyter container jupyterlab-apk8s. Under the file menu of the running Notebook, choose **New** and **Notebook**, and select the **Python 3** kernel from the drop-down list. Enter the Python code from Listing 4-3 into the first input cell and click the **play** button located in the menu bar under the tab, or use the keyboard shortcut **Shift-Enter** (see Figure 4-8).

Listing 4-3. Python communicating with Prometheus

```python
import requests

response = requests.get('http://prometheus-k8s:9090/api/v1/query',
    params={'query': "node_load1"})

if response.status_code == 200:
    print("Got 200 response from Prometheus")

for node_data in response.json()['data']['result']:
    value = node_data['value'][1]
    name = node_data['metric']['instance']
    print(f'Node {name} has a 1m load average of {value}')
```

The newly created Jupyter Notebook, Untitled.ipynb, executes
a single cell that returns the connection status to Prometheus and the
current one-minute load average for each of the Kubernetes nodes in the
dev2 cluster as shown in Figure 4-8.

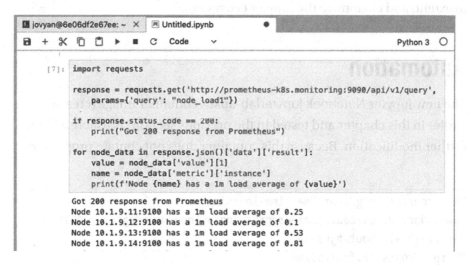

Figure 4-8. *Communicating with Prometheus*

Additional Learning

If you are new to Data Science or Machine Learning, this custom Notebook contains several popular libraries and frameworks for getting started. Popular online courses in artificial intelligence and Machine Learning often use Jupyter Notebooks or MATLAB/Octave. Coursera offers one of the most popular Machine Learning courses[16] using MATLAB/Octave, taught by Andrew Ng, a Stanford professor and co-founder of Google Brain. Udacity offers an introductory Nanodegree course called *API Programming with Python,*[17] heavily utilizing Jupyter Notebooks. Jeremy Howard's[18] fast.ai offers a unique top-down approach in the course *Introduction to Machine Learning for Coders*[19] and the fast.ai Python libraries are included with this custom image.

The Jupyter Notebook environment is not limited to the preinstalled Python libraries; developers and data scientists can use `pip install` to extend the Python environment to suit their needs. The commands `jupyter labextension`[20] and `jupyter serverextension` are also available to extend and customize the Jupyter ecosystem.[21]

Automation

The new Jupyter Notebook jupyterlab-apk8s container image (created earlier in this chapter and tested in the previous section) is usable without further modification. Because this container does not contain proprietary

---

[16]`www.coursera.org/learn/machine-learning`
[17]`www.udacity.com/course/ai-programming-python-nanodegree--nd089`
[18]`www.fast.ai/about/#jeremy`
[19]`http://course18.fast.ai/ml`
[20]`https://jupyterlab.readthedocs.io/en/stable/user/extensions.html`
[21]`https://blog.jupyter.org/99-ways-to-extend-the-jupyter-ecosystem-11e5dab7c54`

code or business logic, it may be uploaded to any public container registry including Docker Hub. The following commands tag the new image with the apk8s Docker Hub account and pushes it to the registry, making it available to the public:

```
docker tag jupyterlab-apk8s:latest \
apk8s/jupyterlab-apk8s:latest
```

```
docker push apk8s/jupyterlab-apk8s:latest
```

Not all containers should be publicly accessible, as they may contain proprietary business logic or data. Aside from the security aspect of private container registries, it is also a good practice to retain control of these assets, along with avoiding vendor lock-in. Fortunately, the open source GitLab (installed in Chapter 2) comes with a built-in container registry.

Building the jupyterlab-apk8s container has been a straightforward yet manual process. The version of the newly built jupyterlab-apk8s container is not coupled to the code that created it. A developer could easily make a change and forget to push a new version for other developers. Automation not only solves the problem of enforcing a coupling between code version and image version, but it also opens up the ability to add test suites and security checks.

The remainder of this chapter uses GitLab CI to automate the building and storage of the jupyterlab-apk8s container defined earlier. The new Data Science group set up earlier in GitLab has been configured to perform GitLab CI operations via GitLab Runners on the new **dev2** cluster. The next section covers writing a GitLab CI configuration for automating a container building and versioning.

GitLab CI

A large number of powerful CI/CD tools are available today. Jenkins, Buildbot, Drone, Concourse, and dozens of other well-designed tools have exposed the high demand for sophisticated and stable methods of automating the complex processes of software integration, delivery, and deployment.

GitLab CI has deep integration with GitLab itself and requires it to run; however, this does not mean a project may be managed only by GitLab. The Git VCS allows multiple remotes, allowing a project to exist in multiple hosted repositories such as GitHub or Bitbucket. GitLab also supports *pull* and *push*-based project synchronization with repository mirroring.[22] Rather than managing another application, this book uses GitLab CI specifically for its integration with GitLab and Kubernetes.

GitLab CI requires a GitLab project and a GitLab Runner. Earlier in this chapter, a GitLab group named Data Science (gitlab.apk8s.dev/ds) was configured along with a GitLab Runner installed after configuring Kubernetes access for the group. Within this new Data Science group, the project jupyterlab-apk8s (gitlab.apk8s.dev/ds/jupyterlab-apk8s) was developed and included a single Dockerfile built and tested in the previous section. Invoking GitLab CI requires one file, .gitlab-ci.yml, covered in the next section.

.gitlab-ci.yml

When any source repository in GitLab project contains a file named .gitlab-ci.yml, the presence of the file invokes GitLab CI, which creates a new Pipeline and begins to run all defined Jobs. Create a file named in the new jupyterlab-apk8s project and add the contents of Listing 4-4.

---

[22]https://docs.gitlab.com/12.1/ce/workflow/repository_mirroring.html

Listing 4-4. GitLab CI pipeline configuration

```
stages:
  - build
  - test
  - deploy

tag_build:
  stage: build
  only:
    - tags@ds/jupyterlab-apk8s
  image:
    # debug version is required for shell
    name: gcr.io/kaniko-project/executor:debug-v0.10.0
    entrypoint: [""]
  script: |
    # configure kaniko
    export KCFG=$(printf '{"auths":{"%s":{"username":"%s","pass
    word":"%s"}}}' \
      "$CI_REGISTRY" "$CI_REGISTRY_USER" "$CI_REGISTRY_PASSWORD")
    echo $KCFG > /kaniko/.docker/config.json

    /kaniko/executor --context $CI_PROJECT_DIR --dockerfile
    $CI_PROJECT_DIR/Dockerfile \
    --destination $CI_REGISTRY_IMAGE:$CI_COMMIT_TAG \
    --destination $CI_REGISTRY_IMAGE:latest
```

The new .gitlab-ci.yml configuration file contains a single job named tag_build. Job names are user defined and may contain any descriptive text. There are three default stages for GitLab CI pipelines: build, test, and deploy. The tag_build job is assigned the stage, build, and only runs when the ds/jupyterlab-apk8s project receives new tags pushed to the project.

GitLab CI/CD pipeline configuration, as shown in Listing 4-4, provides GitLab Runners with build and deployment instructions via rules and scripts. Refer to GitLab's official documentation for detailed information on pipeline configuration.[23]

Kaniko

Building container images from within a Docker container requires mounting the host server's Docker socket. This method has considerable security implications and is challenging to achieve with automated CI/CD solutions such as GitLab CI and Kubernetes. To solve this problem, Google developed the project Kaniko,[24] specifically designed as "a tool to build container images from a Dockerfile, inside a container or Kubernetes cluster."

The `tag_build` job uses a Kaniko image. GitLab CI checks out the specified `git` tag and runs `/kaniko/executor`, specifying the `Dockerfile`. Before the executor is invoked, a Kaniko configuration JSON file is generated at `/kaniko/.docker/config.json`, providing authentication credentials to the `ds/jupyterlab-apk8s` project's container registry.

Integrated Environment Variables

GitLab CI provides an extensive set of environment variables[25] to the image containers specified in a job. The `tag_build` job uses the environment variables `CI_REGISTRY`, `CI_REGISTRY_USER`, and `CI_REGISTRY_PASSWORD` to provide Kaniko with authentication credentials for the `ds/jupyterlab-apk8s` project's container registry. The variable `CI_REGISTRY_IMAGE` is the path to the project-based image—in this case, `reg.gitlab.apk8s.dev/ds/jupyterlab-apk8s`. Lastly, `CI_COMMIT_TAG` is the `git` tag that triggered this job and used to tag the container along with the tag `latest`.

---

[23]https://docs.gitlab.com/ee/ci/yaml/
[24]https://github.com/GoogleContainerTools/kaniko
[25]https://docs.gitlab.com/ce/ci/variables/

Running a Pipeline

A GitLab CI pipeline is triggered once a tag is committed to the
ds/jupyterlab-apk8s repository containing the file .gitlab-ci.yml.
Tag the commit as follows:

```
git commit v0.0.1
```

Push the new tag:

```
git push origin v0.0.1
```

Finally, open a web browser to <gitlab>/ds/jupyterlab-apk8s/
pipelines (see Figure 4-9). Click the pipeline **running** status to view the jobs.

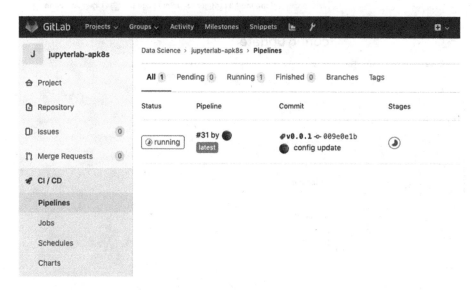

Figure 4-9. *GitLab CI pipelines*

The pipeline detail view (see Figure 4-10) shows job tag_build as
defined in the .gitlab-ci.yml configuration file. Best practices for
container workflows would involve jobs in the test stage, including
functional tests and container security checks.

Container security   There are a wealth of books and resources specializing in CI/CD and container security. Although beyond the scope of this book, tools such as Clair[26] by CoreOS check for container vulnerabilities through static analysis. Cilium,[27] also by CoreOS, secures network connectivity. Both projects are well documented and support Kubernetes deployments.

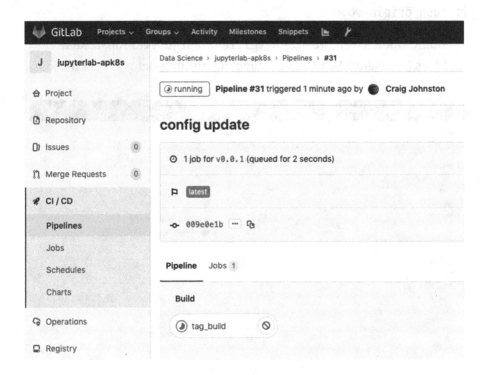

Figure 4-10.   *GitLab CI Pipeline Jobs*

---

[26]https://github.com/coreos/clair
[27]https://github.com/cilium/cilium

Next, click the `tag_build` job to view its process in a web terminal as shown in Figure 4-11. The `jupyterlab-apk8s` image contains a large number of dependencies and may take between 20 and 30 minutes to build.

Figure 4-11. *GitLab CI running job*

Once the build completes, a new image is available in the Data Science group project **jupyterlab-apk8s** registry at `reg.gitlab.apk8s.dev/ds/jupyterlab-apk8s` with the tags `v0.0.1` and `latest` as shown in Figure 4-12.

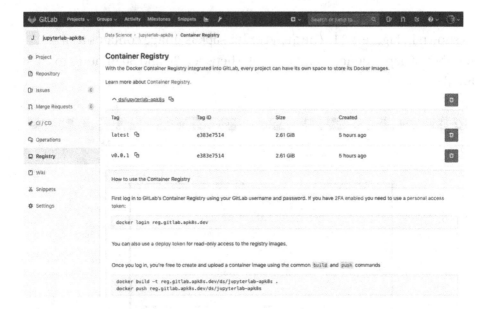

Figure 4-12. *GitLab container registry*

Manual Testing in Kubernetes

The previous sections describe the creation of a GitLab group called
Data Science (ds) and the project **jupyterlab-apk8s**, along with a GitLab
CI configuration that builds a custom Jupyter Notebook container now
available at `reg.gitlab.apk8s.dev/ds/jupyterlab-apk8s:v0.0.1`.

The new Jupyter Notebook is intended for provisioning by JupyterHub,
described later in the chapter on Data Science. Manually testing the new
`jupyterlab-apk8s` image on the **dev2** cluster can be accomplished with a
few imperative commands through the use of `kubectl`.

The GitLab container registry for the `jupyterlab-apk8s` project is
private, and pulls against it from the **dev2** cluster require a Kubernetes
Secret with an access token. Create an access token for the `jupyterlab-`
`apk8s` GitLab project registry by clicking **Settings** in the left-hand
navigation, choose **Repository,** and click the expand button in the **Deploy
Tokens** section.

Create a token with the name **k8s**, skip the **Expires at** field, and check **read_registry** in the Scopes field (see Figure 4-13).

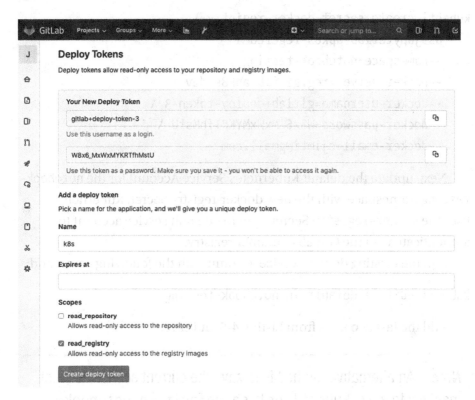

Figure 4-13. *GitLab Deploy Tokens*

Prepare Namespace

Create the Namespace notebook-testing (in the dev2 cluster), indented for testing custom notebooks:

kubectl create namespace notebook-testing

Add a docker-registry Secret with the key and value generated by GitLab. Figure 2-13 shows a generated token with the key gitlab+deploy-token-3 and the value W8x6_MxWxMYKRTfhMstU. Run the following command to create a new secret in the notebook-testing Namespace (change the username, password, server, and email accordingly):

```
kubectl create secret docker-registry \
    ds-jupyterlab-apk8s-regcred \
    --namespace=notebook-testing \
    --docker-server=reg.gitlab.apk8s.dev \
    --docker-username=gitlab+deploy-token-3 \
    --docker-password=W8x6_MxWxMYKRTfhMstU \
    --docker-email=cjimti@gmail.com
```

Next, update the default Kubernetes Service Account for the notebook-testing Namespace with the new docker-registry Secret. Kubernetes uses the docker-registry Secret from the default service account to authenticate with the GitLab container registry.

Edit the existing default service account with the following command:

```
kubectl edit sa default -n notebook-testing
```

Add the last two lines from Listing 4-5 and save.

Note   An alternative method is to save the current service account manifest to a file, kubectl get sa default -n notebook-testing -o yaml > ./sa.yaml, edit sa.yaml, and reapply with kubectl apply -f sa.yml.

Listing 4-5. Editing the notebook-testing default Service Account

```
#...
apiVersion: v1
kind: ServiceAccount
metadata:
  creationTimestamp: "2019-08-01T20:18:34Z"
```

```
name: default
namespace: notebook-testing
resourceVersion: "21353"
selfLink: /api/v1/namespaces/notebook-testing/
serviceaccounts/default
uid: 2240fc34-b050-4ccb-9f96-f4f378842dbd
secrets:
- name: default-token-dhj94
imagePullSecrets:
- name: ds-jupyterlab-apk8s-regcred
```

Run Notebook

The previous section configured the default service account in the
notebook-testing Namespace with the ability to authenticate against the
GitLab registry provided by the ds/jupyterlab-apk8s project. Running
containers for testing means there is little need to save and version
a declarative configuration. Kubectl provides an imperative kubectl
run[28] command that generates a minimal Pod configuration useful for
temporary tasks such as testing, debugging, experimenting, or merely
demonstrating functionality.

The following kubectl command starts a Pod with the name test-
notebook. The Pod is set to remove its configuration when complete and
never automatically restart with the flags --rm=true and --restart=Never.
The environment variable JUPYTER_ENABLE_LAB=yes informs the Jupyter
Notebook to start up in the updated JupyterLab mode.

---

[28]https://kubernetes.io/docs/reference/generated/kubectl/kubectl-
commands#run

145

Issue the following command and observe the output similar to Figure 4-14:

```
kubectl run -i -t test-notebook \
  --namespace=notebook-testing \
  --restart=Never --rm=true \
    --env="JUPYTER_ENABLE_LAB=yes" \
  --image=reg.gitlab.apk8s.dev/ds/jupyterlab-apk8s:v0.0.1
```

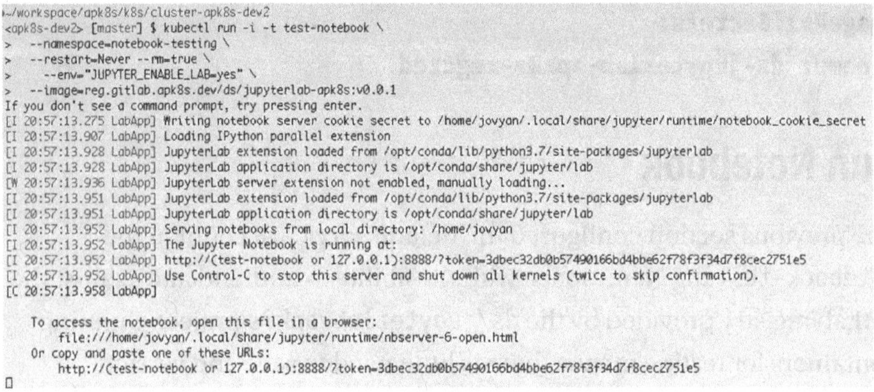

Figure 4-14. *Running a custom Jupyter Notebook*

The container jupyterlab-apk8s is large and depending on network conditions may take several minutes to download, create, and start the Pod. Once the Pod is running, copy the generated token from the output logs as seen in Figure 4-14.

Jupyter Notebooks listen on port 8888 by default. In testing and demonstrations such as this, it is common to port-forward Pod containers directly to a local workstation rather than configure Services and Ingress.

Caution   Jupyter Notebooks intend and purposefully allow remote code execution. Exposing Jupyter Notebooks to public interfaces requires proper security considerations and is reviewed further in the chapters "Indexing and Analytics" and "Platforming AIML".

Port-forward the test-notebook Pod with the following command:

```
kubectl port-forward test-notebook 8888:8888 \
-n notebook-testing
```

Once kubectl has begun forwarding port 8888 on the local workstation to port 8888 in the Pod, use the token provided in the container output (shown in Figure 4-14) to open jupyterlab-apk8s in a web browser. Browse to

```
http://localhost:8888/?token=3db...1e5
```

The new Jupyter Notebook should load and operate the same as it did earlier in this chapter on local testing (see Figure 4-6), only this time within the **dev2** Kubernetes cluster. The next section covers using a GitLab API user token to pull and push files from the notebook repository.

Repository Access

A variety of Machine Learning automation and Serverless platforms use CI/CD components along with VCS (version control system) repositories to build and deploy containerized workloads. The following is a simplistic approach to demonstrating a CI/CD pipeline originating from the cluster, in this case modifying the jupyterlab-apk8s image from within the jupyterlab-apk8s running container.

Create a GitLab **Personal Access Token** from **User Settings** (found in the drop-down menu under the user avatar). The token name is only used for reference. Check the **api** scope and click "Create personal access token" (see Figure 4-15). Record the generated token value, as this is not shown again; however, users may generate new tokens at any time.

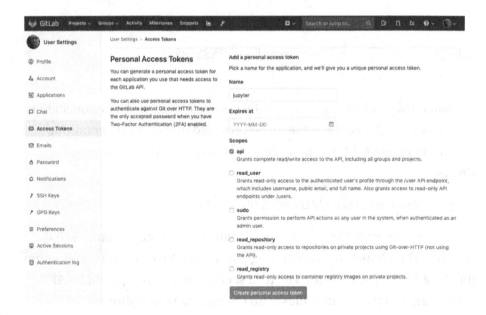

Figure 4-15. *GitLab Deploy Tokens*

Return to the `test-notebook` Pod running the custom Jupyter Notebook `jupyterlab-apk8s` in the web browser. In the Launcher tab, under the section titled **Other**, choose **Terminal**. Once a command prompt is available, clone the source code for `jupyterlab-apk8s`, and replace the token with the one generated earlier:

```
export GL_TOKEN=JDYxbywCZqS_N8zAsB6z
export GL_PROJ=gitlab.apk8s.dev/ds/jupyterlab-apk8s.git
git clone https://oauth2:$GL_TOKEN@$GL_PROJ
```

Caution   Sharing this running Notebook with other developers exposes your personal GitLab token. The chapters "Indexing and Analytics" and "Platforming AIML" demonstrate alternate methods of Notebook and repository access.

Later in this book, the chapter "Platforming Blockchain" uses the Python packages web3 and py-solc to communicate with an in-cluster Ethereum Blockchain network from within a user-provisioned Jupyter Notebook. The chapter "Pipeline" develops test MQTT clients and event listeners using the Python package paho-mqtt. Adding these packages to the custom JupyterLab container ensures a standard set of dependencies are always available to developers. Additional packages are easy to add at runtime.

Note   The jupyterlab-apk8s container is large and contains many packages and applications that may not be used by all developers. It is also likely that a developer will need additional packages. The jupyterlab-apk8s container defined in this book is for demonstration purposes. An optional practice involves creating a basic suit of custom Notebooks focusing on a specific area of development.

Next, open the Dockerfile in the cloned project and edit the RUN layer containing a pip install command. Add the Python packages paho-mqtt, web3, and py-solc as shown in Listing 4-5.

Listing 4-5. Source fragment from Dockerfile

```
# Installs blockchain, data science, and machine learning
# python packages
RUN pip install --no-cache \
    rubix \
    python-gitlab \
    scipy \
    numpy \
    pandas \
    scikit-learn \
```

```
    matplotlib \
    tensorflow \
    torch \
    torchvision \
    fastai \
    octave_kernel \
    jupyterlab-git \
    paho-mqtt \
    web3 \
    py-solc
```

Finally, commit the change, tag the commit v0.1.2, and push it back to the remote:

```
git commit -a -m "Blockchain and IoT packages."
git tag v0.1.2
git push origin v0.1.2
```

Earlier in this chapter, the project `ds/jupyterlab-apk8s` was configured to trigger a GitLab CI pipeline as new tags are pushed to the repository. The container `reg.gitlab.apk8s.dev/ds/jupyterlab-apk8s:v0.1.2` will become available once the CI pipeline completes.

GitOps

GitOps,[29] a process popularized by Weaveworks,[30] is another trending concept within the scope of Kubernetes CI/CD. GitOps involves the use of applications reacting to `git push` events. GitOps focuses primarily on Kubernetes clusters matching the state described by configuration

---

[29]`www.gitops.tech/`
[30]`www.weave.works/`

150

residing in a Git repository. On a simplistic level, GitOps aims to replace kubectl apply with git push. Popular and well-supported GitOps implementations include ArgoCD,[31] Flux,[32] and Jenkins X.[33]

Summary

This chapter presented a high-level introduction to CI/CD concepts and where they can fit from both a development and operations perspective. The use of a single-node (k3s) Kubernetes cluster running at Vultr and a four-node custom Kubernetes cluster running at Scaleway demonstrated multi-cluster, multi-cloud coordination at the application (platform) level. Running multiple small clusters with a well-defined separation of responsibility is an emerging architectural pattern.[34] The chapter developed a custom Jupyter Notebook built with a GitLab CI pipeline and was manually deployed and used to develop its capabilities further.

This chapter did not cover deployment. Deployment is often defined as a final step in the CI/CD pipeline and highly coupled to a specific application and its production requirements.

The overall goal of this chapter is to present CI/CD (in a simplistic manner) as a platform feature, exposing opportunities to expand beyond detached development concerns and integrate this powerful mechanism into the core of an enterprise application platform. New software platforms are extendable, and containerized workloads are natural means to extend

---

[31]https://argoproj.github.io/argo-cd/

[32]https://github.com/fluxcd/flux

[33]https://jenkins-x.io/

[34]https://content.pivotal.io/blog/kubernetes-one-cluster-or-many

platforms developed on Kubernetes. Developing and deploying containers are all possible from within the Kubernetes ecosystem. As demonstrated in this chapter, it is possible to provide a platform that may be extended limitlessly from within itself.

The next chapter covers data, specifically data pipelines into databases, indexes, event queues, and filesystems. Data is central to platform presented in this book, from the collection, analysis, processing, and presentation of data to the generation of new data derived from the inference of artificial intelligence or the results of blockchain transactions on smart contracts triggered by IoT events. The upcoming chapters intend to get started working with data from a platform perspective.

CHAPTER 5

Pipeline

All software platforms operate by communicating data in one form or
another. Data-driven services use data to determine flow (or logic), while
event-driven services listen for events to execute predetermined flow
and logic. In ether sense, these services are communicating data, and
the transmission of data itself is an event. Data-driven vs. event-driven
architectures typically boil down to the meaning and value of the data they
handle, and how the data is acted on, transformed, processed, or analyzed
by services consuming it.

The applications that manage data are often central components in
software platforms. How data is processed and maintained is typically
determined through business logic driven by business requirements. A
mature software platform should provide efficient and flexible application
logic able to accommodate a range of data management requirements,
supporting both data-driven and event-driven implementations.

IoT, Machine Learning, and Blockchain technologies produce
and consume data, each with specific needs: IoT devices produce and
consume high volumes of real-time data while communicating state.
Machine learning often requires extensive, organized catalogs of data.
Finally, Blockchain consumes and emits events as data.

The context of this book and the platform at hand considers data
as generic as possible, being primarily concerned with collection and
distribution and leaving the meaning and value of data to higher-level
application requirements. This chapter focuses on moving data from
publishers to subscribers in data pipelines.

© Craig Johnston 2020
C. Johnston, *Advanced Platform Development with Kubernetes*,
https://doi.org/10.1007/978-1-4842-5611-4_5

Statefulness and Kubernetes

Database management systems (databases) are stateful applications. Traditional monolithic architectures typically revolve around a central database, shared across multiple domains, while microservice architectures favor multiple databases, isolated to specific services and domains. Regardless of the overall system architecture, database applications are stateful, and not all stateful applications can easily exploit the strengths of Kubernetes.

Containerization and the orchestration of containers by Kubernetes are well suited for building extensible systems made up of separate, portable, and scalable components. At the heart of all Kubernetes platforms are the Pods, containerized workloads best treated as ephemeral and stateless. Pods are expected to come and go, scaling up and down based on rules, or unexpectedly terminated and re-spawned when underlying infrastructure fails or undergoes maintenance. Designing components to operate in this fashion realizes the advantage of Kubernetes's robust scaling, performance, redundancy, and self-healing capabilities. Operating stateful applications within this architecture can be challenging. However, many applications can maintain state over a distributed architecture; these applications are ideal for Kubernetes.

Kubernetes is suited for communicating data and events through vast networks of services backed by stateless Pods. However, the storage and retrieval of data is a stateful activity, a concept not as well suited for Kubernetes's ephemeral workloads. Data stored within a Pod is lost when the Pod is removed or replaced. Pods may attach to external Persistent Volumes; however, sharing Persistent Volumes between multiple Pods is not widely supported by storage providers and is challenging to achieve with acceptable performance and stability. Finally, operating a stateful application within a single Pod is neither scalable nor fault-tolerant. Stateful applications (such as databases) that work well with Kubernetes maintain state over a distributed network of nodes.

Kubernetes offers stateful functionality in the form of StatefulSets. StatefulSets are mostly equivalent to Deployments, yet deploy enumerated Pods able to reattach to storage allocated to them through Volume Claim Templates. A StatefulSet creates Pods named with an ordinal index, for example, `PODNAME-0..n`, and provides a stable network ID such as `PODNAME-4.somenamespace.svc.cluster.local`. If a Pod in a StatefulSet has crashed, been upgraded, or rescheduled to another node, Kubernetes creates a new Pod with the same name and network ID and reattaches any persistent volumes previously associated with the Pod name. Even if their workloads are ephemeral, Pods are stateful in concept through persistent naming and storage. Elasticsearch, Cassandra, and Kafka are some examples of data management applications that work well when deployed in multiple stateful Pods. Systems like these manage their data replication, distributed processing, and work around faulty or missing nodes within their self-managed, clustered networks. When properly configured, these applications continue to perform when missing a node (in this case a Pod) and typically provide limitless horizontal scaling. In some respects, Kubernetes makes scaling and managing these applications easier than the traditional methods involving the cumbersome task of provisioning virtual machines or bare-metal servers. In contrast, Kubernetes provides the ability to increment the desired number of Pods by merely editing and reapplying configuration.

Real-Time Data Architecture

A software platform intent on providing Machine Learning, IoT, and Blockchain capabilities requires the ability to collect, transform, process, and manage data, metadata, and metrics. The next few chapters cover a handful of enterprise-grade applications able to operate within a Kubernetes cluster, providing real-time data collection, routing, transformation, indexing, and the management of data and metrics (see Figure 5-1).

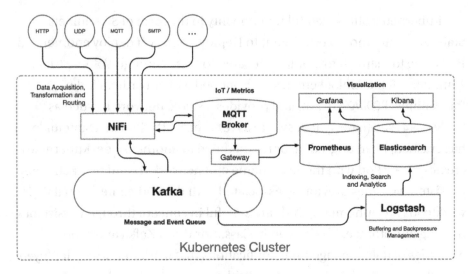

Figure 5-1. *Data management architecture*

The following sections cover the technology used in this chapter to assemble a real-time distributed streaming platform, ready for any form of inbound data and uniquely tailored for IoT.

Message and Event Queues

Web and mobile applications typically operate on a finite set of defined data structures; custom API endpoints authenticate, validate, and persist these objects in structured databases. By contrast, IoT platforms often require the ability to accept a wide range of data types and structures produced by any variety of connected devices. IoT platforms are primarily responsible for the distribution of device state to other devices and services.

Publish and subscribe (also known as Pub/Sub) applications solve the problem of gathering and distributing data (often referred to as events or messages) and connect a near-limitless number of producers to almost any number of interested consumers. This chapter focuses on

implementing the highly available and distributed streaming platform
Apache Kafka for all real-time data and event distribution, along with the
purpose-built MQTT broker, Mosquitto, for IoT.

Distributed Streaming Platform

Apache Kafka bills itself as a distributed streaming platform and acts as a
type of "central nervous system" for real-time data operations within the
platform. Kafka can handle many hundreds of thousands of messages per
second with a half-dozen nodes and proper configuration, a capability far
exceeding most use cases outside of significant data-centric enterprises.
Kafka records message (data) as records within a topic, consisting of a key,
value, and timestamp. Kafka manages the relationship, collection, and
distribution of records through its Consumer, Producer, Streaming, and
Connector APIs.

Kafka provides stable and mature client libraries for all major
programming languages, allowing custom platform components to
operate on data (events and messages) in real time.

MQTT and IoT

MQTT[1] (Message Queuing Telemetry Transport) is a publish/subscribe
messaging protocol designed for IoT and IIoT (Industrial Internet of
Things) implementations. Devices may publish and subscribe to topics
through MQTT brokers and Brokers may be bridged together. MQTT
is designed to be lightweight, able to run in resource-constrained
environments, including Raspberry Pi.[2]

---

[1]https://mqtt.org

[2]https://appcodelabs.com/introduction-to-iot-build-an-mqtt-server-
using-raspberry-pi

Consider an organization with a factory operating thousands of sensors and controllers communicating directly with an on-premises MQTT broker. The organization also subscribes to a cloud-hosted MQTT solution for gathering metrics from remote or isolated devices. Each of these Brokers may be bridged together and communicate bidirectionally with a larger data platform as shown in Figure 5-2.

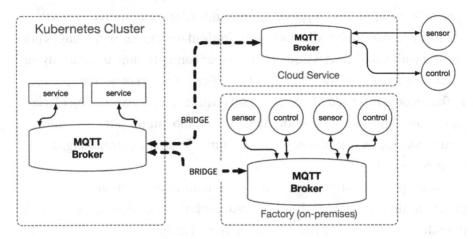

Figure 5-2. *MQTT network*

Mosquitto is a popular open source MQTT broker, configured later in this chapter for in-cluster MQTT operations. Mosquitto can publish and subscribe to any other MQTT compatible broker, typically on-premises or cloud-based SaaS.

Development Environment

This chapter uses the same, inexpensive four-node cluster setup on Scaleway in Chapter 4. The cluster includes one DEV1-M (3 CPU/4G RAM/40G SSD) for the Kubernetes master node and three DEV1-L (4 CPU/8G RAM/80GB SSD) for worker nodes. Configuring and operating Apache Kafka, Apache NiFi, Elasticsearch, and Logstash utilizes the majority of CPU and RAM of this small development cluster. These specifications are an absolute minimum requirement and should be scaled up as desired.

Note   The entire three-node development cluster used in this chapter is equivalent to one 12 core CPU/32GB RAM server instance similar to a single production node in a typical enterprise configuration.

Cluster-Wide Configuration

This chapter uses the same general Kubernetes configuration as detailed in Chapter 3, including Ingress Nginx, Cert Manager, Rook-Ceph, and monitoring configurations. If following along from previous chapters, copy and apply the configuration manifests from the directory `cluster-apk8s-dev1/000-cluster` in Listing 3-15 to `cluster-apk8s-dev3/000-cluster` and create the directory `cluster-apk8s-dev3/003-data` (as shown in Listing 5-1) to hold the manifests used throughout this chapter.

Listing 5-1. Development Cluster configuration layout

```
.
└── cluster-apk8s-dev1
└── cluster-apk8s-dev2
└── cluster-apk8s-dev3
    └── 000-cluster
        ├── 00-ingress-nginx
        ├── 10-cert-manager
        ├── 20-rook-ceph
        └── 30-monitoring
    └── 003-data
```

Note Numerically prefixed directories are a simple convention to infer an intended order of precedence. Configuration manifests may generally be applied in any order.

Data Namespace

Create the directory `cluster-apk8s-dev3/003-data/000-namespace` to contain namespace-wide configuration manifests. This development cluster should be considered single tenant considering its size and use for demonstration. However, containing all data-related functionality in tenant-based Namespaces (e.g., `clientx-data`) allows the opportunity to apply fine-grained role-based access control and networking rules. Since this development cluster has only one tenant, the namespace `data` is suitable. The following configurations apply to all services in the new data Namespace.

Within the `cluster-apk8s-dev3/003-data/000-namespace` directory, create a Kubernetes Namespace in a file named `00-namespace.yml` from Listing 5-2.

Listing 5-2. Data Namespace

```
apiVersion: v1
kind: Namespace
metadata:
  name: data
```

Apply the Namespace configuration:

```
$ kubectl apply -f 00-namespace.yml
```

TLS Certificates

Later in this chapter, secure Ingress configurations are applied for NiFi at
`nifi.data.dev3.apk8s.dev` and Kibana at `kib.data.dev3.apk8s.dev`,
providing external access to their user interfaces. Cert Manager, along with
a ClusterIssuer, should be present in the cluster (see Chapter 3).

Create a Certificate configuration in a file named `05-certs.yml` from
Listing 5-3.

Listing 5-3. Certificates for the data Namespace

```
apiVersion: certmanager.k8s.io/v1alpha1
kind: Certificate
metadata:
  name: data-cert
  namespace: data
spec:
  secretName: data-production-tls
  issuerRef:
    name: letsencrypt-production
    kind: ClusterIssuer
  commonName: data.dev3.apk8s.dev
  dnsNames:
    - data.dev3.apk8s.dev
    - nifi.data.dev3.apk8s.dev
    - kib.data.dev3.apk8s.dev
  acme:
    config:
      - http01:
          ingressClass: nginx
```

```
      domains:
        - data.dev3.apk8s.dev
        - nifi.data.dev3.apk8s.dev
        - kib.data.dev3.apk8s.dev
```

Apply the Certificate configuration:

```
$ kubectl apply -f 05-certs.yml
```

Basic Auth

The development cluster uses Basic Auth[3] (Basic Authentication) as a convenient method of securing Ingress. Using a single Basic Auth secret across Ingresses simplifies the use of authentication during development and can be replaced with more sophisticated methods such as OAuth when required.

Create a file named auth with the utility htpasswd:[4]

```
$ htpasswd -c ./auth sysop
```

Create a generic Kubernetes Secret named sysop-basic-auth with the auth file generated earlier:

```
$ kubectl create secret generic sysop-basic-auth \
--from-file auth -n data
```

---

[3]https://developer.mozilla.org/en-US/docs/Web/HTTP/Authentication
[4]https://httpd.apache.org/docs/2.4/programs/htpasswd.html

Apache Zookeeper

Apache Zookeeper[5] has become a standard for many popular applications requiring distributed coordination, including Hadoop,[6] HBase,[7] Kafka, NiFi, and Elasticsearch. In this chapter, both Kafka and NiFi utilize a shared Zookeeper cluster. Elasticsearch operates as a single node in this environment; however, larger Elasticsearch clusters could also take advantage of a shared Zookeeper.

Zookeeper may be scaled to tolerate a given number of failed nodes; however, some architectures favor multiple isolated installs to avoid single points of failure. Scaled or multiple Zookeeper configurations are a production concern, whereas sharing this service in a development environment makes better use of limited resources.

Create the directory cluster-apk8s-dev3/003-data/010-zookeeper. Within the new 010-zookeeper directory, create a file named 10-service.yml from Listing 5-4.

Listing 5-4. Zookeeper Service

```
apiVersion: v1
kind: Service
metadata:
  name: zookeeper
  namespace: data
spec:
  ports:
    - name: client
      port: 2181
```

---

[5]https://zookeeper.apache.org
[6]https://hadoop.apache.org/
[7]https://hbase.apache.org

```
    protocol: TCP
    targetPort: client
  selector:
    app: zookeeper
  sessionAffinity: None
  type: ClusterIP
```

Apply the Zookeeper Service configuration:

```
$ kubectl apply -f 10-service.yml
```

Zookeeper clients such as Kafka and NiFi manage their relationships to individual nodes. A standard Service definition in Kubernetes is assigned an IP address and most commonly configured to route any communication with that service to any Pod matching a specified selector and port. However, applications such as Zookeeper require the ability for each Zookeeper node (running as a Pod) to communicate with its peers (running as Pods). A standard Kubernetes Service is inadequate for use in a peer-aware cluster as each node must be able to communicate specifically with each other node and not merely any node matching a selector and port. Kubernetes provides this functionality through the concept of a Headless Service,[8] which is a Service without a ClusterIP defined (clusterIP: None). The following service definition creates a Headless Service returning DNS entries for Pods matching the selector app: zookeeper as defined in the StatefulSet described in the next section.

Create a Headless Service configuration in a file named 10-service-headless.yml from Listing 5-5.

---

[8]https://kubernetes.io/docs/concepts/services-networking/service/
#headless-services

Listing 5-5. Zookeeper Headless Service

```
apiVersion: v1
kind: Service
metadata:
  name: zookeeper-headless
  namespace: data
spec:
  clusterIP: None
  ports:
    - name: client
      port: 2181
      protocol: TCP
      targetPort: 2181
    - name: election
      port: 3888
      protocol: TCP
      targetPort: 3888
    - name: server
      port: 2888
      protocol: TCP
      targetPort: 2888
  selector:
    app: zookeeper
  sessionAffinity: None
  type: ClusterIP
```

Apply the Zookeeper Headless Service configuration:

```
$ kubectl apply -f 10-service-headless.yml
```

Next, create a StatefulSet configuration in a file named
40-statefulset.yml from Listing 5-6.

Listing 5-6. Zookeeper StatefulSet

```
apiVersion: apps/v1
kind: StatefulSet
metadata:
  name: zookeeper
  namespace: data
spec:
  podManagementPolicy: OrderedReady
  replicas: 2
  revisionHistoryLimit: 1
  selector:
    matchLabels:
      app: zookeeper
  serviceName: zookeeper-headless
  template:
    metadata:
      labels:
        app: zookeeper
    spec:
      containers:
        - command:
            - /bin/bash
            - -xec
            - zkGenConfig.sh && exec zkServer.sh start-foreground
          env:
            - name: ZK_REPLICAS
              value: "2"
            - name: JMXAUTH
              value: "false"
            - name: JMXDISABLE
              value: "false"
```

```
        - name: JMXPORT
          value: "1099"
        - name: JMXSSL
          value: "false"
        - name: ZK_CLIENT_PORT
          value: "2181"
        - name: ZK_ELECTION_PORT
          value: "3888"
        - name: ZK_HEAP_SIZE
          value: 1G
        - name: ZK_INIT_LIMIT
          value: "5"
        - name: ZK_LOG_LEVEL
          value: INFO
        - name: ZK_MAX_CLIENT_CNXNS
          value: "60"
        - name: ZK_MAX_SESSION_TIMEOUT
          value: "40000"
        - name: ZK_MIN_SESSION_TIMEOUT
          value: "4000"
        - name: ZK_PURGE_INTERVAL
          value: "0"
        - name: ZK_SERVER_PORT
          value: "2888"
        - name: ZK_SNAP_RETAIN_COUNT
          value: "3"
        - name: ZK_SYNC_LIMIT
          value: "10"
        - name: ZK_TICK_TIME
          value: "2000"
      image: gcr.io/google_samples/k8szk:v3
      imagePullPolicy: IfNotPresent
```

```
livenessProbe:
  exec:
    command:
      - zkOk.sh
  failureThreshold: 3
  initialDelaySeconds: 20
  periodSeconds: 10
  successThreshold: 1
  timeoutSeconds: 1
name: zookeeper
ports:
  - containerPort: 2181
    name: client
    protocol: TCP
  - containerPort: 3888
    name: election
    protocol: TCP
  - containerPort: 2888
    name: server
    protocol: TCP
readinessProbe:
  exec:
    command:
      - zkOk.sh
  failureThreshold: 3
  initialDelaySeconds: 20
  periodSeconds: 10
  successThreshold: 1
  timeoutSeconds: 1
resources: {}
terminationMessagePath: /dev/termination-log
terminationMessagePolicy: File
```

```
        volumeMounts:
          - mountPath: /var/lib/zookeeper
            name: data
      dnsPolicy: ClusterFirst
      restartPolicy: Always
      schedulerName: default-scheduler
      securityContext:
        fsGroup: 1000
        runAsUser: 1000
      terminationGracePeriodSeconds: 30
      volumes:
        - emptyDir: {}
          name: data
  updateStrategy:
    type: OnDelete
```

Lastly, apply the Zookeeper StatefulSet configuration:

```
$ kubectl apply -f 40-statefulset.yml
```

Zookeeper, a shared dependency of Kafka and NiFi, is now available on the development cluster. The next section sets up a two-node Apache Kafka cluster.

Apache Kafka

Apache Kafka "is used for building real-time data pipelines and streaming apps. It is horizontally scalable, fault-tolerant, wicked fast, and runs in production in thousands of companies."[9] The following configuration stands up a two-node Kafka cluster, well suited for a small-scale development

---

[9]https://kafka.apache.org

environment and data science activities. As noted earlier, Apache Kafka is the central nervous system of this data-driven platform. In addition to providing stable and feature-rich client libraries in every major programming language, many data management applications have developed first-class connectors to both publish and subscribe to Kafka events including Logstash and NiFi, demonstrated later in this chapter; see Figure 5-3.

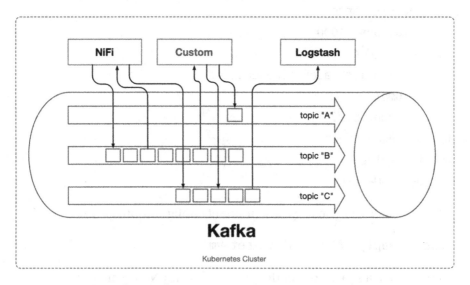

Figure 5-3. *Apache Kafka*

High-performance, low-latency event queues such as Apache Kafka operate at peak efficiency on dedicated, highly optimized, bare-metal servers. Running Kafka in containers, on shared virtual instances with abstracted storage and overlay networks (as the Kubernetes cluster defined in this book), can significantly reduce its efficiency and throughput. However, in some cases, a reduction in optimal performance may not be noticed, or may readily be compensated for through scaling. Operating Kafka within Kubernetes brings numerous advantages, including unified networking, DNS, scaling, self-healing, security, monitoring, and a unified control plane with other components. On a conceptual level, Kafka is one of many components forming a Kubernetes-based data platform described throughout this book. While Kafka itself my not profit significantly from management within Kubernetes, the larger data platform benefits from Kafka's inclusion through a higher cohesion among its essential components.

The following configuration sets up Kafka in a similar fashion to Zookeeper (configured in the previous section) with the addition of persistent volumes, as shown in Figure 5-4.

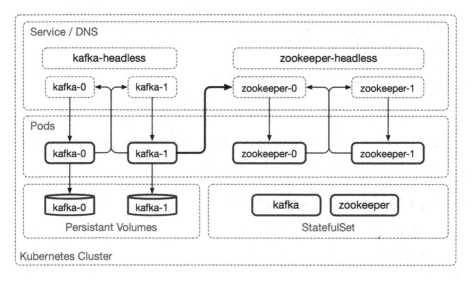

Figure 5-4. *Apache Kafka and Zookeeper Kubernetes configuration*

Create the directory `cluster-apk8s-dev3/003-data/020-kafka`. Within the new `020-kafka` directory, create a file named `10-service.yml` from Listing 5-7.

Listing 5-7. Kafka Service

```
apiVersion: v1
kind: Service
metadata:
  name: kafka
  namespace: data
```

```
spec:
  ports:
    - name: broker
      port: 9092
      protocol: TCP
      targetPort: kafka
  selector:
    app: kafka
  sessionAffinity: None
  type: ClusterIP
```

Apply the Kafka Service configuration:

```
$ kubectl apply -f 10-service.yml
```

Next, create a Headless Service configuration for Kafka in a file named
10-service-headless.yml from Listing 5-8.

Listing 5-8. Kafka Headless Service

```
apiVersion: v1
kind: Service
metadata:
  name: kafka-headless
  namespace: data
spec:
  clusterIP: None
  ports:
    - name: broker
      port: 9092
      protocol: TCP
      targetPort: 9092
```

```
selector:
  app: kafka
sessionAffinity: None
type: ClusterIP
```

Apply the Kafka Headless Service configuration:

```
$ kubectl apply -f 10-service-headless.yml
```

Next, create a StatefulSet configuration for Kafka in a file named 40-statefulset.yml from Listing 5-9.

The following configuration uses a Kafka container maintained by Confluent Inc.[10] Confluent provides commercial support for their open source event-streaming platform built around Kafka. Kafka functionality utilized in this book works with both Confluent's Kafka distribution and the standard, upstream Apache Kafka.

Listing 5-9. Kafka StatefulSet

```
apiVersion: apps/v1
kind: StatefulSet
metadata:
  labels:
    app: kafka
  name: kafka
  namespace: data
spec:
  podManagementPolicy: OrderedReady
  replicas: 2
  revisionHistoryLimit: 1
```

---

[10]https://www.confluent.io

```
selector:
  matchLabels:
    app: kafka
serviceName: kafka-headless
template:
  metadata:
    labels:
      app: kafka
  spec:
    containers:
      - command:
          - sh
          - -exc
          - |
            unset KAFKA_PORT && \
            export KAFKA_BROKER_ID=${HOSTNAME##*-} && \
            export KAFKA_ADVERTISED_LISTENERS=PLAINTEXT:
            //${POD_IP}:9092 && \
            exec /etc/confluent/docker/run
        env:
          - name: POD_IP
            valueFrom:
              fieldRef:
                apiVersion: v1
                fieldPath: status.podIP
          - name: KAFKA_HEAP_OPTS
            value: -Xmx1G -Xms1G
          - name: KAFKA_ZOOKEEPER_CONNECT
            value: zookeeper-headless:2181
          - name: KAFKA_LOG_DIRS
            value: /opt/kafka/data/logs
          - name: KAFKA_OFFSETS_TOPIC_REPLICATION_FACTOR
```

```
    value: "1"
  - name: KAFKA_JMX_PORT
    value: "5555"
image: confluentinc/cp-kafka:5.3.1-1
imagePullPolicy: IfNotPresent
livenessProbe:
  exec:
    command:
      - sh
      - -ec
      - /usr/bin/jps | /bin/grep -q SupportedKafka
  failureThreshold: 3
  initialDelaySeconds: 30
  periodSeconds: 10
  successThreshold: 1
  timeoutSeconds: 5
name: kafka-broker
ports:
  - containerPort: 9092
    name: kafka
    protocol: TCP
readinessProbe:
  failureThreshold: 3
  initialDelaySeconds: 30
  periodSeconds: 10
  successThreshold: 1
  tcpSocket:
    port: kafka
  timeoutSeconds: 5
resources: {}
terminationMessagePath: /dev/termination-log
terminationMessagePolicy: File
```

```
            volumeMounts:
              - mountPath: /opt/kafka/data
                name: datadir
        dnsPolicy: ClusterFirst
        restartPolicy: Always
        schedulerName: default-scheduler
        securityContext: {}
        terminationGracePeriodSeconds: 60
  updateStrategy:
    type: OnDelete
  volumeClaimTemplates:
    - metadata:
        name: datadir
      spec:
        accessModes:
          - ReadWriteOnce
        resources:
          requests:
            storage: 5Gi
        storageClassName: rook-ceph-block
```

Apply the Kafka StatefulSet configuration:

```
$ kubectl apply -f 40-statefulset.yml
```

Kubernetes Pod Disruption Budgets11 limit the number of Pods allowed to be down at any given time with the exception of unplanned outages such as node failures or Pod errors. A PodDisruptionBudget configuration is especially useful for updating a stateful set representing a highly available cluster such as Kafka. With proper configuration and resources, a Kafka cluster may stay entirely operational, while a subset of nodes are offline.

---

[11]https://kubernetes.io/docs/concepts/workloads/pods/
disruptions/#how-disruption-budgets-work

> **Note**   Due to the limited resources of the development environment
> specified in this chapter, the Kafka configuration defined in the
> following is stable, yet not highly available.[12]

Create a PodDisruptionBudget configuration for Kafka in a file named
45-pdb.yml from Listing 5-10.

Listing 5-10. Kafka Pod Disruption Budget

```yaml
apiVersion: policy/v1beta1
kind: PodDisruptionBudget
metadata:
  name: kafka
  namespace: data
  labels:
    app: kafka
spec:
  maxUnavailable: 1
  selector:
    matchLabels:
      app: kafka
```

Lastly, apply the Kafka PodDisruptionBudget configuration:

```
$ kubectl apply -f 45-pdb.yml
```

The new development environment is now running a two-node Kafka
cluster. The next section sets up Pod for testing and debugging.

---

[12]www.loudera.com/documentation/kafka/latest/topics/kafka_ha.html

Kafka Client Utility Pod

Kafka can broker data between nearly every component in this data-driven platform with minimal administrative overhead. However, the Kafka container provided by Confluence contains several useful scripts (see Table 5-1) for testing, backup, security configuration, and general administrative functions. Running a Kafka client utility Pod provides command-line administrative access to this critical platform component.

The Kafka test client Pod runs the same `confluentinc/cp-kafka:5.3.1-1` image as the operational cluster configured earlier. However, the Pod is configured to execute the command `tail -f /dev/null` rather than the standard entry point, keeping `tail` an active process and preventing the Pod from completing.

Create a Kafka test client configuration in a file named `99-pod-test-client.yml` from Listing 5-11.

Listing 5-11. Kafka test client Pod

```
apiVersion: v1
kind: Pod
metadata:
  name: kafka-client-util
  namespace: data
spec:
  containers:
    - command:
        - sh
        - -c
        - exec tail -f /dev/null
      image: confluentinc/cp-kafka:5.3.1-1
      imagePullPolicy: IfNotPresent
      name: kafka
```

```
resources: {}
terminationMessagePath: /dev/termination-log
terminationMessagePolicy: File
```

Apply the Kafka test client Pod configuration:

```
$ kubectl apply -f 99-pod-client-util.yml
```

The container image `confluentinc/cp-kafka:4.1.2-2` running in the Kafka test client Pod comes with the utilities listed in Table 5-1. Run any of the commands listed in Table 5-1 with the `--help` flag for a list of configuration arguments. Cloudera provides detailed documentation on their website: *Kafka Administration Using Command Line Tools.*[13]

Table 5-1. *Kafka client utility scripts*

Script	Description
kafka-acls	User authentication, authorization, and access control list management.
kafka-broker-api-version	List the API versions of all nodes in the cluster.
kafka-configs	Add/remove entity config for a topic, client, user, or broker.
kafka-console-consumer	Used to create, alter, list, and describe topics.
kafka-console-producer	Read data from standard output and write it to a Kafka topic.
kafka-consumer-groups	List the current consumer groups.

(*continued*)

---

[13]`www.cloudera.com/documentation/enterprise/latest/topics/kafka_admin_cli.html`

Table 5-1. (*continued*)

Script	Description
kafka-consumer-offset-checker	Return the number of messages read and written with lag times for each consumer in a specific consumer group.
kafka-consumer-perf-test	Run a consumer performance test on a broker and topic.
kafka-delegation-tokens	Delegation tokens are shared secrets between brokers and clients. Create, describe, renew, and expire tokens.
kafka-delete-records	Delete records from a topic with a given offset.
kafka-log-dirs	Output a JSON object with log information per broker.
kafka-mirror-maker	Replicate the Kafka cluster.[14]
kafka-preferred-replica-election	Rebalance topics.[15]
kafka-producer-perf-test	Run a producer performance test on a broker and topic.
kafka-reassign-partitions	Reassign the Kafka topic partition Leaders to a different Kafka Broker.
kafka-replay-log-producer	Consume messages from one topic and replay (produce) them in another.
kafka-replica-verification	Verify that data is replicated correctly for one or more topics.
kafka-run-class	Provides the ability to call Kafka classes directly; used primarily by the other scripts.

(*continued*)

---

[14]https://cwiki.apache.org/confluence/pages/viewpage.action?pageId=27846330

[15]https://blog.imaginea.com/how-to-rebalance-topics-in-kafka-cluster/

Table 5-1. (*continued*)

Script	Description
kafka-server-start kafka-server-stop	Unused in the context of administering the Confluent distribution.
kafka-streams- application-reset	Reset the internal state of a Kafka Streams[16] application.
kafka-topics	Create, list, configure, and delete topics.
kafka-verifiable- producer kafka-verifiable- consumer	Produce and consume a set number of messages for testing.

TESTING KAFKA

1. Drop into a Bash[17] session on the new Kafka test client Pod.

   ```
   $ kubectl exec -it kafka-client-util bash -n data
   ```

2. From the command-line on the new Pod, create the topic test with **one partition** and **one replica**.

   ```
   # kafka-topics --zookeeper zookeeper-headless:2181 \
   --topic test --create --partitions 1 --replication-factor
   ```

3. List all topics in the Kafka cluster. The new cluster should only have the test topic along with one or more internal topics beginning with two underscores.

   ```
   # kafka-topics --zookeeper zookeeper-headless:2181 --list
   ```

---

[16]https://kafka.apache.org/documentation/streams/
[17]www.gnu.org/software/bash/

4. Listen to the new test topic. kafka-console-consumer printing message to the console.

```
# kafka-console-consumer --bootstrap-server kafka:9092 \
--topic test
```

5. Open an additional Bash session on Kafka test client Pod from a separate terminal.

```
$ kubectl exec -it kafka-client-util bash -n data
```

6. Send a test message with kafka-console-producer utility.

```
# kafka-console-producer --broker-list kafka:9092 \
--topic test
```

7. Type a message and return. Each line of text is sent to the topic as a message and displayed in the terminal running the Kafka console consumer (step 4).

The development environment is now running a two-node Kafka cluster, tested and ready to receive and deliver messages. Consider adding an administrative web interface with Kafka Manager,[18] developed by Yahoo!. LinkedIn developed the Burrow[19] utility to monitor consumer lag times and provide stats over an HTTP endpoint. Cruise-control,[20] also developed by LinkedIn, and DoctorKafka[21] developed by Pinterest automate dynamic workload rebalancing and self-healing. Kafka has a vast and evolving ecosystem of utilities and third-party support.[22]

---

[18]https://github.com/yahoo/kafka-manager
[19]https://github.com/linkedin/Burrow
[20]https://github.com/linkedin/cruise-control
[21]https://github.com/pinterest/doctorkafka
[22]https://cwiki.apache.org/confluence/display/KAFKA/Ecosystem

Kafka is designed to work at an immense scale, as a highly available, fault-tolerant, distributed, general-purpose publish/subscribe system, and this is a great reason to keep it in the center of a data-driven architecture. Kafka can easily handle a tremendous volume[23] of data and metrics from nearly any source, especially IoT devices. However, the next section covers another publish/subscribe application called Mosquitto which implements the MQTT protocol, uniquely designed for IoT.

Mosquitto (MQTT)

Protocols such as MQTT (and AMQP) focus on lightweight client to message broker communications suitable for a wide and growing range of consumer and industrial IoT devices. In contrast, Apache Kafka is a much heavier event queue implementation, able to process and persist tremendous volumes of data. While these systems are similar in concept, adding MQTT capabilities to the data platform in this book demonstrates a variety of protocols and the ability to exchange messages between them.

Imagine a factory where machine states are both controlled and communicated through on-premises MQTT broker; an MQTT broker within a remote data platform acts as a client-bridge and relays these messages to Kafka. Machine Learning models run predictive analysis on a rolling last hour of data from Kafka and make decisions for adjusting a particular machine's state and communicate this decision back through MQTT (see Figure 5-5).

---

[23]https://engineering.linkedin.com/kafka/benchmarking-apache-kafka-2-million-writes-second-three-cheap-machines

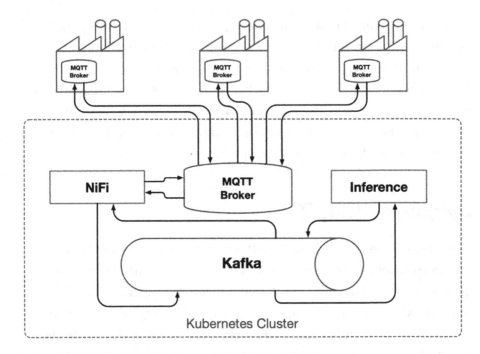

Figure 5-5. *Apache Kafka and MQTT event queues*

Mosquitto[24] is an open source MQTT broker maintained by the Eclipse
Foundation[25] as one of many components offered by the *iot.eclipse.org*
project.

Create the directory cluster-apk8s-dev3/003-data/050-mqtt. Within
the new 050-mqtt directory, create a file named 10-service.yml from
Listing 5-12.

Listing 5-12. Mosquitto MQTT Service

```
apiVersion: v1
kind: Service
metadata:
```

---

[24]https://mosquitto.org/
[25]https://eclipse.org/

```
      name: mqtt
      namespace: data
      labels:
        app: mqtt
    spec:
      selector:
        app: mqtt
      ports:
        - protocol: "TCP"
          port: 1883
          targetPort: 1883
      type: ClusterIP
```

Apply the MQTT Service configuration:

```
$ kubectl apply -f 10-service.yml
```

Next, create a ConfigMap for Mosquitto in a file named 20-configmap.
yml from Listing 5-13. The small configuration file defined here instructs
the server to run as the user mosquitto and listen on port 1883. There is
no encryption or authentication in this example because the server in this
development environment is not exposed directly to the public. See the
online documentation for an extensive list of configuration options.[26]

Caution   Never expose an MQTT broker to the public Internet
without authentication and encryption enabled. All clients should be
trusted. It is highly recommended to employ a VPN or well-configured
firewall to secure remote connections.

---

[26]https://mosquitto.org/man/mosquitto-conf-5.html

Listing 5-13. Mosquitto configuration ConfigMap

```
apiVersion: v1
kind: ConfigMap
metadata:
  name: mqtt
  namespace: data
  labels:
    app: mqtt
data:
  mosquitto.conf: |-
    user mosquitto
    port 1883
```

Apply the Mosquitto configuration ConfigMap:

```
$ kubectl apply -f 20-configmap.yml
```

Next, create a Deployment for Mosquitto in a file named
30-deployment.yml from Listing 5-14. The Mosquitto defined here is
intended to run as a single instance. Scaling Mosquitto for production
often involves provisioning Brokers for a specified client or group of
clients. There are many other open source and commercial MQTT
brokers available, including VerneMQ,[27] a highly available distributed
implementation, and the popular RabbitMQ[28] supporting AMQP,[29]
STOMP,[30] as well as MQTT, both open source and written in Erlang.

---

[27]https://vernemq.com
[28]www.rabbitmq.com
[29]www.amqp.org
[30]https://stomp.github.io

Listing 5-14. Mosquitto Deployment

```
apiVersion: apps/v1
kind: Deployment
metadata:
  name: mqtt
  namespace: data
  labels:
    app: mqtt
spec:
  replicas: 1 # keep at 1 for
  revisionHistoryLimit: 1
  selector:
    matchLabels:
      app: mqtt
  template:
    metadata:
      labels:
        app: mqtt
    spec:
      volumes:
        - name: mqtt-config-volume
          configMap:
            name: mqtt
      containers:
        - name: mqtt
          image: eclipse-mosquitto:1.6.6
          imagePullPolicy: IfNotPresent
          volumeMounts:
            - name: mqtt-config-volume
              mountPath: /mosquitto/config
```

```
    ports:
      - name: mqtt
        containerPort: 1883
```

Apply the Mosquitto Deployment:

```
$ kubectl apply -f 30-deployment.yml
```

An MQTT broker is installed and running in the Kubernetes development cluster. Utilities such as MQTT.fx[31] and mqtt-spy[32] are great for testing and debugging MQTT brokers. The following exercise tests the new Broker utilizing the mosquitto_sub utility on the new Mosquitto Pod along with MQTT.fx operated on a local workstation.

TESTING MOSQUITTO

1. Download and install MQTT.fx version 1.7.1 on a local workstation. Visit https://mqttfx.jensd.de/index.php/download.

2. Drop into a Bash session on the Mosquitto MQTT broker Pod (use kubectl get pods -n data to find its name).

   ```
   $ kubectl exec -it mqtt-6899646f75-g65sf sh -n data
   ```

3. From the command line within the Mosquitto MQTT Pod, begin listening for messages on the dev/test topic.

   ```
   # mosquitto_sub -t dev/apk8s
   ```

4. From the local workstation, use kubectl to port-forward the mqtt Kubernetes Service to the local workstation running MQTT.fx.

   ```
   $ kubectl port-forward svc/mqtt 1883:1883 -n data
   ```

---

[31]https://mqttfx.jensd.de
[32]http://kamilfb.github.io/mqtt-spy/

5. Open MQTT.fx and select "local mosquitto" from the connect drop-down, and then click Connect as shown in Figure 5-6.

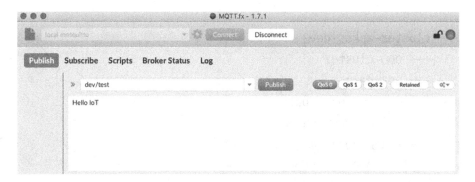

Figure 5-6. *MQTT.fx application running on a local workstation*

6. Provide the same topic; `mosquitto_sub` is listening to from step 3, in this case, `dev/apk8s`. Provide a message in the large text area and click **Publish**.

Note   Simple messaging can also be accomplished with the `mosquitto_pub` utility available alongside `mosquitto_sub`.

---

7. Observe the message printed from the `mosquitto_sub` output.

Summary

The platform now consists of two popular event queues, Kafka and Mosquitto. Kafka is intended as the "central nervous system" of the platform and responsible for the real-time communication of state, metrics, and data, to and from other platform components. Mosquitto provides support for the popular IoT communication protocol MQTT. Listing 5-15 displays an overview of configuration manifests developed in this chapter.

Listing 5-15. Data Pipeline Development Cluster configuration layout

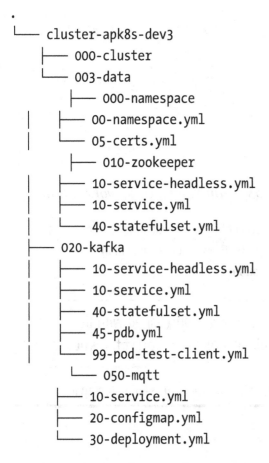

```
.
└── cluster-apk8s-dev3
    ├── 000-cluster
    └── 003-data
        ├── 000-namespace
    │   ├── 00-namespace.yml
    │   └── 05-certs.yml
        ├── 010-zookeeper
    │   ├── 10-service-headless.yml
    │   ├── 10-service.yml
    │   └── 40-statefulset.yml
    ├── 020-kafka
    │   ├── 10-service-headless.yml
    │   ├── 10-service.yml
    │   ├── 40-statefulset.yml
    │   ├── 45-pdb.yml
    │   └── 99-pod-test-client.yml
            └── 050-mqtt
        ├── 10-service.yml
        ├── 20-configmap.yml
        └── 30-deployment.yml
```

The upcoming chapters demonstrate methods of indexing, analysis, visualization, warehousing, and routing data flowing through the queues configured in this chapter.

CHAPTER 6

Indexing and Analytics

A modern, distributed data platform with Kubernetes goes well beyond the collection, storage, and transmission of data. Search, indexing, analyzing, and data science applications are essential elements in data-centric platforms. This chapter focuses on web-scale[1] technologies, an ecosystem that matured outside of the mainline concerns of Big Data.[2] Where Big Data assumes a limited number of simultaneous requests to process nearly unlimited lakes[3] of data, web-scale assumes an eventual unlimited simultaneous demand for data. Web-scale analytics and Big Data are growing closer together and rapidly advancing in combined capabilities. This chapter covers general data indexing, metrics, analytics, and data science built for web-scale architectures. The next chapter covers how Kubernetes fits into the Big Data picture by supporting the development of modern data lakes and warehouses. Kubernetes's ability to construct robust, distributed clusters brings opportunities to bridge the data and control planes of these two distinct problem domains, Big Data at web-scale.

---

[1] Haight, Cameron. "Enter Web-Scale IT." Gartner Blog Network, May 16, 2013. https://blogs.gartner.com/cameron_haight/2013/05/16/enter-web-scale-it/.

[2] Lohr, Steve. "The Origins of 'Big Data': An Etymological Detective Story." Bits Blog (blog), February 1, 2013. https://bits.blogs.nytimes.com/2013/02/01/the-origins-of-big-data-an-etymological-detective-story/.

[3] Dixon, James. "Pentaho, Hadoop, and Data Lakes." James Dixon's Blog (blog), October 14, 2010. https://jamesdixon.wordpress.com/2010/10/14/pentaho-hadoop-and-data-lakes/.

© Craig Johnston 2020
C. Johnston, *Advanced Platform Development with Kubernetes*,
https://doi.org/10.1007/978-1-4842-5611-4_6

This chapter focuses on applications that cover a generic yet capable range of communication, indexing, and data science requirements. Applications focused on a specific problem domain may benefit from technology targeted at a higher level; however, general search, analytics, and data science technologies are often the foundation of a multilayered approach in developing a focused data-driven solution.

Search and Analytics

Data exists as structured, semi-structured and unstructured. Unstructured data includes a variety of data types, such as images, videos, audio, PDFs, and raw text. The next chapter covers the development of data lakes to store unstructured data. However, this chapter is concerned with semi-structured, document-based data supported by Elasticsearch, a document-based data index capable of the storage, retrieval, and analysis of billions of records.

Data Science Environment

In the section "Data Lab," this chapter ties together the operations of data gathering, queueing indexing, and analysis into a data science environment. JupyterHub is configured to provide JupyterLab instances (introduced in Chapter 4) to enhance data science activities by leveraging in-cluster access to Kafka, Elasticsearch, Mosquitto, and more.

Development Environment

Previous chapters utilized generic compute resources from low-cost hosting providers Vultr and Scaleway. This chapter continues the trend by selecting discount compute offerings by Hetzner. Hetzner is another excellent option for constructing low-cost development and experimental Kubernetes clusters.

The Kubernetes cluster in this chapter utilizes one CX21 (2 vCPU/8G RAM/40G SSD) and four CX41 (4 vCPU/16G RAM/160G SSD) instances by Hetzner. Hetzner pricing at the time of this writing puts this cluster at less than four US dollars per day.

Note   Ubuntu server instances on Hetzner do not include kernel headers needed by some packages or the kernel module rbd (required by Ceph). Use the following commands on each Hetzner server to install the kernel headers and load rbd shown in Listing 6-1.

Listing 6-1. Installing kernel headers and the rdb kernel module

```
$ # install kernel headers
$ apt install -y linux-headers-$(uname -r)

$ # load the Ceph rbd kernel module
$ modprobe rbd
```

Labeled as dev4, the custom Kubernetes cluster in this chapter is set up following installation instructions from Chapter 3 along with manifests from Chapter 5. If following along from the previous chapter, duplicate and apply the manifests from cluster-apk8s-dev3 into cluster-apk8s-dev4 as shown in Listing 6-2.

Listing 6-2. Development environment prerequisites

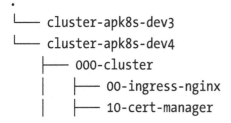

```
.
└── cluster-apk8s-dev3
└── cluster-apk8s-dev4
    ├── 000-cluster
    │   ├── 00-ingress-nginx
    │   ├── 10-cert-manager
```

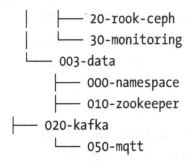

```
|        ├──── 20-rook-ceph
|        └──── 30-monitoring
└──── 003-data
         ├──── 000-namespace
         ├──── 010-zookeeper
├──── 020-kafka
         └──── 050-mqtt
```

TLS Certificates

This chapter uses the subdomains kib for Kibana, auth for Keycloak, and lab for JupyterHub/JupyterLab. Ensure the TLS Kubernetes Secret data-production-tls is available to ingress by generating the certificates. Listing 6-3 lists an example Cert Manager configuration defining the file cluster-apk8s-dev4/003-data/000-namespace/05-certs.yml.

Listing 6-3. cluster-apk8s-dev4 TLS Certificate

```
apiVersion: cert-manager.io/v1alpha2
kind: Certificate
metadata:
  name: data-cert
  namespace: data
spec:
  secretName: data-production-tls
  issuerRef:
    name: letsencrypt-production
    kind: ClusterIssuer
  commonName: data.dev4.apk8s.dev
```

```
dnsNames:
  - data.dev4.apk8s.dev
  - auth.data.dev4.apk8s.dev
  - lab.data.dev4.apk8s.dev
  - kib.data.dev4.apk8s.dev
```

Basic Auth

Create a Kubernetes Secret containing Basic Auth credentials. Later on, Ingress Nginx is configured to use this Secret to secure access to Kibana.

First, create a username/password combination in a file named auth using the htpasswd[4] utility.

```
$ cd cluster-apk8s-dev4/003-data/000-namespace
$ htpasswd -c auth sysop
```

Use the kubectl imperative command create secret to create a Secret named sysop-basic-auth from the auth file structured as expected by Ingress.

```
$ kubectl create secret generic sysop-basic-auth \
    --from-file auth -n data
```

ELK

The ELK stack[5] consists of Elasticsearch, Logstash, and Kibana. ELK is a popular suite of applications for indexing, searching, routing, transforming, and visualizing data. Elasticsearch B.V. maintains this open source stack and offers managed services along with many other popular open source and commercial software.

---

[4]https://httpd.apache.org/docs/current/programs/htpasswd.html
[5]www.elastic.co/what-is/elk-stack

> **Note**   The Elasticsearch B.V. *Elastic License* may be too restrictive
> for platforms-as-a-service (PaaS) offerings that include Elasticsearch.
> Amazon has forked the project and created the *Open Distro*
> *for Elasticsearch*[6] under an Apache 2.0 software license (albeit
> somewhat controversial[7]). Due diligence is a requirement for
> choosing a distribution that suits a particular use case.

Elasticsearch

Elasticsearch is a data indexer and analytics engine based on Apache
Lucene[8] and created as a distributed system designed explicitly for
horizontal scalability and high availability. Elasticsearch accepts any form
of JSON-based data structures, making it well suited for interoperability
with modern web APIs. Elasticsearch can automatically detect many data
types, yet custom templates may also be provided to assert data types for
ambiguous fields that require casting or transformation, such as numbers
represented as strings or date formats. Elasticsearch has extensive features
for data aggregation and statistical analysis and can store data along
with its indexes. Although intended for data indexing and aggregation,
Elasticsearch is a capable NoSQL database.

This chapter sets up a single-node Elasticsearch instance. Production
deployments of Elasticsearch consist of multiple nodes, each dedicated
to a specific task: data nodes store, index, and query data; master nodes
update the cluster state; and client nodes take the form of load balancers,
performing indexing and searching.

---

[6]https://opendistro.github.io/for-elasticsearch/

[7]Leonard, Andrew. "Amazon Has Gone From Neutral Platform to Cutthroat
Competitor, Say Open Source Developers." Medium, April 24, 2019. https://
onezero.medium.com/open-source-betrayed-industry-leaders-accuse-
amazon-of-playing-a-rigged-game-with-aws-67177bc748b7.

[8]https://lucene.apache.org/

Note   Elasticsearch B.V., the official maintainers of Elasticsearch, has developed a solution they call the "Elastic Cloud on Kubernetes,[9]" implementing the Kubernetes Operator pattern for installing and managing Elasticsearch clusters. Consider this solution for production implementations.

Create the directory cluster-apk8s-dev4/003-data/030-elasticsearch. Within the new 030-elasticsearch directory, create a file named 10-service.yml from Listing 6-4.

Listing 6-4. Elasticsearch Service

```
apiVersion: v1
kind: Service
metadata:
  namespace: data
  name: elasticsearch
spec:
  type: ClusterIP
  selector:
    app: elasticsearch
  ports:
    - name: http-es
      port: 9200
      targetPort: http-es
      protocol: TCP
```

Apply the Elasticsearch Service configuration:

```
$ kubectl apply -f 10-service.yml
```

---

[9]www.elastic.co/elasticsearch-kubernetes

Next, create a StatefulSet configuration for Elasticsearch in a file named 40-statefulset.yml from Listing 6-5.

Listing 6-5. Elasticsearch StatefulSet

```
apiVersion: apps/v1
kind: StatefulSet
metadata:
  name: elasticsearch
  namespace: data
  labels:
    app: elasticsearch
spec:
  serviceName: elasticsearch
  replicas: 1 # single-node cluster
  selector:
    matchLabels:
      app: elasticsearch
  template:
    metadata:
      labels:
        app: elasticsearch
    spec:
      initContainers:
        - name: init-sysctl
          image: busybox:1.27.2
          command: ["sysctl", "-w", "vm.max_map_count=262144"]
          securityContext:
            privileged: true
        - name: init-chown
          image: busybox:1.27.2
          command: ["/bin/sh"]
```

```yaml
      args: ["-c", "chown -R 1000:1000 /usr/share/
      elasticsearch/data"]
      securityContext:
        privileged: true
      volumeMounts:
        - name: es-data
          mountPath: /usr/share/elasticsearch/data
containers:
  - name: elasticsearch
    image: docker.elastic.co/elasticsearch/
     elasticsearch:7.1.1
    imagePullPolicy: IfNotPresent
    env:
    - name: "discovery.type"
      value: "single-node"
    - name: "cluster.name"
      value: "apk8s"
    - name: "transport.host"
      value: "127.0.0.1"
    - name: "ES_JAVA_OPTS"
      value: "-Xms512m -Xmx512m"
    - name: "http.host"
      value: "0.0.0.0"
    - name: "http.port"
      value: "9200"
    - name: "http.cors.allow-origin"
      value: "http://localhost:1358"
    - name: "http.cors.enabled"
      value: "true"
    - name: "http.cors.allow-headers"
      value: "X-Requested-With,X-Auth-Token,Content-
      Type,Content-Length,Authorization"
```

```
        - name: "http.cors.allow-credentials"
          value: "true"
      ports:
        - containerPort: 9200
          name: http-es
        - containerPort: 9300
          name: tcp-es
      volumeMounts:
        - name: es-data
          mountPath: /usr/share/elasticsearch/data
  volumeClaimTemplates:
    - metadata:
        name: es-data
      spec:
        storageClassName: rook-ceph-block
        accessModes: [ ReadWriteOnce ]
        resources:
          requests:
            storage: 50Gi
```

Apply the Elasticsearch StatefulSet configuration:

```
$ kubectl apply -f 40-statefulset.yml
```

Use kubectl to port-forward the Elasticsearch Service to a local workstation.

```
$ kubectl port-forward elasticsearch-0 9200:9200 -n data
```

Use curl to check the health of the new single-node Elasticsearch cluster. A successful installation returns a JSON object with the status key reporting the message green.

```
$ curl http://localhost:9200/_cluster/health
```

Elasticsearch is designed to shard[10] and replicate data across a large cluster of nodes. Single-node development clusters only support a single shard per index and are unable to replicate data because there are no other nodes available. Using `curl`, `POST` a (JSON) template to this single-node cluster, informing Elasticsearch to configure any new indexes with one shard and zero replicas.

```
$ cat <<EOF | curl -X POST \
-H "Content-Type: application/json" \
-d @- http://localhost:9200/_template/all
{
  "index_patterns": "*",
  "settings": {
    "number_of_shards": 1,
    "number_of_replicas": 0
  }
}
EOF
```

Logstash

Logstash is the central hub in the Elastic ecosystem. "Logstash is an open-source, server-side data processing pipeline that ingests data from a multitude of sources simultaneously, transforms it, and then sends it to your favorite 'stash.'"[11] This book uses Logstash to inject data into Elasticsearch. Injecting large volumes of data at a high velocity into Elasticsearch can be challenging; however, Logstash buffers data and manages back pressure caused by the indexing process. Logstash has a

---

[10]www.elastic.co/blog/how-many-shards-should-i-have-in-my-elasticsearch-cluster

[11]www.elastic.co/products/logstash

large set of useful input plug-ins, including Apache Kafka, utilized later
in this chapter to index records (events/message) from Kafka topics into
Elasticsearch.

To operate the examples in this chapter, ensure Apache Kafka is
running in the Kubernetes cluster. Review Kafka installation instructions
from Chapter 5 if necessary.

Create the directory cluster-apk8s-dev4/003-data/032-logstash.
Within the new 032-logstash directory, create a file named 10-service.
yml from Listing 6-6.

Listing 6-6. Logstash Service

```
kind: Service
apiVersion: v1
metadata:
  name: logstash
  namespace: data
spec:
  selector:
    app: logstash
  ports:
  - protocol: TCP
    port: 5044
  type: ClusterIP
```

Apply the Logstash Service configuration:

```
$ kubectl apply -f 10-service.yml
```

Next, create a ConfigMap containing Logstash configuration settings in
a file named 30-configmap-config.yml from Listing 6-7. To limit memory
usage in resource-constrained environments (such as the development
cluster defined in this chapter), configure the Java JVM -Xms512m
and -Xmx523m settings to a relatively small number.

Listing 6-7. Logstash configuration ConfigMap

```
apiVersion: v1
kind: ConfigMap
metadata:
  name: logstash-config
  namespace: data
data:
  logstash.yml: |
    http.host: "0.0.0.0"
    xpack.monitoring.enabled: false

  pipelines.yml: |
    - pipeline.id: main
      path.config: "/usr/share/logstash/pipeline"
  log4j2.properties: |
    status = error
    name = LogstashPropertiesConfig

    appender.console.type = Console
    appender.console.name = plain_console
    appender.console.layout.type = PatternLayout
    appender.console.layout.pattern = [%d{ISO8601}][%-5p]
    [%-25c] %m%n

    appender.json_console.type = Console
    appender.json_console.name = json_console
    appender.json_console.layout.type = JSONLayout
    appender.json_console.layout.compact = true
    appender.json_console.layout.eventEol = true

    rootLogger.level = ${sys:ls.log.level}
    rootLogger.appenderRef.console.ref = ${sys:ls.log.format}_
    console
```

```
jvm.options: |
  ## JVM configuration

  -Xms512m
  -Xmx523m

  -XX:+UseParNewGC
  -XX:+UseConcMarkSweepGC
  -XX:CMSInitiatingOccupancyFraction=75
  -XX:+UseCMSInitiatingOccupancyOnly
  -Djava.awt.headless=true
  -Dfile.encoding=UTF-8
  -Djruby.compile.invokedynamic=true
  -Djruby.jit.threshold=0
  -XX:+HeapDumpOnOutOfMemoryError
  -Djava.security.egd=file:/dev/urandom
```

Apply the Logstash configuration ConfigMap:

```
$ kubectl apply -f 30-configmap-config.yml
```

Logstash processes events in three stages: input, filter, and output. The configuration in Listing 6-8 demonstrates the use of a Kafka input plug-in to consume data from topic message and metrics. The output configuration checks for the existence of a Kafka topic and, if found, routes the data from the topic into a corresponding index prepended with the current day.

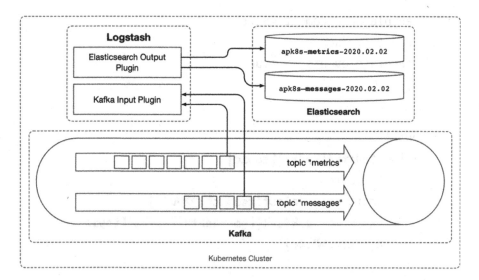

Figure 6-1. *Kafka to Elasticsearch Logstash pipeline configuration*

Create a ConfigMap containing Logstash pipeline settings in a file named 30-configmap-pipeline.yml from Listing 6-8.

Listing 6-8. Logstash pipeline configuration ConfigMap

```
apiVersion: v1
kind: ConfigMap
metadata:
  name: logstash-pipeline
  namespace: data
data:
  logstash.conf: |
    input {
      kafka {
        bootstrap_servers => "kafka-headless:9092"
        topics => [ "messages", "metrics"]
        auto_offset_reset => "latest"
        auto_commit_interval_ms => "500"
```

```
        enable_auto_commit => true
        codec => json
        decorate_events => true
    }
  }

  output {
    if [@metadata][kafka][topic] {
      elasticsearch {
          hosts => [ "elasticsearch:9200" ]
          index => "apk8s-%{[@metadata][kafka][topic]}-
          %{+YYYY.MM.dd}"
      }
    }
  }
}
```

Apply the Logstash pipeline configuration ConfigMap:

```
$ kubectl apply -f 30-configmap-pipeline.yml
```

Lastly, create a Logstash Deployment in a file named 40-deployment.
yml from Listing 6-9.

Listing 6-9. Logstash Deployment

```
apiVersion: apps/v1
kind: Deployment
metadata:
  name: logstash
  namespace: data
  labels:
    app: logstash
spec:
  replicas: 1
```

```
selector:
  matchLabels:
    app: logstash
template:
  metadata:
    labels:
      app: logstash
  spec:
    containers:
    - name: logstash
      image: docker.elastic.co/logstash/logstash:7.1.1
      ports:
      - containerPort: 5044
      env:
      - name: ES_VERSION
        value: 7.1.1
      volumeMounts:
      - name: config-volume
        mountPath: /usr/share/logstash/config
      - name: logstash-pipeline-volume
        mountPath: /usr/share/logstash/pipeline
    volumes:
    - name: config-volume
      configMap:
        name: logstash-config
    - name: logstash-pipeline-volume
      configMap:
        name: logstash-pipeline
```

Apply the Logstash Deployment:

```
$ kubectl apply -f 40-deployment.yml
```

The cluster is now running a single Logstash instance, easily scalable by incrementing the replicas as desired. Starting with a single node is useful for early debugging.

As configured earlier, the Logstash pipeline accepts JSON data input from the Kafka topic messages and metrics. The output configuration instructs Logstash to populate Elasticsearch indexes based on the topic name and day.

Note   Refer to Chapter 5 for instructions on setting up Apache Kafka and the `kafka-test-client` Pod required for examples in this chapter.

Test the new Logstash pipeline by echoing a simple JSON message to the `kafka-console-producer` script provided by the `kafka-test-client`.

```
$ kubectl -n data exec -it kafka-test-client -- \
bash -c "echo '{\"usr\": 1, \"msg\": \"Hello ES\" }' | \
kafka-console-producer --broker-list kafka:9092 \
--topic messages"
```

Use `kubectl` to port-forward the Elasticsearch Service to a local workstation.

```
$ kubectl port-forward elasticsearch-0 9200:9200 -n data
```

Next, ensure that Logstash correctly routed the data event from the Kafka topic messages into the correct index. Use `curl` to get all records for the index pattern `apk8s-messages-*`. The following command returns all records from indexes beginning with `apk8s-messages-`:

```
$ curl http://localhost:9200/apk8s-messages-*/_search
Example response:
{
    "took": 1,
```

```
    "timed_out": false,
    "_shards": {
        "total": 1,
        "successful": 1,
        "skipped": 0,
        "failed": 0
    },
    "hits": {
        "total": {
            "value": 1,
            "relation": "eq"
        },
        "max_score": 1.0,
        "hits": [
            {
                "_index": "apk8s-messages-2020.03.02",
                "_type": "_doc",
                "_id": "IDn7mXABZUrIUU7qdxAr",
                "_score": 1.0,
                "_source": {
                    "@version": "1",
                    "usr": 1,
                    "@timestamp": "2020-03-02T06:42:38.545Z",
                    "msg": "Hello ES"
                }
            }
        ]
    }
}
```

Earlier in this chapter, the template all was defined to match all
indexes and set default sharding and replication. Additional templates
could be added to define data types for fields on specific or sets of indexes.

However, when no templates match fields or indexes, Elasticsearch makes a best-effort guess at the data types. Review the default mapping generated for the new index with the following curl command:

```
$ curl http://localhost:9200/apk8s-messages-*/_mapping
```

In the case of Elasticsearch 7.1.1 configured in this cluster, the field user received the numeric assignment *long*, and field msg indexed as *text*.

Logstash's ability to buffer and manage back pressure from the Elasticsearch indexing operations can play a vital role in platforms consuming and processing tremendous amounts of data at a very high velocity. Even in the small cluster defined in this chapter, Logstash may scale[12] to a dozen or more nodes, each one consuming and buffering data into this single Elasticsearch node.

Kibana

Kibana is the front-end component of the ELK stack and integrates seamlessly with Elasticsearch and is an excellent tool for debugging, development, and visualizations of Elasticsearch data. However, Kibana is also limited to working exclusively with Elasticsearch. Modern analytics, visualizations, and dashboards often require the collection, processing, and visualization of data from a variety of providers. It is not uncommon to utilize Kibana as internal development and debugging utility for Elasticsearch while employing more general solutions for visualization and analysis across the platform at large.

Create the directory cluster-apk8s-dev4/003-data/034-kibana. Within the new 034-kibana directory, create a file named 10-service.yml from Listing 6-10.

---

[12]www.elastic.co/guide/en/logstash/current/deploying-and-scaling.html

Listing 6-10. Kibana Service

```
apiVersion: v1
kind: Service
metadata:
  name: kibana
  namespace: data
  labels:
    app: kibana
spec:
  selector:
    app: kibana
  ports:
    - protocol: "TCP"
      port: 80
      targetPort: 5601
  type: ClusterIP
```

Apply the Kibana Service:

```
$ kubectl apply -f 10-service.yml
```

Next, create a ConfigMap containing Kibana configuration settings in a file named 20-configmap.yml from Listing 6-11.

Listing 6-11. Kibana configuration ConfigMap

```
apiVersion: v1
kind: ConfigMap
metadata:
  name: kibana
  namespace: data
  labels:
    app: kibana
data:
```

```
kibana.yml: |-
  server.name: kib.data.dev4.apk8s.dev
  server.host: "0"
  elasticsearch.hosts: http://elasticsearch:9200
```

Apply the Kibana ConfigMap:

```
$ kubectl apply -f 20-configmap.yml
```

Next, create a Kibana Deployment in a file named 30-deployment.yml from Listing 6-12.

Listing 6-12. Kibana Deployment

```
apiVersion: apps/v1
kind: Deployment
metadata:
  name: kibana
  namespace: data
  labels:
    app: kibana
spec:
  replicas: 1
  revisionHistoryLimit: 1
  selector:
    matchLabels:
      app: kibana
  template:
    metadata:
      labels:
        app: kibana
    spec:
      volumes:
        - name: kibana-config-volume
```

```
    configMap:
      name: kibana
  containers:
    - name: kibana
      image: docker.elastic.co/kibana/kibana-oss:7.1.1
      imagePullPolicy: IfNotPresent
      volumeMounts:
        - name: kibana-config-volume
          mountPath: /usr/share/kibana/config
      env:
        - name: CLUSTER_NAME
          value: apk8s
      ports:
        - name: http
          containerPort: 5601
```

Apply the Kibana Deployment:

```
$ kubectl apply -f 30-deployment.yml
```

Next, create an Ingress for Kibana in a file named 50-ingress.yml from Listing 6-13.

Listing 6-13. Kibana Ingress

```
apiVersion: networking.k8s.io/v1beta1
kind: Ingress
metadata:
  name: kibana
  namespace: data
  labels:
    app: kibana
  annotations:
    nginx.ingress.kubernetes.io/auth-type: basic
```

```
        nginx.ingress.kubernetes.io/auth-secret: sysop-basic-auth
        nginx.ingress.kubernetes.io/auth-realm: "Authentication
        Required"
spec:
  rules:
    - host: kib.data.dev4.apk8s.dev
      http:
        paths:
          - backend:
              serviceName: kibana
              servicePort: 5601
            path: /
  tls:
    - hosts:
      - kib.data.dev4.apk8s.dev
      secretName: data-production-tls
```

Apply the Kibana Ingress:

```
$ kubectl apply -f 50-ingress.yml
```

The following ingress exposes Kibana to the public at *https://kib.data.dev4.apk8s.dev* and uses Basic Auth for security. The secret `sysop-basic-auth` contains the username and password for Basic Auth.

If following along, the new Elasticsearch instance contains only a single record. The remainder of this chapter demonstrates provisioning JupyterLab environments capable of communicating data to and from the Elasticsearch configured in this chapter and Kafka configured in the previous.

Data Lab

This chapter and the previous bring the essential capabilities of a data-driven platform, including event streams with Kafka, IoT message brokering by Mosquitto, data routing, and transformation in Logstash and persistent indexed data through Elasticsearch. The remainder of this chapter creates a user-provisioned data laboratory connected to these systems directly within the cluster as shown in Figure 6-2.

JupyterLab, first introduced in Chapter 4, brings a robust and extendable suite of data science capabilities along with a command-line terminal. Operating JupyterLab within the cluster creates an incredibly efficient environment for both traditional data science, analytics, and experimentation, along with opportunities for development and operations through closer interaction with the Kubernetes API.

The following sections demonstrate the setup of a Kubernetes Namespace, sample RBAC, and ServiceAccount permissions allowing JupyterLab access to Kubernetes resources. JupyterHub[13] is configured to provision JupyterLab environments, authenticating against Keycloak.

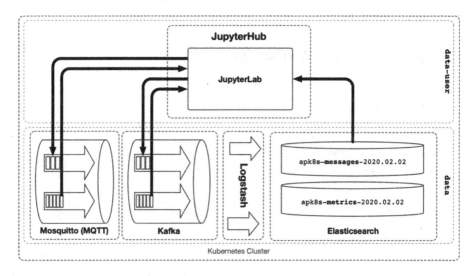

Figure 6-2. *JupyterLab in the data-lab Namespace*

---

[13]https://jupyterhub.readthedocs.io/en/stable/

Keycloak

Keycloak[14] is a free, open source identity and access management application sponsored by Red Hat. Keycloak provides the ability to create and manage user accounts, or connect to an existing LDAP or Active Directory. Third-party applications may authenticate users through OpenID Connect, OAuth 2.0, and SAML 2.0.

Keycloak provides a turnkey solution for identity management and third-party authentication well suited to the requirements of the data platform described in this book. The following section implements a single-node Keycloak instance, used later in this chapter for JupyterHub to authenticate users before provisioning JupyterLab instances for them.

Create the directory `cluster-apk8s-dev4/003-data/005-keycloak`. Within the new `005-keycloak` directory, create a file named `10-service.yml` from Listing 6-14.

Listing 6-14. Keycloak Web Service

```
apiVersion: v1
kind: Service
metadata:
  name: web-keycloak
  namespace: data
spec:
  selector:
    app: web-keycloak
  ports:
    - name: http-web
      protocol: "TCP"
```

---

[14]www.keycloak.org/

```
      port: 8080
      targetPort: http-web
   type: ClusterIP
```

Apply the Keycloak Web Service:

```
$ kubectl apply -f 10-service.yml
```

Next, create a Secret containing Keycloak administrator credentials in a file named 15-secret.yml from Listing 6-15.

Listing 6-15. Keycloak administrator and keystore credentials

```
apiVersion: v1
kind: Secret
metadata:
  name: keycloak
  namespace: data
  labels:
    app: keycloak
type: Opaque
stringData:
  keycloak_user: "sysop"
  keycloak_password: "verystrongpassword"
  keystore_password: "anotherverystrongpassword"
```

Apply the Keycloak Secret:

```
$ kubectl apply -f 10-service.yml
```

Next, create a Keycloak Deployment in a file named 30-deployment. yml from Listing 6-16.

Listing 6-16. Keycloak deployment

```
apiVersion: apps/v1
kind: StatefulSet
metadata:
  name: web-keycloak
  namespace: data
spec:
  serviceName: web-keycloak
  replicas: 1
  revisionHistoryLimit: 1
  selector:
    matchLabels:
      app: web-keycloak
  template:
    metadata:
      labels:
        app: web-keycloak
    spec:
      initContainers:
        - name: keycloak-init-chown
          image: alpine:3.10.1
          imagePullPolicy: IfNotPresent
          volumeMounts:
            - name: keycloak-db
              mountPath: /data
          command: ["chown"]
          args: ["-R","1000:1000","/data"]
      containers:
        - name: web-keycloak
          image: jboss/keycloak:6.0.1
          imagePullPolicy: IfNotPresent
```

```
env:
  - name: PROXY_ADDRESS_FORWARDING
    value: "true"
  - name: KEYCLOAK_HOSTNAME
    value: "auth.data.dev4.apk8s.dev"
  - name: KEYCLOAK_USER
    valueFrom:
      secretKeyRef:
        name: keycloak
        key: keycloak_user
  - name: KEYCLOAK_PASSWORD
    valueFrom:
      secretKeyRef:
        name: keycloak
        key: keycloak_password
  - name: KEYSTORE_PASSWORD
    valueFrom:
      secretKeyRef:
        name: keycloak
        key: keystore_password
ports:
  - name: http-web
    containerPort: 8080
volumeMounts:
  - name: keycloak-db
    mountPath: /opt/jboss/keycloak/standalone/data
volumeClaimTemplates:
  - metadata:
      name: keycloak-db
    spec:
      storageClassName: rook-ceph-block
```

```
        accessModes: [ ReadWriteOnce ]
        resources:
          requests:
            storage: 5Gi
```

Apply the Keycloak Deployment:

```
$ kubectl apply -f 30-deployment.yml
```

Lastly, create an Ingress for Keycloak in a file named 50-ingress.yml from Listing 6-17.

Listing 6-17. Keycloak Ingress

```
apiVersion: networking.k8s.io/v1beta1
kind: Ingress
metadata:
  name: web-auth
  namespace: data
  labels:
    app: web-auth
spec:
  rules:
  - host: auth.data.dev4.apk8s.dev
    http:
      paths:
      - backend:
          serviceName: web-keycloak
          servicePort: 8080
        path: /
  tls:
  - hosts:
    - auth.data.dev4.apk8s.dev
    secretName: data-production-tls
```

Apply the Keycloak Ingress:

```
$ kubectl apply -f 50-ingress.yml
```

Realm, Client, and User

Keycloak provides identity management and authentication to multiple tenants through the configuration of realms.[15] JupyterHub is configured later on in this chapter to authenticate users using Oauth2,[16] belonging to the realm datalab. A Keycloak client associated with a realm grants access to applications such as JupyterHub looking to authenticate users. This section sets up a realm, client, and user used to provision JupyterLab servers later in this chapter.

Using a web browser, visit the new Ingress *https://auth.data.dev4.apk8s.dev/auth/* as set up in the previous section. Log in to Keycloak using the sysop credential defined in Listing 6-15. After logging in, master is the default realm shown in the upper left of the user interface and depicted in Figure 6-3. Open the "Add realm" menu by clicking the drop-down to the right of the realm title and create the new realm datalab.

---

[15]www.keycloak.org/docs/latest/server_admin/index.html#_create-realm
[16]https://oauth.net/2/

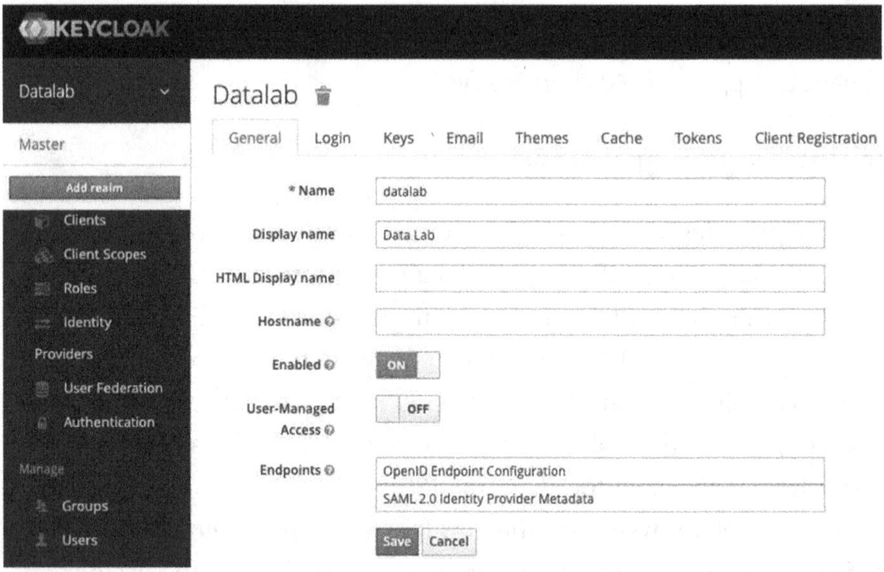

Figure 6-3. *Add realm*

Next, navigate to Clients in the left-hand navigation of the new Datalab realm. Click Create and fill in the "Add Client" form to add a new client named datalab shown in Figure 6-4.

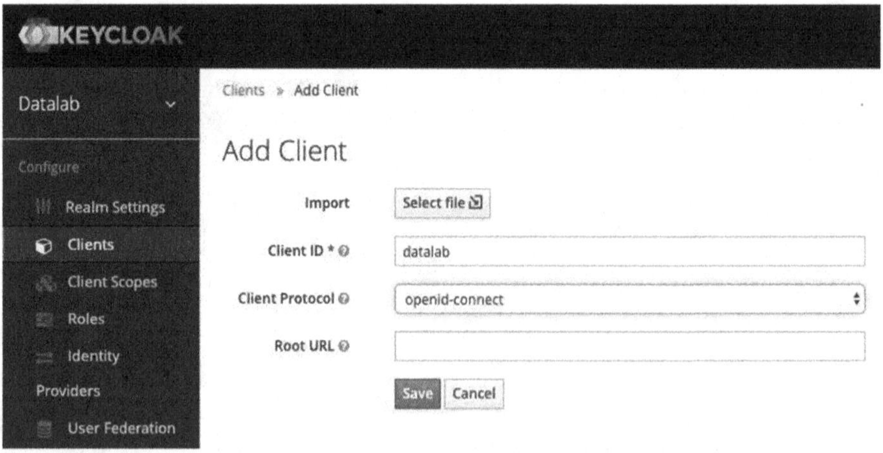

Figure 6-4. *Add client*

After adding the new datalab client, click the Credentials tab to retrieve the generated secret, as shown in Figure 6-5. JupyterHub is later configured to use the client ID datalab and the generated secret for permission to authenticate users against the Keycloak datalab realm.

Figure 6-5. *Client credentials*

Configure the new datalab client (under the Setting tab) by switching Authorization Enabled to *on*. Provide Valid Redirect URIs, in this case, https://lab.data.dev4.apk8s.dev/hub/oauth_callback later defined in the "JupyterHub" section. Review Figure 6-6.

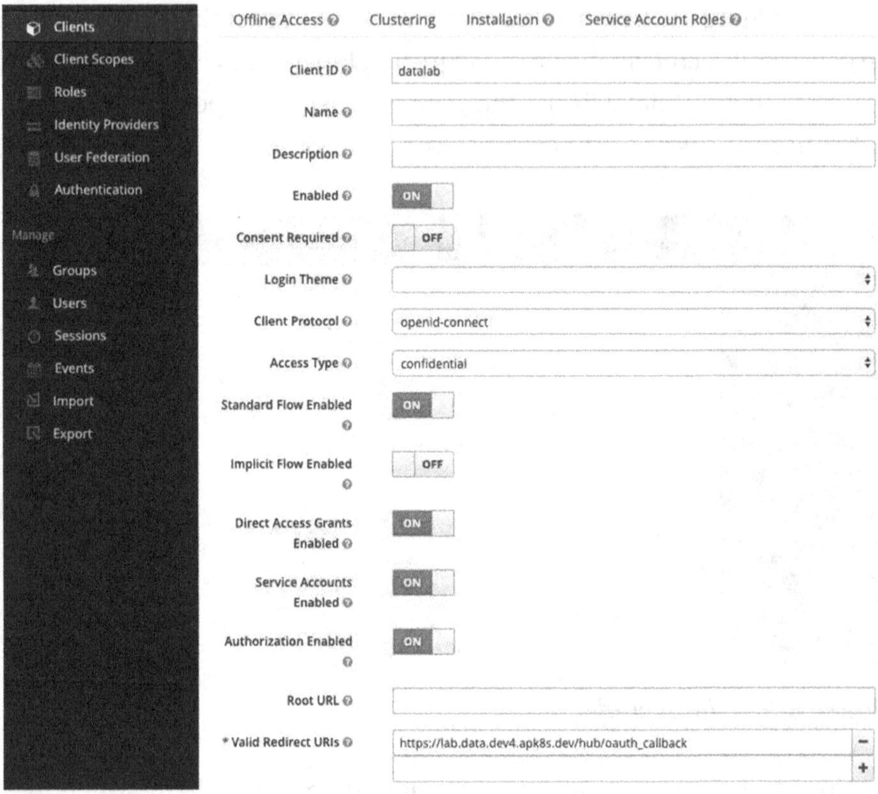

Figure 6-6. *Client configuration*

Finally, create one or more users in the datalab realm by choosing Users under the Manage section of the left-hand menu. After adding a user, assign a password under the Credentials tab. Use a strong password; any users assigned to this realm are later given access to a JupyterLab environment with permissions to read and write data and execute code from within the cluster.

Namespace

Most Kubernetes objects are associated with a Namespace, including Pods, Deployments, StatefulSets, Jobs, Ingresses, Services, and more, in other words: "A *Namespace* defines a logically named group for multiple *Kind*s of resources."[17] Namespaces not only aid in organizing configured objects, they also provide options for security, resource allocation, and resource constraints.

Tip   Use Kubernetes ResourceQuota[18] objects for fine-grain restriction to resources for a given Namespace, including the total number of Pods and PersistentVolumeClaims allowed, CPU, memory, and storage class restrictions.

This section sets up the Namespace data-lab along with a ServiceAccount and RBAC permissions used by JupyterLab and JupyterHub.

Create the directory cluster-apk8s-dev4/005-data-lab/000-namespace to contain namespace-wide configuration manifests. Next, create a Kubernetes Namespace in a file named 00-namespace.yml from Listing 6-18.

Listing 6-18. data-lab Namespace

```
apiVersion: v1
kind: Namespace
metadata:
  name: data-lab
```

Apply the Namespace configuration:

```
$ kubectl apply -f 00-namespace.yml
```

The default service account assigned to Pods in this cluster does not have access to the Kubernetes API. The following creates a service account assigned to JupyterLab Pods provisioned by JupyterHub.

---

[17]https://github.com/kubernetes/community/blob/master/contributors/design-proposals/architecture/namespaces.md#design
[18]https://kubernetes.io/docs/concepts/policy/resource-quotas/

Create the file 05-serviceaccount.yml from Listing 6-19.

Listing 6-19. data-lab ServiceAccount

```
apiVersion: v1
kind: ServiceAccount
metadata:
  name: data-lab
  namespace: data-lab
```

Apply the ServiceAccount configuration:

```
$ kubectl apply -f 05-serviceaccount.yml
```

Next, create a Role for the new datalab ServiceAccount, later assigned to JupyterLab, and a Role for the hub ServiceAccount, later used by JupyterHub. Create the file 07-role.yml from Listing 6-20.

Listing 6-20. data-lab and hub Roles for the data-lab Namespace

```
apiVersion: rbac.authorization.k8s.io/v1beta1
kind: Role
metadata:
  name: data-lab
  namespace: data-lab
rules:
  - apiGroups: [""]
    resources: ["pods","events","services"]
    verbs: ["get","watch","list","endpoints","events"]
---
apiVersion: rbac.authorization.k8s.io/v1
kind: Role
metadata:
  name: hub
  namespace: data-lab
```

```
rules:
  - apiGroups: [""]
    resources: ["pods", "persistentvolumeclaims"]
    verbs: ["get","watch","list","create","delete"]
  - apiGroups: [""]
    resources: ["events"]
    verbs: ["get", "watch", "list"]
```

Note   Kubernetes interprets "" (apiGroups: [""]) as the core API group.[19,20]

Apply the Roles configuration:

```
$ kubectl apply -f 07-role.yml
```

Lastly, csreate RoleBinding objects associating the new Roles to their corresponding ServiceAccounts. Create the file 08-rolebinding.yml from Listing 6-21.

Listing 6-21. data-lab and hub RoleBindings

```
apiVersion: rbac.authorization.k8s.io/v1beta1
kind: RoleBinding
metadata:
  name: data-lab
  namespace: data-lab
roleRef:
  apiGroup: rbac.authorization.k8s.io
  kind: Role
  name: data-lab
```

---

[19]https://kubernetes.io/docs/concepts/overview/kubernetes-api/
#api-groups
[20]https://kubernetes.io/docs/reference/access-authn-authz/
rbac/#role-examples

```
subjects:
  - kind: ServiceAccount
    name: data-lab
    namespace: data-lab
---
apiVersion: rbac.authorization.k8s.io/v1beta1
kind: RoleBinding
metadata:
  name: hub
  namespace: data-lab
roleRef:
  apiGroup: rbac.authorization.k8s.io
  kind: Role
  name: hub
subjects:
  - kind: ServiceAccount
    name: hub
    namespace: data
```

Apply the RoleBinding configuration:

```
$ kubectl apply -f 08-rolebinding.yml
```

JupyterHub

JupyterHub "spawns, manages, and proxies multiple instances of the single-user Jupyter notebook server."[21] This section installs JupyterHub into the development cluster and configures it to authenticate users with

---

[21]Project Jupyter team. "JupyterHub Documentation." October 21, 2019. https://jupyterhub.readthedocs.io/en/stable/

Keycloak and spawn JupyterLab (notebook) servers into the `data-lab`
Namespace. Additionally, the `data-lab` Role defined in the previous
section grants JupyterHub limited access to the Kubernetes API.

Zero to JupyterHub[22] with Kubernetes is a stable JupyterHub Helm
chart with comprehensive and detailed documentation. Although much
of this book opts to utilize plain YAML files for learning and clarity,
JupyterHub is a complex system that is well abstracted by this chart while
providing any necessary configuration overrides.

Note   Helm is a successful and well-maintained package manager
for Kubernetes, yet also under rapid development; therefore, consult
the official documentation[23] for simple install instructions along with
the *additional notes*[24] *from Zero to JupyterHub.*

Create the directory `cluster-apk8s-dev4/003-data/100-jupterhub`
to contain the `values.yml` manifest used by Helm. Populate with the
contents of Listing 6-22.

Note the following bolded elements in the `values.yml` Helm
configuration:

1.   Within the `proxy` section, set the `secretToken` to
       a 32-character string of random hex values. The
       official documentation recommends using the
       following command:

       $ openssl rand -hex 32.[25]

---

[22]https://zero-to-jupyterhub.readthedocs.io/en/latest/
[23]https://helm.sh/docs/
[24]https://zero-to-jupyterhub.readthedocs.io/en/latest/setup-helm.html
[25]www.openssl.org/

2. Within the `singleuser` section, note the container image apk8s/`datalab`. A variety[26] of Jupyter Notebook images may be used here; however, in this case, the specified image represents a highly customized version developed in Chapter 4.

3. Within the `hub` section, `extraConfig` is used to inject additional configuration not directly exposed by the Helm chart. In this case, the configuration instructs KubeSpawner[27] to spawn JupyterLab Pods in the `data-lab` Namespace and configured to use the `data-lab` ServiceAccount defined earlier in this chapter.

    Additionally, within the `hub` section, `extraEnv` is used to populate environment variables required by the `GenericOAuthenticator` defined later in values.yml. Note the Keycloak realm `datalab`, created earlier in this chapter and defined in the environment variables **OAUTH2_AUTHORIZE_URL** and **OAUTH2_TOKEN_URL**.

4. Within the `auth` section, the `GenericOAuthenticator`[28] is configured with a `client_id` and `client_secret` set up earlier in the Keycloak `datalab` realm. Note the datalab realm is part of the `token_url` and `userdata_url` paths.

---

[26]https://jupyter-docker-stacks.readthedocs.io/en/latest/using/selecting.html

[27]https://jupyterhub-kubespawner.readthedocs.io/en/latest/spawner.html

[28]https://github.com/jupyterhub/oauthenticator

Listing 6-22. JupyterHub Helm values

```
proxy:
  secretToken: "large_random_hex_string"
  service:
    type: ClusterIP

singleuser:
  image:
    name: apk8s/datalab
    tag: v0.0.5
  defaultUrl: "/lab"
  storage:
    dynamic:
      storageClass: rook-ceph-block
      capacity: 10Gi

hub:
  image:
    name: jupyterhub/k8s-hub
    tag: 0.9-dcde99a
  db:
    pvc:
      storageClassName: rook-ceph-block
  extraConfig:
    jupyterlab: |-
      c.Spawner.cmd = ['jupyter-labhub']
      c.KubeSpawner.namespace = "data-lab"
      c.KubeSpawner.service_account = "data-lab"
    jupyterhub: |-
      c.Authenticator.auto_login = True
  extraEnv:
```

```
      OAUTH2_AUTHORIZE_URL: https://auth.data.dev4.apk8s.dev/
      auth/realms/datalab/protocol/openid-connect/auth
      OAUTH2_TOKEN_URL: https://auth.data.dev4.apk8s.dev/auth/
      realms/datalab/protocol/openid-connect/token
      OAUTH_CALLBACK_URL: https://lab.data.dev4.apk8s.dev/hub/
      oauth_callback

scheduling:
  userScheduler:
    enabled: true
    replicas: 2
    logLevel: 4
    image:
      name: gcr.io/google_containers/kube-scheduler-amd64
      tag: v1.14.4

auth:
  type: custom
  custom:
    className: oauthenticator.generic.GenericOAuthenticator
    config:
      login_service: "Keycloak"
      client_id: "datalab"
      client_secret: "from_keycloak_client_config"
      token_url: https://auth.data.dev4.apk8s.dev/auth/
      realms/datalab/protocol/openid-connect/token
      userdata_url: https://auth.data.dev4.apk8s.dev/auth/
      realms/datalab/protocol/openid-connect/userinfo
      userdata_method: GET
      userdata_params: {'state': 'state'}
      username_key: preferred_username
```

Add the JupyterHub repository[29] to Helm and update.

```
$ helm repo add jupyterhub \
    https://jupyterhub.github.io/helm-chart/
```

```
$ helm repo update
```

Install (or upgrade/update) the JupyterHub Helm package.

```
$ helm upgrade --install lab-hub jupyterhub/jupyterhub \
    --namespace="data" \
    --version="0.9-dcde99a" \
    --values="values.yml"
```

Note   JupyterHub takes several minutes to pull and initialize large containers. You may need to rerun the Helm command should it time out during install.

Finally, configure an Ingress for the JupyterHub web proxy in a file named 50-ingress.yml from Listing 6-23.

Listing 6-23. JupyterHub Ingress

```
apiVersion: networking.k8s.io/v1beta1
kind: Ingress
metadata:
  name: jupyterhub
  namespace: data
spec:
  rules:
    - host: lab.data.dev4.apk8s.dev
```

---

[29]https://zero-to-jupyterhub.readthedocs.io/en/latest/setup-jupyterhub/setup-helm.html

```
    http:
      paths:
        - backend:
            serviceName: proxy-public
            servicePort: 80
          path: /
  tls:
    - hosts:
      - lab.data.dev4.apk8s.dev
      secretName: data-production-tls
```

Apply the Ingress configuration:

```
$ kubectl apply -f 50-ingress.yml
```

JupyterHub is configured to run in the cluster and in the Namespace data and configured to spawn single-user JupyterLab servers (Pods) in the data-lab namespace. After applying configuration JupyterHub may take several minutes to boot as it must preload large JupyterLab images. Once JupyterHub has fully booted, launch a new JupyterLab instance (with a user created in Keycloak under the datalab realm) by visiting *https:// lab.data.dev4.apk8s.dev*.

JupyterLab

First introduced in Chapter 5, JupyterLab is "the next-generation web-based user interface for Project Jupyter,"[30] a feature-rich data science environment. Project Jupyter began in 2014 and has seen massive adoption; in 2018, there were over 2.5 million[31] Jupyter notebooks shared

---

[30]Project Jupyter. "JupyterLab Documentation." 2019. `https://jupyterlab. readthedocs.io/`.

[31]Perkel, Jeffrey M. "Why Jupyter Is Data Scientists' Computational Notebook of Choice." Nature 563 (October 30, 2018): 145–46. `https://doi.org/10.1038/ d41586-018-07196-1`.

publicly on GitHub. Kubernetes is a natural fit for provisioning and serving JupyterLab environments through JupyterHub, as demonstrated in the previous section.

Streamlining the development of machine learning and statistical models has driven the success of Project Jupyter. Many data science activities, such as machine learning, require static, immutable data sets to achieve reproducible results from experimentation. However, operating Jupyter environments with static data alongside real-time event streams, indexes, and the full power of Kubernetes distributed computing is an opportunity to offer a variety of data science functionality directly in the center of a data platform.

The following sections demonstrate brief examples of working directly with the data and control plane from within the cluster, connecting JupyterLab notebooks with the Kubernetes API, Kafka, Elasticsearch, and Mosquitto MQTT.

Kubernetes API

The default JupyterLab environment includes a CLI (command-line interface) terminal, and the customized JupyterLab (developed in Chapter 4) used in this chapter provides kubectl. Figure 6-7 demonstrates kubectl communicating with the Kubernetes API to retrieve a list of pods running in the current namespace. kubectl is permitted access to the Kubernetes API through a custom service account and RBAC configuration applied earlier in this chapter.

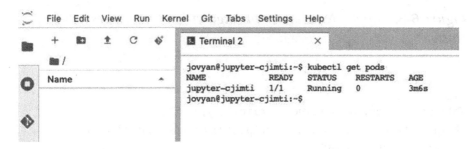

Figure 6-7. *Running kubectl in a JupyterLab terminal*

Figure 6-8 depicts communication with the Kubernetes API through code running in a Python-based Jupyter Notebook, using the official Python client library for Kubernetes.[32] Extending permissions to the service account used by JupyterLab Pod can allow Python to perform any Kubernetes API operation, for example, the creation of Pods, Jobs,[33] CronJobs,[34] or Deployments related to data science, analytics, or ETL activities.

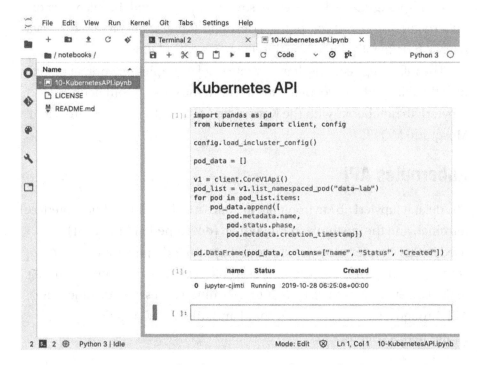

Figure 6-8. *Jupyter Notebook running Python Kubernetes API in cluster*

---

[32]https://github.com/kubernetes-client/python

[33]https://kubernetes.io/docs/concepts/workloads/controllers/
jobs-run-to-completion/

[34]https://kubernetes.io/docs/concepts/workloads/controllers/cron-jobs/

Creating, managing, and monitoring Kubernetes resources from within Kubernetes has facilitated significant progress in automating machine learning, deep learning, and deployment of artificial intelligence–based solutions. Kubeflow (described in Chapter 1) is one such application, a "Machine Learning Toolkit for Kubernetes,"[35] that takes full advantage of the Kubernetes API to automate many of the complex tasks related to machine learning.

Kafka

Figure 6-9 depicts a Python-based Jupyter Notebook publishing simulated device sensor data to the Kafka topic `metrics`. Producing and consuming data from Kafka topics requires only a few lines of code. Kafka is a powerful conduit for communicating events and data between services, including Jupyter Notebooks. Earlier in this chapter, Logstash is configured to consume events from select Kafka topics and deliver them to Elasticsearch for indexing and longtime persistence. The next section demonstrates retrieving the data produced in Figure 6-9 from its destination in Elasticsearch.

---

[35]`www.kubeflow.org`

Figure 6-9. *Jupyter Notebook running a Python Kafka producer*

Elasticsearch

Figure 6-10 depicts a simple match_all query against any Elasticsearch index beginning with apk8s-metrics-. The query demonstrated in this example may be built up to perform advanced search, filtering,[36] and aggregations[37] across billions of records.[38]

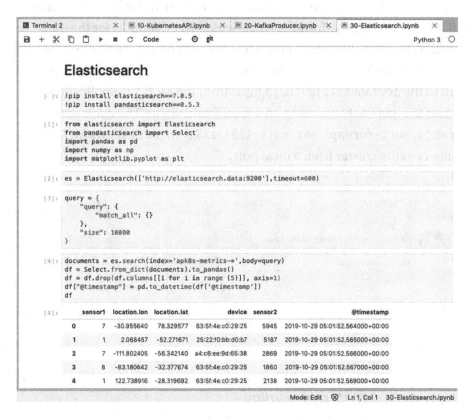

Figure 6-10. *Jupyter Notebook Elasticsearch with Python*

---

[36]www.elastic.co/guide/en/elasticsearch/reference/current/query-filter-context.html

[37]www.elastic.co/guide/en/elasticsearch/reference/current/search-aggregations.html

[38]Batlogg, Jodok. "Querying 24 Billion Records in 900ms." Elastic Blog. 2012. www.elastic.co/videos/querying-24-billion-records-in-900ms.

The results of data mining Elasticsearch can form new indexes or export as CSV-based data sets to package and share along with machine learning results.

Mosquitto (MQTT)

MQTT is a popular choice for IoT communication and metrics collection. Chapter 5 introduced Mosquitto to provide MQTT support for the data pipeline. Figure 6-12 depicts only a few lines of code that need to consume events from an MQTT topic. This example displays test JSON messages sent to the dev/apk8s/lightbulb topic from the MQTT.fx application, shown in Figure 6-11, running on a local workstation. The command kubectl port-forward svc/mqtt 1883:1883 -n data allows MQTT.fx to connect to the cluster from a local port.

Figure 6-11. *MQTT testing utility*

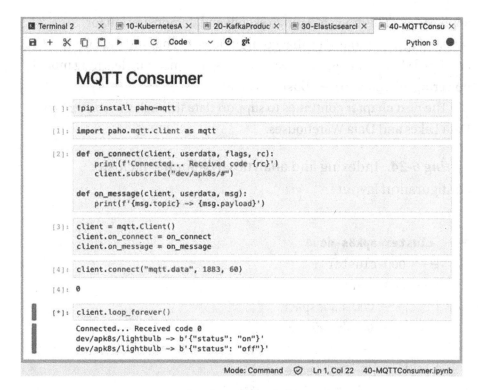

Figure 6-12. *Jupyter Notebook Python MQTT consumer*

Summary

This chapter configured and demonstrated the ELK stack (Elasticsearch, Logstash, and Kibana) to provide enterprise-grade data pipelining, indexing, analysis, and persistence. The cluster now supports SSO, identity management, and authorization through Keycloak, initially used by JupyterHub to authenticate users and provision JupyterLab instances with limited access to the Kubernetes API. If you are following along, the structure of Kubernetes manifests should look similar to Listing 6-24.

This book should demonstrate the power Kubernetes gives platform architects, software developers, researchers, and even hobbyists to construct modern data platforms quickly, from a diverse set of best-in-class applications. This book is a rough sketch and demonstration for developing novel solutions that communicate events and data from IoT, and Blockchain and Big Data technologies, into machine learning models, powering inference-based business logic.

The next chapter continues to support data through the concepts of Data Lakes and Data Warehouses.

Listing 6-24. Indexing and analytics development cluster configuration layout

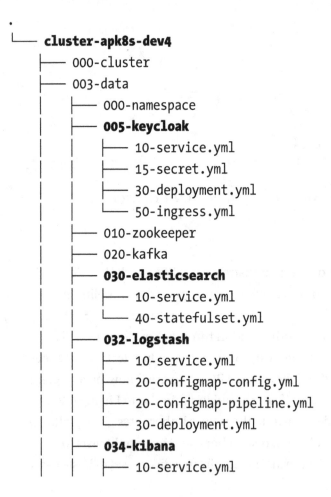

```
.
└── cluster-apk8s-dev4
    ├── 000-cluster
    ├── 003-data
    │   ├── 000-namespace
    │   ├── 005-keycloak
    │   │   ├── 10-service.yml
    │   │   ├── 15-secret.yml
    │   │   ├── 30-deployment.yml
    │   │   └── 50-ingress.yml
    │   ├── 010-zookeeper
    │   ├── 020-kafka
    │   ├── 030-elasticsearch
    │   │   ├── 10-service.yml
    │   │   └── 40-statefulset.yml
    │   ├── 032-logstash
    │   │   ├── 10-service.yml
    │   │   ├── 20-configmap-config.yml
    │   │   ├── 20-configmap-pipeline.yml
    │   │   └── 30-deployment.yml
    │   ├── 034-kibana
    │   │   ├── 10-service.yml
```

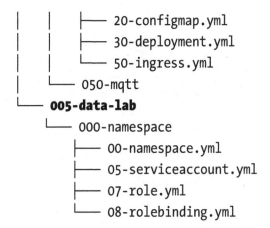

```
|       |       ├── 20-configmap.yml
|       |       ├── 30-deployment.yml
|       |       └── 50-ingress.yml
|       └── 050-mqtt
└── 005-data-lab
        └── 000-namespace
                ├── 00-namespace.yml
                ├── 05-serviceaccount.yml
                ├── 07-role.yml
                └── 08-rolebinding.yml
```

CHAPTER 7

Data Lakes

The concepts of data warehouses, data marts, and data lakes have become commonplace in many enterprises. Big Data technology has enabled organizations to collect, store, and process an ever-growing stream of data. IoT, social media, and the digital transformation of every aspect of business only continue to increase the volume and velocity of data available to organizations.

Traditionally, Big Data concepts have focused on the problem of managing massive volumes and varieties of collected data for large organizations or projects specific to data collection and analysis. Big Data technologies, especially Apache Hadoop and its ecosystem, enable organizations to consume and store all data produced or related to their organization. However, many Big Data solutions came before the rise in the availability and popularity of containers and container orchestration, specifically Kubernetes. In the past, engaging Big Data technologies typically meant provisioning dedicated clusters and often a team to operate and maintain them. A single chapter on data lakes and warehouses can hardly scratch the surface of this vibrant and mature ecosystem. The following exercises aim to demonstrate a minute set of Big Data concepts at a small scale, leveraging the advantage of Kubernetes in unifying the control plane between static and transactional data and any variety of workloads.

All data contains some value to an organization; the cost of extracting that value has always been the challenge, whether it be analysts poring over regional sales reports or purchasing managers auditing inventory levels. Yet over the last two decades, the volume and frequency of available

© Craig Johnston 2020
C. Johnston, *Advanced Platform Development with Kubernetes,*
https://doi.org/10.1007/978-1-4842-5611-4_7

data have increased dramatically, from consumer and industrial IoT to social media, IT systems, and custom applications producing torrents of data. Big organizations needed a solution to a Big Data problem. In 2006 the Hadoop project tackled these issues though clustering any number of commodity servers into a Big Data solution. Hadoop Distributed File System (HDFS), along with its implementation of MapReduce concepts, allows data to be limitlessly gathered into vast "lakes" and analyzed at their source. Hadoop is a valuable and powerful technology for many organizations. However, many Hadoop capabilities are achievable within Kubernetes, including highly distributed workloads, fault tolerance, and self-healing, along with the benefit of a much more extensive and rapidly expanding ecosystem. Kubernetes is not Big Data technology, yet the next Big Data capable systems are likely to spring from it.

This chapter does not attempt to convince enterprises with established Big Data management applications to consider moving them into Kubernetes; instead, the goal aims to lay a foundation for implementing these concepts into a variety of new application platforms developed atop Kubernetes.

Data Processing Pipeline

Figure 7-1 depicts a typical data processing pipeline consisting of raw and processed data storage, an event system, a metadata system, and application workloads for analysis and transformation. Most of the architecture depicted and later described in this chapter is not explicitly designed for Kubernetes nor has any dependency on Kubernetes to operate. However, wrapping these specialized clusters within a Kubernetes cluster establishes a unified control plain, networking, monitoring, security policies, and fine-grained resource management, including provisioning and limiting storage, memory, and CPU. Although technologies such as Elasticsearch, Kafka, MQTT, and other enterprise solutions require extensive knowledge to configure and manage them effectively in demanding production environments, Kubernetes abstracts the underlying infrastructure common to all.

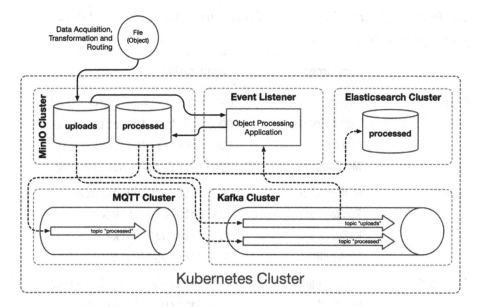

Figure 7-1. *Object processing pipeline*

Development Environment

This chapter builds up data processing and management capabilities from previous chapters by including MinIO for object storage and Apache Cassandra as a key/value store for object metadata, raw data warehousing, and processed data.

The following exercises utilize the inexpensive Hetzner cluster mentioned in Chapter 6, including one CX21 (2 vCPU/8G RAM/40G SSD) for the Kubernetes master node and four CX41 (4 vCPU/16G RAM/160G SSD) instances for worker nodes, yet any equivalent infrastructure will accommodate. Additionally, this chapter leverages applications and cluster configurations installed in Chapters 3, 5, and 6; see Table 7-1. This chapter organizes configuration manifests for the new cluster dev5, under the folder cluster-apk8s-dev5.

Table 7-1. *Key applications and configurations assembled from previous chapters*

	Resources	Organization
Chapter 3	Ingress	000-cluster/00-ingress-nginx
	Cert Manager	000-cluster/10-cert-manager
	Storage	000-cluster/20-rook-ceph
	Monitoring	000-cluster/30-monitoring
Chapter 5	Namespace	003-data/000-namespace
	Zookeeper	003-data/010-zookeeper
	Kafka	003-data/020-kafka
	Mosquitto	003-data/050-mqtt
Chapter 6	Elasticsearch	003-data/030-elasticsearch
	Logstash	003-data/032-logstash
	Kibana	003-data/034-kibana
	Keycloak	003-data/005-keycloak
	JupyterHub	005-data-lab/000-namespace
		003-data/100-jupyterhub

The remainder of this chapter focuses on reading and writing data to a modern concept of data lakes as object storage implemented by MinIO. MinIO's ability to emit events related to the addition, status, and deletion of objects (files) makes it a compelling addition to any data processing pipeline. Finally, this chapter demonstrates the rapid prototyping of applications reacting to object-related events produced by MinIO into Kafka and MQTT utilizing Python-based Jupyter Notebooks running within JupyterLab instances.

Data Lake as Object Storage

Transactional databases, data warehouses, and data marts are all technologies that intend to store and retrieve data in known structures. Organizations often need to store new and varied types of data, often whose form is not known or suitable for structured data systems. The concept of managing this idea of unlimited data in any conceivable form is known as a Data Lake. Traditionally, filesystems and block storage solutions store most file-based data that an organization wishes to gather and maintain outside of its database management systems. Filesystems and block storage systems are challenging to scale, with varying degrees of fault tolerance, distribution, and limited support for metadata and analytics.

HDFS (Hadoop Distributed File System) has been a popular choice for organizations needing the conceptual advantage of a Data Lake. HDFS is complicated to set up and maintain, typically requiring dedicated infrastructure and one or more experts to keep it operational and performant.

This chapter builds a Data Lake with Object Storage, implemented with MinIO. MinIO provides a distributed, fault-tolerant object storage system compatible with Amazon S3. MinIO is horizontally scalable and supports objects up to five terabytes, with no limit to the number of objects it may store. These capabilities alone meet the basic conceptual requirements of a data lake. However, MinIO is extensible though its support for events and a powerful S3-compatible query system.

MinIO Operator

A Kubernetes Operator is a type of resource manager and, in this case, installing and managing one or more MinIO clusters.

> **Note**   The concept of a Kubernetes Operator came about in 2016.
> CoreOS began developing custom resource definitions representing
> controllers aimed at managing the life cycle of stateful applications
> and called them Operators. Operators go beyond the limited
> concerns of package managers and installers such as Helm by
> managing pre- and post-install conditions, monitoring, and runtime
> operations. Operators are custom Kubernetes resources and
> installed declaratively like any other resource, or through a package
> manager such as Helm. After acquiring CoreOs, Red Hat released the
> Operator Framework[1] in 2018 and later launched OperatorHub[2] with
> contributors Amazon, Microsoft, and Google.

The MinIO project offers an official Kubernetes Operator. The
following configuration installs the MinIO operator, managing the new
custom resource definition Tenant used for declaring new MinIO clusters.

Create the directory cluster-apk8s-dev5/000-cluster/22-minio to
contain the MinIO operator installation documentation. Next, create a file
named README.md from Listing 7-1.

Listing 7-1. MinIO operator installation documentation

```
# MinIO Operator Installation

see: https://github.com/minio/operator

Quick Start:
```shell script
kubectl apply -k github.com/minio/operator
```
```

---

[1]https://github.com/operator-framework
[2]https://operatorhub.io/

Apply the MinIO operator configuration:

```
$ kubectl apply -k github.com/minio/operator
```

The Kubernetes cluster now contains the Namespace minio-system with a ServiceAccount and Deployment named minio-operator. "Operators are clients of the Kubernetes API that act as controllers for a custom resource,"[3] in this case, the new resource type Tenant. The next section sets up a MinIO cluster by declaring a Tenant resource.

MinIO Cluster

MinIO is an S3-compatible object storage system, able to provide a type of Data Lake capability to the platform. The small Minio cluster defined in Listing 7-2 includes four nodes, supporting an essential level of high availability. The Tenant resource describes four MinIO nodes with ten gigabytes each, using the rook-ceph-block storage class created in Chapter 3. The standard storage configuration uses half the available disks (in this case, persistent volumes) for data and the other half for parity, allowing full read/write activity with the loss of one node and ready-only activity at the loss of two nodes. This configuration is sufficient for a small development cluster or proof of concept.

Generate a large random string for both the username and password sections of the Secret defined in Listing 7-2. This username and password are equivalent to AWS S3 credentials and may be used in any S3-compatible client to interact with MinIO.

Create the directory cluster-apk8s-dev5/003-data/070-minio to contain the MinIO cluster configuration. Next, create a file named 90-cluster.yml from Listing 7-2.

---

[3]https://kubernetes.io/docs/concepts/extend-kubernetes/operator/

Listing 7-2. MinIO cluster configuration

```
apiVersion: v1
kind: Secret
metadata:
  namespace: data
  name: minio-creds-secret
type: Opaque
stringData:
  accesskey: REPLACE_WITH_STRONG_PASSWORD
  secretkey: REPLACE_WITH_STRONG_PASSWORD
---
apiVersion: minio.min.io/v1
kind: Tenant
metadata:
  name: minio
  namespace: data
spec:
  metadata:
    annotations:
      prometheus.io/path: /minio/prometheus/metrics
      prometheus.io/port: "9000"
      prometheus.io/scrape: "true"
  image: minio/minio:RELEASE.2020-08-18T19-41-00Z
  serviceName: minio-internal-service
  zones:
    - name: "zone-0"
      servers: 4
      volumesPerServer: 1
      volumeClaimTemplate:
        metadata:
          name: miniodata
        spec:
```

```
      storageClassName: rook-ceph-block
      accessModes:
        - ReadWriteOnce
      resources:
        requests:
          storage: 10Gi
## Secret with credentials to be used by MinIO instance.
credsSecret:
  name: minio-creds-secret
podManagementPolicy: Parallel
requestAutoCert: false
certConfig:
  commonName: ""
  organizationName: []
  dnsNames: []
liveness:
  initialDelaySeconds: 10
  periodSeconds: 1
  timeoutSeconds: 1
```

Apply the MinIO cluster configuration:

```
$ kubectl apply -f 90-cluster.yml
```

After applying the cluster configuration, including the Secret and
Tenant resources, MinIO is accessible within the Kubernetes cluster at the
Service address minio-internal-service:9000 or the Headless Service
address minio-hl:9000.

An Ingress configuration, as shown in Listing 7-3, provides external
access to MinIO. MinIO is compatible with AWS S3 object storage service;
therefore, existing systems capable of interacting with the AWS S3 may
utilize the new minio.data.dev5.apk8s.dev as an alternative endpoint.

Next, create a file named 50-ingress.yml from Listing 7-3.

Listing 7-3. MinIO cluster Ingress

```
apiVersion: networking.k8s.io/v1beta1
kind: Ingress
metadata:
  name: minio
  namespace: data
  annotations:
    cert-manager.io/cluster-issuer: letsencrypt-production
    nginx.ingress.kubernetes.io/proxy-body-size: "0"
    nginx.ingress.kubernetes.io/proxy-read-timeout: "600"
    nginx.ingress.kubernetes.io/proxy-send-timeout: "600"
spec:
  rules:
    - host: minio.data.dev5.apk8s.dev
      http:
        paths:
          - backend:
              serviceName: minio-internal-service
              servicePort: 9000
            path: /
  tls:
    - hosts:
        - minio.data.dev5.apk8s.dev
      secretName: minio-data-tls
```

Apply the Ingress configuration for new MinIO cluster:

```
$ kubectl apply -f 50-ingress.yml
```

In addition to the S3-compatible API, MinIO serves as a useful and attractive web-based user interface accessible from a web browser at https://minio.data.dev5.apk8s.dev/.

The next section configures the command-line MinIO Client, used to create buckets, configure the MinIO server, and set up notification events.

MinIO Client

The MinIO Client[4] is a command-line utility for interacting with a MinIO Cluster (and mostly compatible with AWS S3). The MinIO Client supports any operation related to object storage, from creating buckets and listing objects to full administrative and configuration capabilities. In the next section, the MinIO Client is used to configure object state–related notifications on the buckets created in the following.

Refer to the MinIO Client Quickstart Guide for installation instructions for any particular workstation. After installing the MinIO Client (mc) on a local workstation, create an alias for the new cluster called apk8s-dev5 using the Ingress host defined in Listing 7-3 and the credentials defined in Listing 7-2:

```
$ mc config host add apk8s-dev5 \
    https://minio.data.dev5.apk8s.dev \
    username password
```

Create the buckets, upload, processed, and twitter used later in this chapter and the next:

```
$ mc mb apk8s-dev5/upload
$ mc mb apk8s-dev5/processed
$ mc mb apk8s-dev5/twitter
```

---

[4]https://docs.min.io/docs/minio-client-complete-guide

List the three new buckets:

```
$ mc ls apk8s-dev5
```

The MinIO Client can easily copy files from a local workstation or AWS S3, Google Cloud Storage, and more. Start by creating new host aliases or listing existing aliases:

```
$ mc config host list
```

The MinIO Client is a powerful utility for manual interaction with the object storage cluster. For programmatic control over the object cluster, MinIO provides SDKs for JavaScript, Java, Python, Golang, .NET, and Haskell. The MinIO Cluster is also compatible with the AWS S3 API and many libraries such as Amazon's Boto3 for Python, AWS.S3 class for JavaScript, or s3 package for Golang. Boto3 is used later in this chapter to process CSV files.

The next section leverages MinIO's ability to emit events related to objects.

MinIO Events

Object-related event notifications provide a sophisticated form of extensibility to a data-centric platform by allowing any number of services to consume these notifications and perform tasks. MinIO supports the configuration of object-state notification to AMQP,[5] Elasticsearch, Kafka, MQTT, MySQL, NATS,[6] NSQ,[7] PostgreSQL, Redis, and webhooks.[8]

---

[5]www.amqp.org/

[6]https://nats.io/

[7]https://nsq.io/

[8]www.programmableweb.com/news/what-are-webhooks-and-how-do-they-enable-real-time-web/2012/01/30

The following exercise configures MinIO with the ability to notify Elasticsearch, Kafka, and MQTT, leveraging the technologies installed in Chapters 5 and 6. After configuring the connection settings for Elasticsearch, Kafka, and MQTT, the MinIO servers require a restart; however, after this initial configuration, no further restarts are needed when configuring any number of notification settings.

Begin configuring MinIO by requesting the current configuration and saving it as JSON file. Use the MinIO Client command-line utility (mc) installed in the previous section.

Create a directory for the MinIO server configuration:

```
$ cd ./005-cluster-apk8s-dev5/003-data
$ mkdir -p ./070-minio/cfg
```

Next, get the existing server configuration as a JSON file (the previous section describes configuring the apk8s-dev5 alias). The following multiline command pipes the JSON output to Python to format it for easier editing:

```
$ mc admin config get apk8s-dev5 | \
    python -m json.tool > config.json
```

Under the "notify" section of the config.json, edit the sections for Elasticsearch, Kafka, and MQTT to match Listing 7-4.

Listing 7-4. MinIO server external connection configuration

```
"elasticsearch": {
        "1": {
            "enable": true,
            "format": "namespace",
            "index": "processed",
            "url": "http://elasticsearch:9200"
        }
    },
```

```
"kafka": {
        "1": {
            "brokers": ["kafka-headless:9092"],
            "enable": true,
            "sasl": {
                "enable": false,
                "password": "",
                "username": ""
            },
            "tls": {
                "clientAuth": 0,
                "enable": false,
                "skipVerify": false
            },
            "topic": "upload"
        }
    },
    "mqtt": {
        "1": {
            "broker": "tcp://mqtt:1883",
            "enable": true,
            "keepAliveInterval": 0,
            "password": "",
            "qos": 0,
            "queueDir": "",
            "queueLimit": 0,
            "reconnectInterval": 0,
            "topic": "processed",
            "username": ""
        }
    },
```

Apply the edited config.json and restart the MinIO server:

```
$ mc admin config set apk8s-dev5 < config.json
$ mc admin service restart apk8s-dev5
```

MinIO produces event notification types related to the creation, deletion, and access to objects, as shown in Table 7-2. MinIO supports event notification configurations by bucket and supports fine-grained filtering by type of event, object name prefix, or object name suffix.

Table 7-2. *MinIO supported object events*

Category	Event
Creation	s3:ObjectCreated:Put
	s3:ObjectCreated:Post
	s3:ObjectCreated:Copy
	s3:ObjectCreated:CompleteMultipartUpload
Deletion	s3:ObjectRemoved:Delete
Access	s3:ObjectAccessed:Get
	s3:ObjectAccessed:Head

The next section demonstrates a method for processing object-related events within Kubernetes.

Process Objects

JupyterLab, as set up in Chapter 6, provides a convenient and productive environment for data science activities, primarily due to its proximity to in-cluster data and event sources. On the same note, JupyterLab running within Kubernetes simplifies the ability to experiment with combining data-based events, cluster-based data, and the Kubernetes API. Jupyter Notebooks are a useful tool for quickly building and documenting complex prototypes.

The following exercise prototypes an event listener, creates and places a large CSV file into a MinIO bucket, compresses the CSV by generating a Kubernetes Job, and demonstrates the extraction of data from a compressed CSV.

Configure Notifications

First, configure MinIO to notify Kafka and MQTT topics when particular bucket events occur, specifically at the creation of any object in the upload bucket with the suffix .csv and the creation of any object in the processed bucket with the suffix .gz. In this exercise, the use of both Kafka and MQTT only intends to illustrate a variety of event queues:

```
$ mc event add apk8s-dev5/upload \
      arn:minio:sqs::1:kafka \
--event put --suffix=".csv"

$ mc event add apk8s-dev5/processed \
      arn:minio:sqs::1:mqtt \
--event put --suffix=".gz"
```

Additionally, configure MinIO to keep an index of documents in Elasticsearch, describing the state of all objects in the processed bucket:

```
$ mc event add apk8s-dev5/processed \
      arn:minio:sqs::1:elasticsearch \
```

Event Notebook

Open a JupyterLab environment and start a Python Notebook for testing the new bucket notification events produced by MinIO. In the first cell, ensure the kafka-python library is available:

```
!pip install kafka-python==1.4.7
```

Import the standard JSON library to parse MinIO notifications, the KafkaConsumer[9] class from the kafka-python library, and lastly, the clear_ output function from IPython.display to assist in clearing cell output between loops:

```
import json
from kafka import KafkaConsumer
from IPython.display import clear_output
```

Connect the KafkaConsumer to the upload topic on the Kafka cluster in the data Namespace. Set the group_id to data-bucket-processor:

```
consumer = KafkaConsumer('upload',
    bootstrap_servers="kafka-headless.data:9092",
    group_id='data-bucket-processor')
```

Finally, create a for loop on consumer messages. The loop continues infinitely, replacing the last event with the current event:

```
for msg in consumer:
    jsmsg = json.loads(msg.value.decode("utf-8"))
    clear_output(True)
    print(json.dumps(jsmsg, indent=4))
```

Test the event listener by creating and uploading a test CSV file to the upload bucket from a local workstation:

```
$ touch test.csv
$ mc cp test.csv apk8s-dev5/upload
```

The JupyterLab event notebook should now display an s3:ObjectCreated:Put event notification similar to Listing 7-5.

---

[9]https://kafka-python.readthedocs.io/en/master/apidoc/KafkaConsumer.html

Listing 7-5. Example bucket event notification

```
{
    "EventName": "s3:ObjectCreated:Put",
    "Key": "upload/test.csv",
    "Records": [
        {
            "eventVersion": "2.0",
            "eventSource": "minio:s3",
            "awsRegion": "",
            "eventTime": "2019-12-27T08:27:40Z",
            "eventName": "s3:ObjectCreated:Put",
            "userIdentity": {
                "principalId": "3Fh36b37coCN3w8GAMO7"
            },
            "requestParameters": {
                "accessKey": "3Fh36b37coCN3w8GAMO7",
                "region": "",
                "sourceIPAddress": "0.0.0.0"
            },
            "responseElements": {
                "x-amz-request-id": "15E42D02F9784AD2",
                "x-minio-deployment-id": "0e8f8...",
                "x-minio-origin-endpoint":
                "http://10.32.128.13:9000"
            },
            "s3": {
                "s3SchemaVersion": "1.0",
                "configurationId": "Config",
                "bucket": {
                    "name": "upload",
                    "ownerIdentity": {
```

```
                "principalId": "3Fh36b378GAMO7"
            },
            "arn": "arn:aws:s3:::upload"
        },
        "object": {
            "key": "test.csv",
            "eTag": "d41d8cd98f998ecf8427e",
            "contentType": "text/csv",
            "userMetadata": {
                "content-type": "text/csv",
                "etag": "d41d8cd90998ecf8427e"
            },
            "versionId": "1",
            "sequencer": "15E42D02FD98E21B"
        }
    },
    "source": {
        "host": "0.0.0.0",
        "port": "",
        "userAgent": "MinIO (darwin"
    }
  }
 ]
}
```

Test Data

Python is an excellent tool for gathering, normalizing, and even generating data. The following exercise produces a CSV file containing one million fictitious blood donors, each consisting of a fake email address, name, blood type, birthday, and state. Lastly, the script uploads the generated CSV data into the upload bucket on the new MinIO cluster.

This section continues the use of an in-cluster JupyterLab environment; however, this is not a requirement. Create a new Jupyter Notebook in JupyterLab in the Kubernetes cluster, or create a Python script on a local workstation.

The example Python script uses the Faker Python library to create fake data and MinIO Client library for connecting to MinIO. Ensure the development environment contains the required dependencies by adding the following pip install directives to the first cell of the Jupyter Notebook:

```
!pip install Faker==2.0.3
!pip install minio==5.0.1
```

In the next cell, import the following libraries:

```
import os
from faker import Faker
from minio import Minio
from minio.error import ResponseError
```

In the next cell, add the following code to open a file named donors. csv, write an initial header for the data, and create a while loop with one million increments:

```
%%time
fake = Faker()

f_customers = open("./donors.csv","w+")
f_customers.write(
    "email, name, type, birthday, state\n"
)

i = 0
while i < 1000000:
    fp = fake.profile(fields=[
        "name",
```

```
        "birthdate",
        "blood_group"])

    st = fake.state()
    bd = fp["birthdate"]
    bg = fp["blood_group"]
    ml = fake.ascii_safe_email()

    f_customers.write(
        f'{ml},{fp["name"]},{bg},{bd},{st}\n'
    )
    i += 1

f_customers.close()
```

In the last cell of the Jupyter Notebook, connect to the MinIO cluster set up earlier in this chapter and upload the newly generated donors. csv into the upload bucket; replace **username** and **password** with values defined in the MinIO Cluster setup:

Note   If developing from a local workstation, replace 'minio-internal-service.data:9000' with 'minio.data.dev5. apk8s.dev' and secure=False with secure=True.

```
%%time
minioClient = Minio('minio-internal-service.data:9000',
                    access_key='username',
                    secret_key='password',
                    secure=False)

try:
    with open("./donors.csv", 'rb') as file_data:
        file_stat = os.stat('./donors.csv')
```

```
minioClient.put_object('upload',
                       'donors.csv',
                       file_data,
                       file_stat.st_size,
                       content_type='application/csv')

except ResponseError as err:
    print(err)
```

If the Event Notebook from the previous section is running, a new event named s3:ObjectCreated:CompleteMultipartUpload with the key upload/donors.csv will be displayed. The MinIO cluster now holds a roughly 60-megabyte object containing test data, representing fake blood donors, their email, name, birthdate, blood type, and state.

At this point, the event system could trigger a wide range of data processing actions. The next section uses a custom data compression application to demonstrate a typical object processing flow.

Containerized Application

On Kubernetes, all workloads execute within a container within a Pod. The last few exercises used a Pod running a JupyterLab container to execute code written in a Jupyter Notebook, an excellent method for experimenting, building a proof of concept, or rapid prototyping. As the prototyping process iterates toward a stable production system, identify independent units of work, develop and wrap them in containers, test, version, and make them available for orchestration.

The following exercise develops a generic object compressor in Go, builds and versions a container, and makes that container publicly available on Docker Hub. On a local workstation, ensure Go version 1.13+ and Docker 19+ are present. Use new or existing accounts on GitLab and Docker Hub (both free) to store the source code and resulting container.

Create a folder for a new Go application on a local workstation; this example uses the folder ~/workspace/apk8s/compressor. From within the new folder, initialize Go Modules[10] (replace with any custom Git repository):

```
$ go mod init github.com/apk8s/compressor
```

Note   As of Go 1.14,[11] Go Modules are ready for production use and considered the official dependency management system for Go. All developers are encouraged to use Go Modules for new projects along with migrating any existing projects.

Create the directory cmd to store the main Go source—a convention typically used to signify a command-line application rather than components of a shared library. Create a file named compressor.go in the cmd directory and populate it with the source from Listing 7-6.

Listing 7-6. Go application: compressor

```go
package main

import (
        "bufio"
        "compress/gzip"
        "flag"
        "io"
        "log"
        "os"
```

---

[10]https://github.com/golang/go/wiki/Modules
[11]https://golang.org/doc/go1.14

```
    minio "github.com/minio/minio-go/v6"
)

var (
    endpoint        = os.Getenv("ENDPOINT")
    endpointSSL     = os.Getenv("ENDPOINT_SSL")
    accessKeyID     = os.Getenv("ACCESS_KEY_ID")
    accessKeySecret = os.Getenv("ACCESS_KEY_SECRET")
)

func main() {
    var (
        fmBucket = flag.String("f", "", "From bucket.")
        toBucket = flag.String("t", "", "To bucket.")
        fmObjKey = flag.String("k", "", "From key.")
    )
    flag.Parse()

    useSSL := true
    if endpointSSL == "false" {
        useSSL = false
    }

    mc, err := minio.New(
        endpoint, accessKeyID,
        accessKeySecret, useSSL)
    if err != nil {
        log.Fatalln(err)
    }

    obj, err := mc.GetObject(
        *fmBucket,
```

```
        *fmObjKey,
        minio.GetObjectOptions{},
)
if err != nil {
        log.Fatalln(err)
}

log.Printf("Starting download stream %s/%s.",
        *fmBucket,
        *fmObjKey)

// synchronous in-memory pipe
pipeR, pipeW := io.Pipe()

// reads from object, writes to pipe
bufIn := bufio.NewReader(obj)

// gzip buffers to memory and flushes on close
gzW, err := gzip.NewWriterLevel(pipeW, 3)
if err != nil {
        log.Fatalln(err)
}

go func() {
        log.Printf("Compress and stream.")
        n, err := bufIn.WriteTo(gzW)
        if err != nil {
                log.Fatalln(err)
        }
        gzW.Close()
        pipeW.Close()
        log.Printf("Compressed: %d bytes", n)
}()
```

```
    // data will not be sent until gzW.Close() and
    // the gzip buffer flushes
    log.Print("BEGIN PutObject")
    _, err = mc.PutObject(
        *toBucket, *fmObjKey+".gz",
        pipeR, -1, minio.PutObjectOptions{})
    if err != nil {
        log.Fatalln(err)
    }
    log.Print("COMPLETE PutObject")

}
```

The new Go application defined earlier connects to a MinIO cluster, compresses an object, and places the compressed output in a new object in a separate bucket. This application is only a simplistic example of object processing, utilizing the Go programming language to create a small, statically compiled binary with no external operating system dependencies.

Test the new compressor application on a local workstation by setting the following environment variables; replace the endpoint, username, and password with values defined earlier in this chapter:

```
$ export ENDPOINT=minio.data.dev5.apk8s.dev
$ export ACCESS_KEY_ID=username
$ export ACCESS_KEY_SECRET=password
```

Compile and execute the compressor application configured with the buckets upload and processed along with the object upload/donors.csv generated and added to MinIO in the previous section:

```
$ go run ./cmd/compressor.go -f upload -k donors.csv -t processed
```

After completing execution, a new object containing a compressed version of the donors.csv named donors.csv.gz is available in the processed bucket and is about 20 megabytes. Additionally, MinIO sent a message to the MQTT cluster on the topic processed and added a new document to the Elasticsearch index processed. Refer to Chapters 5 and 6 on exploring MQTT (Mosquitto) and Elasticsearch.

Next, this chapter uses the Docker Hub organization apk8s to store and serve public containers. Set up a free Docker Hub account or ensure access to a suitable container registry for the following exercise.

Within the folder ~/workspace/apk8s/compressor representing the compressor project, create the file Dockerfile and populate it with the contents of Listing 7-7.

Listing 7-7. Dockerfile for the compressor application

```
FROM golang:1.13.3 AS builder

WORKDIR /go/src

COPY . /go/src

RUN go mod download

RUN CGO_ENABLED=0 \
    GOOS=linux \
    GOARCH=amd64 \
    GO111MODULE=on \
    go build -ldflags "-extldflags -static" \
        -o /go/bin/compressor /go/src/cmd

RUN echo "nobody:x:65534:65534:Nobody:/:" > /etc_passwd

FROM scratch

ENV PATH=/bin
```

```
COPY --from=builder /etc/ssl/certs/ca-certificates.crt /etc/
ssl/certs/
COPY --from=builder /etc_passwd /etc/passwd
COPY --from=builder /go/bin/compressor /bin/compressor

WORKDIR /

USER nobody
ENTRYPOINT ["/bin/compressor"]
```

The new Dockerfile represents a multistage build process. The first stage uses the golang:1.13.3 container named builder to download dependencies and compile a static binary. The builder container also creates an /etc_passwd file to support the user Nobody assigned to execute the binary in the following scratch container, defined as the second stage of the Docker build.

In addition to being a tiny container, weighing in at about ten megabytes, this scratch-based container (Listing 7-7) executes a single binary as the user Nobody, no other user accounts, and no operating system. This method reduces the attack surface to the binary itself, along with the libraries used to compile it. An exploit allowing an attacker to escape the container would do so as the relatively benign user Nobody. There is no perfect security; however, any reduction in potential attack surfaces and complexity reduces the cumulative effect of running hundreds of thousands of containers in a production system.

Lastly, build, tag, and push the container to Docker Hub or any suitable container registry:

```
$ docker build -t apk8s/compressor:v0.0.1 .
$ docker push apk8s/compressor:v0.0.1
```

Test the new container, first by ensuring the environment variables ENDPOINT, ACCESS_KEY_ID, and ACCESS_KEY_SECRET are still exported in the current shell (as defined earlier), and then execute the following command:

```
$ docker run -e ENDPOINT=$ENDPOINT \
    -e ACCESS_KEY_ID=$ACCESS_KEY_ID \
    -e ACCESS_KEY_SECRET=$ACCESS_KEY_SECRET \
    apk8s/compressor:v0.0.1 \
    -f=upload -k=donors.csv -t=processed
```

The new container is ready to run in the Kubernetes cluster and process objects, in this case compressing them. However, the goal of this exercise is to demonstrate the ease of developing small, focused applications and the part they play in a Kubernetes-based data platform. The next section demonstrates how one might prototype an event-based deployment of this (or any) new object processing container.

Programmatic Deployments

The declarative configuration for the desired state of a compute cluster is the idiomatic method for deploying applications in Kubernetes. This book has primarily used YAML directly to define the desired state or used Helm to populate and apply YAML templates indirectly. Even imperative commands such as kubectl run[12] invoke declarative-style API calls under the hood. The exercise in this section develops a prototype application within a Jupyter Notebook that listens for MinIO bucket events and processes objects by defining Kubernetes Jobs and applying them with Kubernetes API.

Before attaching any execution to an event stream, the following exercise uses an in-cluster Jupyter Notebook provided by the JupyterLab environment provisioned by JupyterHub set up in Chapter 6 to develop a prototype Kubernetes Job deployer.

---

[12]https://kubernetes.io/docs/tasks/manage-kubernetes-objects/imperative-command/

When specifying a serviceAccount for a container within a Pod, Kubernetes mounts its associated access token into /var/run/secrets/kubernetes.io/serviceaccount, along with the cluster certificate ca.crt. Pods without a serviceAccount specified mount the default service account for the namespace they are running in. Chapter 6 configured a service account and role named data-lab with extended permissions to the Kubernetes API for use by the JupyterLab container. Ensure the following permissions, **pods/log**, **jobs**, and **jobs/status** (as shown in Listing 7-8) are available to the data-lab Role assigned to the data-lab ServiceAccount in the data-lab Namespace.

Listing 7-8. Update 005-data-lab/000-namespace/07-role.yml

```
apiVersion: rbac.authorization.k8s.io/v1beta1
kind: Role
metadata:
  name: data-lab
  namespace: data-lab
rules:
  - apiGroups: ["","batch"]
    resources: ["pods",
                "pods/log",
                "events",
                "services",
                "jobs",
                "jobs/status"]
    verbs: ["delete",
            "create",
            "get",
            "watch",
            "list",
            "endpoints",
            "patch",
            "events"]
```

Visit the JupyterLab environment `lab.data.dev5.apk8s.dev` set up in Chapter 6. Add and execute the following code samples in individual cells to test and experiment with each step.

Add a cell to install the latest Python Kubernetes client library:[13]

```
!pip install kubernetes
```

Import the following dependencies:

```
from os import path
import yaml
import time
from kubernetes import client, config
from kubernetes.client.rest import ApiException
from IPython.display import clear_output
```

Create a collection of environment variables using the class V1EnvVar[14] for later use with the compressor container. Replace the username and password with values defined earlier in this chapter in the "MinIO Cluster" section. The ENDPOINT_SSL setting is false for the current in-cluster configuration:

```
envs = [
    client.V1EnvVar("ENDPOINT", "minio-internal-service.
    data:9000"),
    client.V1EnvVar("ACCESS_KEY_ID", "username"),
    client.V1EnvVar("ACCESS_KEY_SECRET", "password"),
    client.V1EnvVar("ENDPOINT_SSL", "false"),
]
```

---

[13]https://github.com/kubernetes-client/python
[14]https://github.com/kubernetes-client/python/blob/master/kubernetes/
docs/V1EnvVar.md

Using the class V1Container,[15] configure a container with the image apk8s/compressor:v0.0.1 built and tagged in the previous section. The compressor application requires the environment variables configured previously along with arguments -f specifying the bucket to process from, -k for the object key, and -t for the destination bucket:

```
container = client.V1Container(
    name="compressor",
    image="apk8s/compressor:v0.0.1",
    env=envs,
    args=["-f=upload",
          "-k=donors.csv",
          "-t=processed"])
```

Using the classes V1PodTemplateSpec,[16] V1ObjectMeta,[17] and V1PodSpec,[18] configure a Pod to run the previously configured container:

```
podTmpl = client.V1PodTemplateSpec(
    metadata=client.V1ObjectMeta(
        labels={"app": "compress-donors"}
    ),
    spec=client.V1PodSpec(
        restart_policy="Never",
        containers=[container]))
```

---

[15]https://github.com/kubernetes-client/python/blob/master/kubernetes/docs/V1Container.md

[16]https://github.com/kubernetes-client/python/blob/master/kubernetes/docs/V1PodTemplateSpec.md

[17]https://github.com/kubernetes-client/python/blob/master/kubernetes/docs/V1ObjectMeta.md

[18]https://github.com/kubernetes-client/python/blob/master/kubernetes/docs/V1PodSpec.md

Kubernetes provides the Job resource for Pods intended to run until completed. Jobs only restart a Pod if it exits with a nonzero return. Using the classes V1Job,[19] V1ObjectMeta, and V1JobSpec,[20] configure a Job with the previously configured Pod:

```
job = client.V1Job(
    api_version="batch/v1",
    kind="Job",
    metadata=client.V1ObjectMeta(
        name="compress-donors"
    ),
    spec=client.V1JobSpec(
        template=podTmpl,
        backoff_limit=2)
)
```

Next, configure the Python client and load the Kubernetes Batch API responsible for managing Job resources. The method load_incluster_ config() configures the Python client to utilize the Kubernetes configuration available to the Pod running the current JupyterLab environment.

```
config.load_incluster_config()
batch_v1 = client.BatchV1Api()
```

Use the Kubernetes Batch API to apply the Job configuration:

```
resp = batch_v1.create_namespaced_job(
    body=job,
    namespace="data-lab")
```

---

[19]https://github.com/kubernetes-client/python/blob/master/kubernetes/docs/V1Job.md

[20]https://github.com/kubernetes-client/python/blob/master/kubernetes/docs/V1JobSpec.md

After executing the code in the previous Jupyter Notebook cell, Kubernetes creates a Job named compress-donors in the data-lab Namespace. After successful execution, the Job remains with status Completed. However, any failures result in two retries as configured earlier with the backoff_limit directive. In either case, the code in Listing 7-9 polls the state of the configured Job and removes it after completion; if the Job returns an error, the final code displays the logs from the Pod associated with the Job. Add the code from Listing 7-9 to the final cell of the Jupyter Notebook and execute it.

Listing 7-9. Monitor Job state and cleanup

```
completed = False

while completed == False:
    time.sleep(1)

    try:
        resp = batch_v1.read_namespaced_job_status(
            name="compress-donors",
            namespace="data-lab", pretty=False)
    except ApiException as e:
        print(e.reason)
        break

    clear_output(True)
    print(resp.status)

    if resp.status.conditions is None:
        continue

    if len(resp.status.conditions) > 0:

        clear_output(True)
        print(resp.status.conditions)
```

```python
if resp.status.conditions[0].type == "Failed":
    print("FAILED -- Pod Log --")
    core_v1 = client.CoreV1Api()
    pod_resp = core_v1.list_namespaced_pod(
        namespace="data-lab",
        label_selector="app=compress-donors",
        limit=1
    )

    log_resp = core_v1.read_namespaced_pod_log(
        name=pod_resp.items[0].metadata.name,
        namespace='data-lab')

    print(log_resp)

print("Removing Job...")
resp = batch_v1.delete_namespaced_job(
    name="compress-donors",
    namespace="data-lab",
    body=client.V1DeleteOptions(
        propagation_policy='Foreground',
        grace_period_seconds=5))
break
```

This book leaves the remaining event-based object processing exercise to the reader. Combine the event notebook defined earlier in this chapter with the programmatic deployment of Jobs for processing objects defined earlier. This combination creates a prototyping framework for nearly any form of event-based data processing, including analysis, normalization, the generation of derivative and synthetic data, and housekeeping tasks such as organization and compression demonstrated earlier.

Serverless Object Processing

Automating the processes developed in the previous section is the central focus of Serverless[21] (or functions as a service) technologies briefly covered here.

Cloud vendors offer solutions that abstract away all the complicated moving parts that support the compiling, execution, scaling, and error handling for any isolated workload small and focused enough to be considered a function. Building critical business logic with AWS Lambda,[22] Azure Functions,[23] or Google Cloud Functions[24] is an effective method for rapid development or small teams looking to offload as much operational complexity as possible. However, these Serverless products do come at the cost of strong vendor lock-in and trust that their supporting product line remains a priority for the vendor into the future.

Within the Kubernetes ecosystem,[25] a growing list of Serverless technologies provides both a cloud-native and vendor-neutral approach. Kubeless,[26] OpenFaaS,[27] Fission,[28] Apache OpenWhisk,[29] and Nuclio[30] all provide turnkey Serverless platforms well suited for public cloud or custom Kubernetes cluster. The project Knative[31] provides a flexible

---

[21]https://martinfowler.com/articles/serverless.html

[22]https://aws.amazon.com/lambda/

[23]https://azure.microsoft.com/en-us/services/functions/

[24]https://cloud.google.com/functions/

[25]https://landscape.cncf.io/format=serverless

[26]https://kubeless.io/

[27]www.openfaas.com/

[28]https://fission.io/

[29]https://openwhisk.apache.org/

[30]https://nuclio.io/

[31]https://knative.dev/

platform of components for developing new Serverless-based platforms. Chapter 8 demonstrates the use of OpenFaaS for Serverless-style data transformation.

With Kubernetes abstracting low-level infrastructure concerns, MinIO providing object storage and access, along with a robust Serverless platform automating deployments and the execution of event-based object processing, the Data Lake described in this book is capable of satisfying many enterprise requirements when scaled for production.

Summary

This chapter assembled a type of Data Lake, specifically the upload bucket, responsible for the ingestion of any form and quantity of data[32] with the ability to scale nearly without limit. Data Lakes satisfy any organization's desire to acquire or retain data before the identification of any specific purpose. Data Lakes are not merely flat data storage engines; they must support the ability to provide controlled access for a variety of stakeholders, support tooling for exploration and analysis, and scale in both processing power and volume when needed. MinIO makes an excellent choice for building Data Lakes within Kubernetes. MinIO's S3-compatible API, along with an event notification system supporting a wide variety of external systems, provides a broad and capable platform in which to build modern Data Lakes.[33] Additionally, this chapter demonstrated the power and convenience of leveraging in-cluster Jupyter Notebooks for the rapid prototyping of event-based object processing.

---

[32]www.dataversity.net/data-lakes-101-overview/
[33]https://blog.minio.io/modern-data-lake-with-minio-part-1-716a49499533

Once any data within a Data Lake is organized, processed, or transformed, the concepts of data warehousing emerge. Data Warehouses are critical components for business intelligence, analytics, and data science activities, including machine learning. The next chapter superimposes and extends the capabilities in this chapter with data warehousing concepts.

CHAPTER 8

Data Warehouses

This chapter on Data Warehouses extends from the previous chapter covering the development of a modern Data Lake with the distributed object storage system MinIO. Data Lakes store a wide variety of data forms, while Data Warehouses manage a wide variety of data sources. Data Warehouses provide access to data catalogs, metadata, indexes, key/value stores, message queues, event streams, document, and relational databases, including Data Lakes. The line between Data Lakes and Data Warehouses is not always clear; this book distinguishes the concept of data warehousing as any managed collection of sources containing data that is either processed, organized, indexed, cataloged, or otherwise identified with a purpose.

Open Source Data Lake management systems such as Delta Lake[1] bring ACID transactions, metadata, unified streaming, and batch data, while Kylo[2] offers a robust user interface for data ingestion, preparation, and discovery. These sophisticated Data Lake applications begin to blur the line between a vast, formless Data Lake and the well-organized, Warehouse. However, the results of these systems are likely candidates for higher-level Data Warehouse concepts.

Data lakes are indiscriminate in their collection of data; when organizations acquire data of any kind, the need to store it may arise before the business case for its use. When the value and purpose for a set of data is understood, it may then be processed, schemas developed, attributes

---

[1] https://delta.io/
[2] https://kylo.io/

© Craig Johnston 2020

C. Johnston, *Advanced Platform Development with Kubernetes*,
https://doi.org/10.1007/978-1-4842-5611-4_8

indexed, values normalized, and metadata catalogued for the awareness of interested services or human analysts. Data Warehouses expose access to real-time event and message data and collections of historical data, readied for decision support systems, business intelligence, analytics, machine learning, and inference.

Data and Data Science

The concepts related to supporting Data Science activities are broad, along with an endless array of techniques and implementations focused on providing data-driven decision making by humans or machines. Data platforms facilitate the ingestion, access, and management of data, and within them, Data Warehouses offer a catalog of data sources, schema, and metadata.

In the field of Data Science, Machine Learning activities often pose a particularly demanding set of requirements on data. Ten researchers from Google contributed to a research paper titled "Hidden Technical Debt in Machine Learning Systems."[3] The paper illustrates a typical set of infrastructure dependencies and their relative footprint within the scope of Machine Learning. The infrastructure supporting Machine Learning includes Configuration, Data Collection, Feature Extraction, Data Verification, Machine Resource Management, Analysis Tools, Process Management Tools, Serving Infrastructure, and Monitoring (see Figure 8-1). Additionally, many other Data Science activities require much of this resource, including business intelligence and analytics.

---

[3]Sculley, D., Gary Holt, Daniel Golovin, Eugene Davydov, Todd Phillips, Dietmar Ebner, Vinay Chaudhary, Michael Young, Jean-François Crespo, and Dan Dennison. "Hidden Technical Debt in Machine Learning Systems." In Advances in Neural Information Processing Systems 28, edited by C. Cortes, N. D. Lawrence, D. D. Lee, M. Sugiyama, and R. Garnett, 2503–2511. Curran Associates, Inc., 2015. http://papers.nips.cc/paper/5656-hidden-technical-debt-in-machine-learning-systems.pdf.

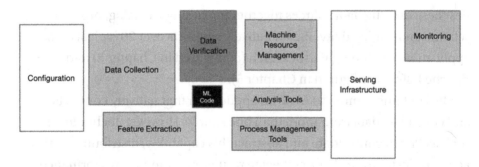

Figure 8-1. *Machine Learning infrastructure*[3]

The next section introduces a foundation of a modest yet highly functional modern Data Warehouse capable of much, if not all, of the functionality required for most Data Science activities, including Machine Learning.

Data Platform

Constructing a modern Data Warehouse in Kubernetes provides an abstraction from low-level infrastructure, a unified control plane, standardized configuration management, holistic monitoring, role-based access control, network policies, and compatibility with the rapidly growing landscape[4] of cloud-native technologies.

This chapter installs and configures three new data sources: MySQL[5] cluster representing a common RDBMS database, Apache Cassandra[6] as a wide-column distributed NoSQL database, and Apache Hive[7] capable of projecting a schema atop the S3-compatible object storage set up in the previous chapter. Presto,[8] a distributed SQL query engine for Big Data,

---

[4]https://landscape.cncf.io/
[5]www.mysql.com/
[6]https://cassandra.apache.org/
[7]https://hive.apache.org/
[8]https://prestodb.io/

ties these existing data sources together into a single catalog, providing schema and connectivity. Presto natively supports over 20 typical data applications, including Elasticsearch (configured in Chapter 6) and Apache Kafka (configured in Chapter 5).

It is not uncommon to write an application that natively connects and consumes data from more than one source. However, technologies such as Presto consolidate and abstract this capability, distribute queries across a cluster to workers, aggregate results, and monitor performance. Centralized access to a vast warehouse of data from Presto reduces technical debt across specialized systems (see Figure 8-2) by managing diverse connectivity requirements and schema management.

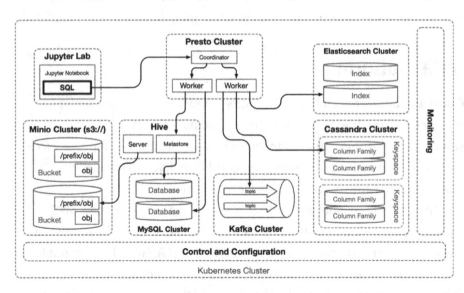

Figure 8-2. *Presto distributed SQL joining multiple data sources*

Development Environment

The following exercises continue to utilize small clusters mentioned in the previous chapters, including one 2 vCPU/8G RAM/40G SSD for the Kubernetes master node and four 4 vCPU/16G RAM/160G SSD instances for Kubernetes worker nodes. The concepts and configurations in this chapter are scaled down to fit this economically minded experimentation and development cluster.

This chapter leverages applications and cluster configurations defined in Chapters 3, 5, and 6 and the new MinIO cluster from Chapter 7 (see Table 7-1). This chapter continues to organize configuration manifests under the folder `cluster-apk8s-dev5`.

Data and Metadata Sources

Data Warehouses not only provide access to historical data from a variety of sources, but they also assist in the ingestion, development, and description of data sets. This section installs MySQL, utilized later by Apache Hive for metadata storage, and is demonstrated in this book by projecting schema atop objects in MinIO. Additionally, this chapter installs Apache Cassandra to further demonstrate the operation of diverse data management systems in Kubernetes, along with leveraging the combinatorial effect of data warehousing concepts.

MySQL

MySQL is a tremendously popular database. According to a 2019 Stack Overflow developer survey, 54% of respondents use MySQL.[9] These results are not surprising, with tens of thousands of websites launched daily powered by MySQL-backed content management systems such as WordPress and Drupal.[10] WordPress claims that it powers 35% of the Internet;[11] if this claim is accurate, it is safe to assume a significant portion of all online data (expressed as website content) is served by MySQL databases.

---

[9]https://insights.stackoverflow.com/survey/2019#technology-_-databases
[10]www.drupal.org/
[11]https://wordpress.com/activity/

The Data Warehouse application Apache Hive requires a database to store and manage metadata. Hive can use MySQL (among many other databases) for metadata. Platform support for MySQL may serve as both a possible data source and a functional dependency of the Data Warehouse (see Figure 8-2).

MySQL, along with most of the traditional database systems, predates Kubernetes, and even cloud-native concepts. Turnkey solutions for configuring and maintaining the challenging requirements of stateful database workloads are rapidly evolving. This section installs a MySQL Kubernetes Operator and defines the desired state of a new MySQL cluster.

MySQL Operator

This section configures the stable, well-documented, and actively maintained MySQL Kubernetes Operator by Presslabs.[12] The MySQL Operator defines a new custom resource represented by the custom resource definition (CRD) MysqlCluster.

If following along from previous chapters, the platform developed in this book set up a Rook Ceph Operator in Chapter 3 defining and managing the resource CephCluster and a MinIO Operator in Chapter 7 defining and managing the resource Tenant. Like previous Operators, the new MySQL Operator extends Kubernetes, therefore giving the platform developed throughout this book the ability to quickly deploy and manage one or more MySQL clusters in one or more Namespaces.

The following configuration installs the MySQL Operator in the new Namespace mysql-operator and can manage MysqlCluster resources created in any Namespace. Organize the Namespace configuration and install documentation at the cluster level. Create the directory cluster-apk8s-dev5/000-cluster/25-mysql-operator to contain the MySQL operator Namespace configuration and documentation. Next, create a file

---

[12]https://github.com/presslabs/mysql-operator

named 00-namespace.yml with contents from Listing 8-1. Additionally, create a file named README.md to document the Helm commands performed next.

Listing 8-1. MySQL operator Namespace

```
apiVersion: v1
kind: Namespace
metadata:
  name: mysql-operator
```

Apply the MySQL operator Namespace configuration:

```
$ kubectl apply -f 00-namespace.yml
```

Next add the Presslabs charts repository to Helm:

```
$ helm repo add presslabs \
https://presslabs.github.io/charts
```

Finally, install the mysql-operator. Configure the operator to use the rook-ceph-block storage class as set up in Chapter 3:

```
$ helm install presslabs/mysql-operator \
  --set orchestrator.persistence.storageClass=rook-ceph-block \
  --name mysql-operator \
  --namespace mysql-operator
```

The new mysql-operator is ready to install and manage MySQL clusters defined in MysqlCluster resources described in the next section. Additionally, the mysql-operator exposes GitHub's MySQL Orchestrator as the Service mysql-operator:80 in the mysql-operator Namespace. Orchestrator is a MySQL management and visualization tool, providing topology discovery, refactoring, and recovery capabilities.[13]

---

[13]https://github.com/github/orchestrator

Access Orchestrator by port-forwarding the Service and visiting it in a browser:

```
$ kubectl port-forward service/mysql-operator \
8080:80 -n mysql-operator
```

MySQL Cluster

The following section defines a small, two-node MySQL cluster named mysql in the data Namespace. Initially, this chapter uses MySQL as a metadata back end for Apache Hive and later on for demonstrating complex joins between diverse data sources with Presto.

Create the directory cluster-apk8s-dev5/003-data/080-mysql to contain the MySQL cluster configuration. Next, create a file named 90-cluster.yml from Listing 8-2.

Listing 8-2. MySQL cluster configuration

```
apiVersion: v1
kind: Secret
metadata:
  name: mysql-credentials
  namespace: data
type: Opaque
stringData:
  ROOT_PASSWORD: strongpassword
  USER: hive
  PASSWORD: strongpassword
  DATABASE: objectmetastore
---
apiVersion: mysql.presslabs.org/v1alpha1
kind: MysqlCluster
metadata:
  name: mysql
```

```
  namespace: data
spec:
  replicas: 2
  secretName: mysql-credentials
  volumeSpec:
    persistentVolumeClaim:
      accessModes: ["ReadWriteOnce"]
      storageClassName: "rook-ceph-block"
      resources:
        requests:
          storage: 1Gi
```

Apply the MySQL cluster configuration:

```
$ kubectl apply -f 90-cluster.yml
```

Apache Cassandra

Apache Cassandra is a high-performance, highly available, wide-column database. The addition of Cassandra to the data platform described in this book rounds out the data access and storage capabilities by providing a web-scale database solution. Netflix is one of the more notable and public Cassandra users, "Netflix is using Cassandra on AWS as a key infrastructure component of its globally distributed streaming product." Netflix has posted benchmarks demonstrating one million plus writes per second.

Cassandra's peer-to-peer design means there are no master nodes to overwhelm or outgrow, allowing Cassandra to scale linearly in both data volume and velocity. These characteristics provide capabilities that bridge many of the volume requirements of Big Data with high-velocity wide-column store data.

The following section configures the Rook Cassandra Operator used to prepare and manage one or more Cassandra clusters within Kubernetes.

Cassandra Operator

Rook[14] is a well-established provider of data storage operators for Kubernetes. This book covers the Rook Ceph Operator in Chapter 3. The Rook Cassandra Operator extends Kubernetes with the new custom resource definition `Cluster`, under the API namespace `cassandra.rook.io`.

The Rook Cassandra Operator[15] supports cluster settings allowing the specification of the desired Cassandra version, container image repository, annotations, and the option to utilize Scylla,[16] a Cassandra-compatible alternative written in C++. Scylla claims performance of 1,000,000s of OPS per node and the ability to scale out to hundreds of nodes with 99% latency of less than one millisecond. Rook's compatibility with both Scylla and Cassandra databases facilitates experimenting with both solutions. Additionally, the Rook Cassandra Operator supports the definition of Cassandra's physical topology enabling the specification of data center and rack configuration for each cluster.

Create the directory `cluster-apk8s-dev5/000-cluster/23-rook-cassandra` to contain the Rook Cassandra operator configuration. Next, create a file named `00-operator.yml` from Listing 8-3.

Listing 8-3. Rook Cassandra operator

```
apiVersion: v1
kind: Namespace
metadata:
  name: rook-cassandra-system
---
```

---

[14]https://rook.io/
[15]https://rook.io/docs/rook/v1.2/cassandra-cluster-crd.html
[16]www.scylladb.com/

```yaml
apiVersion: apiextensions.k8s.io/v1beta1
kind: CustomResourceDefinition
metadata:
  name: clusters.cassandra.rook.io
spec:
  group: cassandra.rook.io
  names:
    kind: Cluster
    listKind: ClusterList
    plural: clusters
    singular: cluster
  scope: Namespaced
  version: v1alpha1
  validation:
    openAPIV3Schema:
      properties:
        spec:
          type: object
          properties:
            version:
              type: string
              description: "Version of Cassandra"
            datacenter:
              type: object
              properties:
                name:
                  type: string
                  description: "Datacenter Name"
                racks:
                  type: array
                  properties:
```

```
            name:
              type: string
            members:
              type: integer
            configMapName:
              type: string
            storage:
              type: object
              properties:
                volumeClaimTemplates:
                  type: object
              required:
                - "volumeClaimTemplates"
            placement:
              type: object
            resources:
              type: object
              properties:
                cassandra:
                  type: object
                sidecar:
                  type: object
              required:
                - "cassandra"
                - "sidecar"
            sidecarImage:
              type: object
          required:
            - "name"
            - "members"
            - "storage"
```

```
                - "resources"
          required:
            - "name"
      required:
        - "version"
        - "datacenter"

---
apiVersion: rbac.authorization.k8s.io/v1
kind: ClusterRole
metadata:
  name: rook-cassandra-operator
rules:
  - apiGroups: [""]
    resources: ["pods"]
    verbs: ["get", "list", "watch", "delete"]
  - apiGroups: [""]
    resources: ["services"]
    verbs: ["*"]
  - apiGroups: [""]
    resources: ["persistentvolumes", "persistentvolumeclaims"]
    verbs: ["get", "delete"]
  - apiGroups: [""]
    resources: ["nodes"]
    verbs: ["get"]
  - apiGroups: ["apps"]
    resources: ["statefulsets"]
    verbs: ["*"]
  - apiGroups: ["policy"]
    resources: ["poddisruptionbudgets"]
    verbs: ["create"]
  - apiGroups: ["cassandra.rook.io"]
```

```yaml
      resources: ["*"]
      verbs: ["*"]
  - apiGroups: [""]
      resources: ["events"]
      verbs: ["create","update","patch"]
---
apiVersion: v1
kind: ServiceAccount
metadata:
  name: rook-cassandra-operator
  namespace: rook-cassandra-system
---
kind: ClusterRoleBinding
apiVersion: rbac.authorization.k8s.io/v1
metadata:
  name: rook-cassandra-operator
roleRef:
  apiGroup: rbac.authorization.k8s.io
  kind: ClusterRole
  name: rook-cassandra-operator
subjects:
- kind: ServiceAccount
  name: rook-cassandra-operator
  namespace: rook-cassandra-system
---
  apiVersion: apps/v1
  kind: StatefulSet
  metadata:
    name: rook-cassandra-operator
    namespace: rook-cassandra-system
    labels:
```

```
    app: rook-cassandra-operator
spec:
  replicas: 1
  serviceName: "non-existent-service"
  selector:
    matchLabels:
      app: rook-cassandra-operator
  template:
    metadata:
      labels:
        app: rook-cassandra-operator
    spec:
      serviceAccountName: rook-cassandra-operator
      containers:
      - name: rook-cassandra-operator
        image: rook/cassandra:v1.1.2
        imagePullPolicy: "Always"
        args: ["cassandra", "operator"]
        env:
        - name: POD_NAME
          valueFrom:
            fieldRef:
              fieldPath: metadata.name
        - name: POD_NAMESPACE
          valueFrom:
            fieldRef:
              fieldPath: metadata.namespace
```

Apply the Cassandra operator configuration:

```
$ kubectl apply -f 00-operator.yml
```

Cassandra Cluster

This section creates a three-node Apache Cassandra cluster, used later to demonstrate the powerful convergence of web-scale wide-column store databases and Big Data systems expressed with the Presto distributed SQL query engine. The following configuration defines a Kubernetes Role, ServiceAccount, and RoleBinding in the data Namespace for use in the Cassandra cluster. The Cassandra cluster is named apk8s and configured in a single virtual rack named r1. More extensive and sophisticated clusters should define multiple data centers and racks distributed within Kubernetes clusters by setting the placement values of nodeAffinity, podAffinity, podAntiAffinity, and tolerations.

Create the directory cluster-apk8s-dev5/003-data/060-cassandra to contain the Cassandra cluster configuration. Next, create a file named 15-rbac.yml from Listing 8-4.

Listing 8-4. Rook Cassandra RBAC configuration

```
apiVersion: rbac.authorization.k8s.io/v1
kind: Role
metadata:
  name: cassandra-member
  namespace: data
rules:
  - apiGroups: [""]
    resources: ["pods"]
    verbs: ["get"]
  - apiGroups: [""]
    resources: ["services"]
    verbs: ["get","list","patch","watch"]
  - apiGroups: ["cassandra.rook.io"]
    resources: ["clusters"]
```

```
    verbs: ["get"]
---
apiVersion: v1
kind: ServiceAccount
metadata:
  name: cassandra-member
  namespace: data
---
apiVersion: rbac.authorization.k8s.io/v1
kind: RoleBinding
metadata:
  name: cassandra-member
  namespace: data
roleRef:
  apiGroup: rbac.authorization.k8s.io
  kind: Role
  name: cassandra-member
subjects:
  - kind: ServiceAccount
    name: cassandra-member
    namespace: data
```

Apply the Cassandra cluster RBAC configuration:

```
$ kubectl apply -f 15-rbac.yml
```

The small Cassandra cluster defined next is constrained to one virtual rack with no specified Kubernetes Node or affinity or tolerations. The following configuration restricts each node in the Cassandra cluster to one CPU and 2 gigabytes of memory.

Create a file named 90-cluster.yml from Listing 8-5.

Listing 8-5. Rook Cassandra cluster configuration

```
apiVersion: cassandra.rook.io/v1alpha1
kind: Cluster
metadata:
  name: cassandra
  namespace: data
spec:
  version: 3.11.1
  mode: cassandra
  datacenter:
    name: apk8s
    racks:
      - name: r1
        members: 3
        storage:
          volumeClaimTemplates:
            - metadata:
                name: cassandra-data
              spec:
                storageClassName: rook-ceph-block
                resources:
                  requests:
                    storage: 5Gi
        resources:
          requests:
            cpu: 1
            memory: 2Gi
          limits:
            cpu: 1
            memory: 2Gi
```

Apply the Cassandra cluster configuration:

```
$ kubectl apply -f 90-cluster.yml
```

Apache Hive

Apache Hive is Data Warehouse software initially developed by Facebook and later given to the Apache Software Foundation. Organizations such as Netflix[17] and FINRA[18] use Hive to query massive volumes of structured data across distributed storage systems, including Hadoop's HDFS and Amazon S3. Hive simplifies the complex MapReduce jobs typically required for querying Big Data by providing a standard SQL interface. While Hive is not a database, it delivers the ability to project schema onto any structured data stored in HDFS or S3-compatible storage. Amazon's AWS offers the product Elastic MapReduce, including a version of Hive as a service.[19]

Apache Hive enables organizations to harness enormous quantities of structured data not managed by formal database management systems, steady streams of IoT data, exports from legacy systems, and ad hoc data ingestion. Apache Hive reduces the complexity and effort to perform Data Science activities, including business analytics, business intelligence, and Machine Learning, by providing an SQL interface, metadata, and schema onto a vast Data Lake.

Containerization

This section creates a custom Apache Hive container configured to use MySQL for the storage of schema and metadata related to objects residing in an S3-compatible distributed storage system, such as the MinIO cluster configured in Chapter 7. Apache Hive, like many Big Data applications,

---

[17]www.youtube.com/watch?v=Idu9OKnAOis
[18]https://technology.finra.org/opensource.html#bigdata
[19]https://docs.aws.amazon.com/emr/latest/ReleaseGuide/emr-hive.html

evolved outside the Cloud-Native and Kubernetes ecosystems, therefore requiring a bit more effort in onboarding it into the cluster. The following starts with building a custom container suitable for use with Kubernetes and local experimentation.

Create the directory apk8s-hive to contain the necessary components and configuration for a new Apache Hive Docker container.[20] Next, create the directory src, and download and uncompress both Apache Hive and its main dependency Apache Hadoop:

```
$ mkdir -p apk8s-hive/src
$ cd apk8s-hive

$ curl -L http://mirror.cc.columbia.edu/pub/software/apache/
hive/hive-3.1.2/apache-hive-3.1.2-bin.tar.gz -o ./src/apache-
hive-3.1.2-bin.tar.gz

$ curl -L http://archive.apache.org/dist/hadoop/common/
hadoop-3.1.2/hadoop-3.1.2.tar.gz -o ./src/hadoop-3.1.2.tar.gz

$ tar -xzvf ./src/apache-hive-3.1.2-bin.tar.gz -C ./src
$ tar -xzvf ./src/hadoop-3.1.2.tar.gz -C ./src
```

Next, extend Apache Hive's capabilities by adding JAR files containing the functionality needed for connecting to S3-compatible object storage and MySQL for schema and metadata management:

```
$ export HIVE_LIB=$(pwd)/src/apache-hive-3.1.2-bin/lib
$ export MIRROR=https://repo1.maven.org/maven2

$ curl $MIRROR/org/apache/hadoop/hadoop-aws/3.1.1/hadoop-aws--
3.1.1.jar -o $HIVE_LIB/hadoop-aws-3.1.1.jar

$ curl $MIRROR/com/amazonaws/aws-java-sdk/1.11.406/aws-java-
sdk-1.11.307.jar -o $HIVE_LIB/aws-java-sdk-1.11.307.jar
```

---

[20]https://github.com/apk8s/hive

```
$ curl $MIRROR/com/amazonaws/aws-java-sdk-core/1.11.307/
aws-java-sdk-core-1.11.307.jar -o $HIVE_LIB/aws-java-sdk-
core-1.11.307.jar

$ curl $MIRROR/com/amazonaws/aws-java-sdk-dynamodb/1.11.307/
aws-java-sdk-dynamodb-1.11.307.jar -o $HIVE_LIB/aws-java-sdk-
dynamodb-1.11.307.jar

$ curl $MIRROR/com/amazonaws/aws-java-sdk-kms/1.11.307/
aws-java-sdk-kms-1.11.307.jar -o $HIVE_LIB/aws-java-sdk-
kms-1.11.307.jar

$ curl $MIRROR/com/amazonaws/aws-java-sdk-s3/1.11.307/aws-java-
sdk-s3-1.11.307.jar -o $HIVE_LIB/aws-java-sdk-s3-1.11.307.jar

$ curl $MIRROR/org/apache/httpcomponents/httpclient/4.5.3/
httpclient-4.5.3.jar -o $HIVE_LIB/httpclient-4.5.3.jar

$ curl $MIRROR/joda-time/joda-time/2.9.9/joda-time-2.9.9.jar -o
$HIVE_LIB/joda-time-2.9.9.jar

$ curl $MIRROR/mysql/mysql-connector-java/5.1.48/mysql-
connector-java-5.1.48.jar -o $HIVE_LIB/mysql-connector-
java-5.1.48.jar
```

Hive, like many Java-based applications, uses XML files for configuration, in this case, hive-site.xml. However, packaging configuration values containing sensitive authentication tokens, passwords, and environment-specific services locations would be an anti-pattern causing security concerns and limiting container reusability. Mounting a configuration file from a filesystem (or ConfigMaps in the case of Kubernetes) is a standard method of configuring containers and provides considerable flexibility for admins or developers using the container; however, this method limits the ability to leverage values from existing Secrets and ConfigMap values available in Kubernetes. The technique described in this section creates a configuration file template to be populated by the container with environment variables at runtime.

Create a file named `hive-site-template.xml` with the contents from Listing 8-6.

Listing 8-6. Apache Hive configuration template `hive-site-template.xml`

```
<configuration>
    <property>
        <name>javax.jdo.option.ConnectionURL</name>
<value>jdbc:mysql://MYSQL_ENDPOINT/objectmetastore?createDataba
seIfNotExist=true&useSSL=false</value>
    </property>
    <property>
        <name>javax.jdo.option.ConnectionDriverName</name>
        <value>com.mysql.jdbc.Driver</value>
    </property>
    <property>
        <name>javax.jdo.option.ConnectionUserName</name>
        <value>MYSQL_USER</value>
    </property>
    <property>
        <name>javax.jdo.option.ConnectionPassword</name>
        <value>MYSQL_PASSWORD</value>
    </property>
    <property>
        <name>fs.s3a.endpoint</name>
        <value>S3A_ENDPOINT</value>
    </property>
    <property>
        <name>fs.s3a.access.key</name>
        <value>S3A_ACCESS_KEY</value>
    </property>
```

```
<property>
    <name>fs.s3a.secret.key</name>
    <value>S3A_SECRET_KEY</value>
</property>
<property>
    <name>fs.s3a.path.style.access</name>
    <value>S3A_PATH_STYLE_ACCESS</value>
</property>
</configuration>
```

Create a shell script named entrypoint.sh as the container's initial process. The entry point script uses sed to replace values in the hive-site.xml configuration file with values from the environment variables passed in through the container runtime, defined in the previous section. After applying the configuration, the script runs the utility schematool to add any MySQL database and tables Hive requires to store schema and metadata. Finally, the entry point script starts both a Hive server and a Hive Metastore[21] server.

Create a Bash[22] script named entrypoint.sh with the contents from Listing 8-7 used as the entry point for the new container.

Listing 8-7. Apache Hive container entrypoint.sh script

```
#!/bin/bash

# provide ample time for other services to come online
sleep 10

# configuration file location
HIVE_CONF="/opt/hive/conf/hive-site.xml"
```

---

[21]https://cwiki.apache.org/confluence/display/Hive/AdminManual+Metasto
re+3.0+Administration
[22]www.gnu.org/software/bash/manual/

```
# template replacements
for v in \
    MYSQL_ENDPOINT \
    MYSQL_USER \
    MYSQL_PASSWORD \
    S3A_ENDPOINT \
    S3A_ACCESS_KEY \
    S3A_SECRET_KEY \
    S3A_PATH_STYLE_ACCESS; do

    sed -i'' "s/${v}/${!v//\//\\/}/g" $HIVE_CONF
done

# add metastore schema to mysql
$HIVE_HOME/bin/schematool -dbType mysql -initSchema
$HIVE_HOME/bin/hiveserver2 start &
$HIVE_HOME/bin/hiveserver2 --service metastore
```

Next, create a Dockerfile with the contents from Listing 8-8.

Listing 8-8. Apache Hive entrypoint.sh

```
FROM ubuntu:16.04

ENV HADOOP_HOME /opt/hadoop
ENV HIVE_HOME /opt/hive
ENV JAVA_HOME /usr/lib/jvm/java-8-openjdk-amd64

RUN apt-get update \
 && apt-get install -y --reinstall build-essential \
 && apt-get install -y \
    curl ssh rsync vim \
    net-tools openjdk-8-jdk python2.7-dev \
    libxml2-dev libkrb5-dev libffi-dev \
```

```
    libssl-dev libldap2-dev python-lxml \
    libxslt1-dev libgmp3-dev libsasl2-dev \
    libsqlite3-dev libmysqlclient-dev

ADD src/hadoop-3.1.2 /opt/hadoop
ADD src/apache-hive-3.1.2-bin /opt/hive

COPY ./hive-site-template.xml /opt/hive/conf/hive-site.xml

ADD entrypoint.sh /
RUN chmod 775 /entrypoint.sh

ENTRYPOINT ["/entrypoint.sh"]

EXPOSE 9083
EXPOSE 10000
EXPOSE 10002
```

Ensure the custom Apache Hive containerization project contains all the necessary files specified earlier, as shown in Listing 8-9. Next, build the container defined in the Dockerfile for local testing:

```
$ docker build -t apk8s-hive-s3m:3.1.2 .
```

Listing 8-9. Apache Hive containerization files

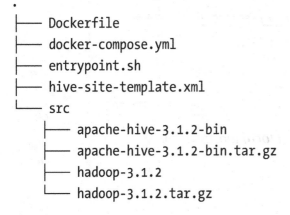

```
.
├── Dockerfile
├── docker-compose.yml
├── entrypoint.sh
├── hive-site-template.xml
└── src
        ├── apache-hive-3.1.2-bin
        ├── apache-hive-3.1.2-bin.tar.gz
        ├── hadoop-3.1.2
        └── hadoop-3.1.2.tar.gz
```

Create a version tag and push the new container to a public registry (or create the tag after the testing the container as performed in the following section):

```
$ docker tag apk8s-hive-s3m:3.1.2 \
apk8s/hive-s3m:3.1.2-1.0.0
```

Local Hive Testing

This section tests the Hive container built in the previous section by creating a database and table schema mapped to the MinIO (S3) bucket test. Create the bucket test in the MinIO cluster defined in Chapter 7. Later in this book, Hive is used to catalog object locations as data sources and project schema onto them. The following demonstrates the creation of a data source by creating a schema in Hive mapped to the empty bucket test (see Figure 8-3).

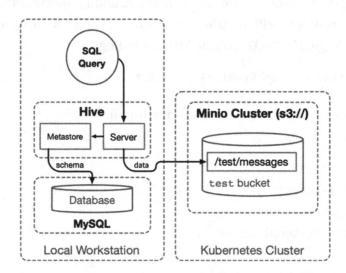

Figure 8-3. *Testing Hive on a local workstation*

After building the new container apk8s-hive-s3m:3.1.2, as described in the previous section, create a Docker Compose[23] file for local testing on the workstation used to build the container. Create the file docker-compose.yml with the contents from Listing 8-10. Set the environment variables S3A_ACCESS_KEY and S3A_SECRET_KEY to the MinIO credentials established in Chapter 7. The Docker Compose configuration defines a mysql:8.0.18 database container along with the Apache Hive container apk8s-hive-s3m:3.1.2 built previously.

Listing 8-10. Apache Hive docker-compose.yml

```
version: "3"

services:
  mysql:
    container_name: mysql
    image: mysql:8.0.18
    command: --default-authentication-plugin=mysql_native_
password
    restart: always
    environment:
      MYSQL_ROOT_PASSWORD: demo
    ports:
      - "3306:3306"
  hive-metastore:
    container_name: hive
    image: apk8s-hive-s3m:3.1.2
    environment:
      MYSQL_ENDPOINT: "mysql:3306"
      MYSQL_USER: "root"
```

---

[23]https://docs.docker.com/compose/

```
    MYSQL_PASSWORD: "demo"
    S3A_ENDPOINT: "https://obj.data.dev5.apk8s.dev"
    S3A_ACCESS_KEY: "miniouser"
    S3A_SECRET_KEY: "miniopassword"
    S3A_PATH_STYLE_ACCESS: "true"
  ports:
    - "9083:9083"
    - "10000:10000"
    - "10002:10002"
  depends_on:
    - mysql
```

Run the new Docker Compose container stack:

```
$ docker-compose up
```

After starting Docker Compose, the new Apache Hive container connects to MySQL, creating a database and tables used to store schema and metadata defined later. The Apache Hive container exposes three ports: HiveServer2 listens on port 10000, providing SQL access over thrift/JDBC; Hive Metastore listens on port 9083, allowing access to metadata and tables over the thrift protocol; and Hive provides a web interface on port 10002 for performance monitoring, debugging, and observation.

Begin testing Apache Hive by executing the command-line application available within the running container:

```
$ docker exec -it hive /opt/hive/bin/hive
```

Create a database named test:

```
hive> CREATE DATABASE IF NOT EXISTS test;
OK
```

Create a table in the test database named message using the empty bucket test (create the bucket in MinIO if it does not exist):

```
hive> CREATE TABLE IF NOT EXISTS test.message (
    >         id int,
    >     message string
    > )
    > row format delimited fields terminated by ','
    > lines terminated by "\n" location 's3a://test/messages';
```

Insert a record into the new test.message table:

```
hive> INSERT INTO test.message
    > VALUES (1, "Hello MinIO from Hive");
```

Select the data back from MinIO (S3):

```
hive> SELECT * FROM test.message;
OK
1       Hello MinIO from Hive
```

The previous test created a type of distributed database capable of cataloging and querying petabytes of data from a distributed, highly scalable MinIO object storage system. The preceding exercise is capable of modeling existing data, provided that all data in the specified bucket and prefix (/test/messages/) has the same structure. This powerful concept allows organizations to begin collecting structured data and apply a schema in the future, once the need to access it arises.

The next section brings the power of Apache Hive to the Kubernetes platform, progressing in this book. Running Hive in Kubernetes brings all the advantages provided by container management, networking, monitoring, and logical proximity to all the services within the data platform.

Modern Data Warehouse

This book considers modern Data Warehouses and Data Lakes as an open (employing containerization), cloud-native platform, the cloud represented by Kubernetes (container orchestration), and the platform as an ever-growing collection of data management applications exposed through APIs and graphical user interfaces with the ability to deploy business logic within.

Many organizations and applications require access to a variety of data sources, from common RDBMS databases to distributed document, object, and key stores—resulting from trends in Digital Transformation, IoT, and Data Science activities such as Machine Learning. Correlating data from various sources is a common practice; however, depending on the relationships between these sources, the process can be challenging. Migrating all data sources to a commercial Data Warehouse may be cost-prohibitive, impose unacceptable limitations, or result in vendor lock-in. Constructing a modern, cloud-native, vendor-neutral Data Warehouse on Kubernetes may open up new possibilities even alongside commercial applications and PaaS offerings. A tremendous amount of functionality and flexibility is achieved with little effort and capital, starting small with a near-limitless ability to scale.

This section adds Presto and Apache Hive to Kubernetes, applying new layers atop the data platform developed throughout this book. Presto and Hive demonstrate the ability to represent and combine data sources such as MinIO (S3), Cassandra, MySQL, and several more, creating a centralized data access point with distributed query execution.

Hive

This section deploys the custom Apache Hive container developed earlier in the chapter. Hive supplies SQL-like capabilities atop Apache Hadoop, extending its use to a broader range of data analytics, analysis, and management applications. Hadoop's Big Data capabilities are traditionally associated with the Hadoop Distributed File System (HDFS). However, the custom container developed earlier extends Hive with the ability to use S3-compatible object storage as a modern alternative to Hadoop's HDFS. Apache Hive creates a Data Warehouse within a broader Data Lake, as shown in Figure 8-4.

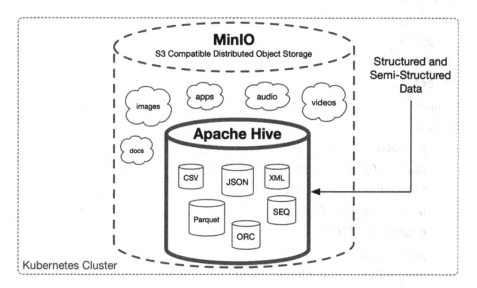

Figure 8-4. *Apache Hive warehousing structured and semi-structured data*

Kubernetes Configuration

The following configuration defines a hive Kubernetes Service backed by a hive Deployment implementing the custom image apk8s/hive-s3m:3.1.2-1.0.0 developed earlier in the chapter. The new Hive container uses MySQL to store schema, defining structured and semi-structured objects stored in MinIO (S3).

Create the directory cluster-apk8s-dev5/003-data/085-hive to contain the Apache Hive Kubernetes configurations. Next, create a file named 10-service.yml from Listing 8-11.

313

Listing 8-11. Apache Hive Service

```
apiVersion: v1
kind: Service
metadata:
  name: hive
  namespace: data
  labels:
    app: hive
spec:
  selector:
    app: hive
  ports:
    - protocol: "TCP"
      port: 10000
      targetPort: tcp-thrift
      name: tcp-thrift
    - protocol: "TCP"
      port: 9083
      targetPort: tcp-thrift-meta
      name: tcp-thrift-meta
    - protocol: "TCP"
      port: 10002
      targetPort: http-hwi
      name: http-hwi
  type: ClusterIP
```

Apply the Apache Hive Service configuration:

```
$ kubectl apply -f 10-service.yml
```

Next, create a file named 30-deployment.yml from Listing 8-12. The following deployment sets the environment variables MYSQL_USER and MYSQL_PASSWORD from the secret mysql-credentials defined earlier in this chapter as part of the MySQL cluster configuration. Chapter 7 configured MinIO with the secret minio-creds-secret, which supplies values for S3A_ACCESS_KEY and S3A_SECRET_KEY environment variables in this custom Hive deployment.

Listing 8-12. Apache Hive Deployment

```
apiVersion: apps/v1
kind: Deployment
metadata:
  name: hive
  namespace: data
  labels:
    app: hive
spec:
  replicas: 1
  revisionHistoryLimit: 1
  selector:
    matchLabels:
      app: hive
  template:
    metadata:
      labels:
        app: hive
    spec:
      containers:
        - name: hive
          image: apk8s/hive-s3m:3.1.2-1.0.0
          imagePullPolicy: IfNotPresent
          env:
            - name: MYSQL_ENDPOINT
              value: "mysql:3306"
            - name: MYSQL_USER
              valueFrom:
```

```
        secretKeyRef:
          name: mysql-credentials
          key: USER
  - name: MYSQL_PASSWORD
    valueFrom:
      secretKeyRef:
        name: mysql-credentials
        key: PASSWORD
  - name: S3A_ENDPOINT
    value: "http://minio:9000"
  - name: S3A_ACCESS_KEY
    valueFrom:
      secretKeyRef:
        name: minio-creds-secret
        key: accesskey
  - name: S3A_SECRET_KEY
    valueFrom:
      secretKeyRef:
        name: minio-creds-secret
        key: secretkey
  - name: S3A_PATH_STYLE_ACCESS
    value: "true"
ports:
  - name: tcp-thrift-meta
    containerPort: 9083
  - name: tcp-thrift
    containerPort: 10000
  - name: http-hwi
    containerPort: 10002
```

Apply the Apache Hive Deployment:

```
$ kubectl apply -f 30-deployment.yml
```

Test Data

As demonstrated previously in this chapter, Apache Hive provides the ability to project schema onto empty buckets, allowing for the creation of ad hoc yet well-structured data sets. While Hive is not itself a database, it can create massively scalable object-based databases atop distributed object storage, in this case the S3-compatible MinIO. Hive provides the ability to store schema supporting existing structured and semi-structured objects of a given type.

The following exercise creates a new blood donor example data set introduced in Chapter 7, consisting of one million records distributed across one thousand CSV files. Each record contains the comma-separated values for email, name, blood type, birthday, and state of fictional donors.

Create a new Jupyter Notebook by running JupyterLab as configured in Chapter 6; in this case, browse to a custom equivalent of https://lab.data.dev5.apk8s.dev/. Add each of the following code segments to their own cell.

Note   The following exercise is executable as a plain Python 3 script on a local workstation by replacing minio-internal-service.data:9000 with minio.data.dev5.apk8s.dev:443 (the MinIO cluster ingress set up in Chapter 7) and secure=False to secure=True.

In the first cell of a Python-based Jupyter Notebook, ensure the installation of Faker and minio libraries as follows:

```
!pip install Faker==2.0.3
!pip install minio==5.0.1
```

Import the following Python libraries:

```
import os
import datetime
from faker import Faker
```

```
from minio import Minio
from minio.error import (ResponseError,
                         BucketAlreadyOwnedByYou,
                         BucketAlreadyExists)
```

Create a function returning a tuple with a single record of fictitious donor information:

```
fake = Faker()

def makeDonor():
    fp = fake.profile(fields=[
        "name",
        "birthdate",
        "blood_group"
    ])

    return (
        fake.ascii_safe_email(),
        fp["name"],
        fp["blood_group"],
        fp["birthdate"].strftime("%Y-%m-%d"),
        fake.state(),
    )
```

Create a MinIO API client and create the bucket exports:

```
bucket = "exports"
mc = Minio('minio-internal-service.data:9000',
           access_key='<accesskey>',
           secret_key='<secretkey>',
           secure=False)
```

```
try:
    mc.make_bucket(bucket)
except BucketAlreadyOwnedByYou as err:
    pass
except BucketAlreadyExists as err:
    pass
except ResponseError as err:
    raise
```

Finally, create a file named with a data time, containing one thousand donor records. Upload the file to the MinIO bucket exports with the prefix donors/ (e.g., donors/20200205022452.csv). Repeat this process one thousand times for a total of one million records for testing.

```
for i in range(1,1001):
    now = datetime.datetime.now()
    dtstr = now.strftime("%Y%m%d%H%M%S")
    filename = f'donors/{dtstr}.csv'
    tmp_file = f'./tmp/{dtstr}.csv'

    with open(tmp_file,"w+") as tf:
        tf.write("email,name,type,birthday,state\n")
        for ii in range(1,1001):
            line = ",".join(makeDonor()) + "\n"
            tf.write(line)

        mc.fput_object(bucket, filename, tmp_file,
                    content_type='application/csv')

    os.remove(tmp_file)
    print(f'{i:02}: {filename}')
```

Create Schema

Test the new custom Apache Hive deployment by executing the hive command-line interface within the running Pod.

First, create a bucket in MinIO named hive.

Get the custom Apache Hive Pod name:

```
$ kubectl get pods -l app=hive -n data
```

Execute the hive command:

```
$ kubectl exec -it hive-8546649b5b-lbcrn \
/opt/hive/bin/hive -n data
```

From within the running hive command, create a database named exports:

```
hive> CREATE DATABASE exports;
```

Next, create the table exports.donors:

```
hive> CREATE TABLE exports.donors (
>       email string,
>       name string,
>       blood_type string,
>       birthday date,
>       state string
> )
> row format delimited fields terminated by ','
> lines terminated by "\n"
> location 's3a://exports/donors';
```

This chapter uses a custom Apache Hive container to project schema onto the distributed object-store. While the single Hive container is capable of executing queries through ODBC/thrift exposed over the hive:1000 Kubernetes Service, a more extensive Hive cluster is necessary for executing production workloads directly against Hive. However, the next section uses a Presto cluster for distributed query execution and only uses Hive to supply schema from its metadata server exposed through the Service hive:9083.

The next section demonstrates the use of Presto to connect structured data collected in the MinIO distributed object storage using Hive along a variety of other data sources, including the RDBMS MySQL and the key/value database Apache Cassandra.

Presto

Presto is the final component of the modern Data Warehouse defined in this book. According to the official website prestodb.io, "Presto is an open source distributed SQL query engine for running interactive analytic queries against data sources of all sizes ranging from gigabytes to petabytes." Although Hive is also a distributed SQL query engine cable of querying vast quantities of data, Presto connects to a broader range of data sources, including Apache Hive (as shown in Figure 8-5). Aside from Presto's high-performance querying capabilities, it provides a central catalog of data sources.

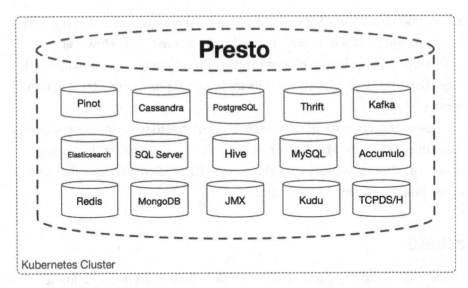

Figure 8-5. *Presto distributed SQL query across multiple data sources*

Presto reduces the amount of application logic needed to retrieve data from multiple sources, both through a standard SQL abstraction and removing the need for the client-side joining of data (in some cases considered an anti-pattern[24]). Presto provides SQL abstraction across all its supported data sources, performs distributed query execution, and includes monitoring and observability. Presto supports client libraries for Go,[25] C,[26] Java,[27] Node.js,[28] PHP,[29] Ruby,[30] R,[31] and Python.[32] A growing set of

---

[24]www.batey.info/cassandra-anti-pattern-distributed.html,
www.slideshare.net/chbatey/webinar-cassandra-antipatterns-45996021

[25]https://github.com/prestodb/presto-go-client

[26]https://github.com/easydatawarehousing/prestoclient/tree/master/C

[27]https://prestodb.io/docs/current/installation/jdbc.html

[28]https://github.com/tagomoris/presto-client-node

[29]https://github.com/Xtendsys-labs/PhpPrestoClient

[30]https://github.com/treasure-data/presto-client-ruby

[31]https://github.com/prestodb/RPresto

[32]https://github.com/prestodb/presto-python-client

web-based GUI clients, visualization, and dashboard applications support Presto, including the new business intelligence application Apache Superset, from the creators of Apache Airflow (see Figure 8-6).

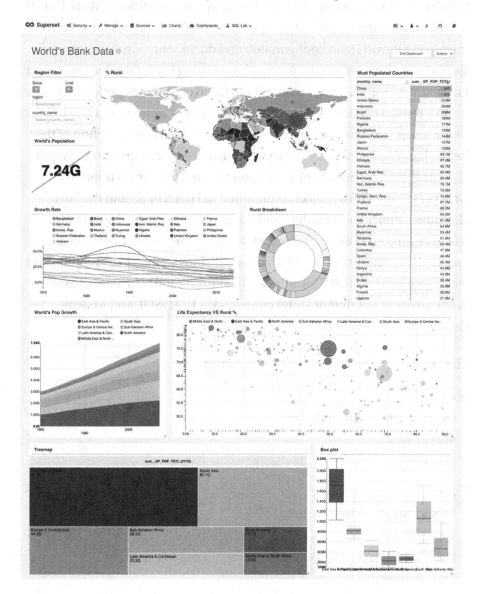

Figure 8-6. *Apache Superset (image from* https://superset. apache.org*)*

Kubernetes Configuration

This chapter installs a Presto cluster with two workers and a coordinator in Kubernetes using a stable open source Helm chart by When I Work Data.[33]

Create the directory `cluster-apk8s-dev5/003-data/095-presto` to contain the Presto Helm configuration and documentation. Next, create a file named `values.yml` with contents from Listing 8-13. Additionally, create a file named `README.md` to document the Helm commands performed next.

In Presto, a catalog represents a top-level data source. Note the four data sources (known as connectors) defined in the catalog section of the Helm chart configuration values.yml. The first two, `obj.properties` and `hive.properties`, use the hive-hadoop2 connector. Presto uses Hive for access to data files (objects) contained in HDFS or S3 and the Hive Metastore service for metadata and schema representing the data files. The `hive.properties` configuration demonstrates the use of the custom Apache Hive container (installed in the previous section) for its Metastore service backed by MySQL. Additionally, the `cassandra.properties` and `mysql.properties` demonstrate connections to MySQL and Apache Cassandra as configured in this chapter.

Listing 8-13. Presto Helm configuration

```
presto:
  environment: "production"
  workers: 2
  logLevel: "INFO"

image:
  repository: "wiwdata/presto"
  tag: "0.217"
  pullPolicy: "IfNotPresent"
```

---

[33]https://github.com/wiwdata/presto-chart

```
service:
  type: ClusterIP

catalog:
  obj.properties: |
    connector.name=hive-hadoop2
    hive.metastore=file
    hive.metastore.catalog.dir=s3://metastore/
    hive.allow-drop-table=true
    hive.s3.aws-access-key= miniobucketuserid
    hive.s3.aws-secret-key= miniobucketuserpassword
    hive.s3.endpoint=http://minio:9000
    hive.s3.path-style-access=true
    hive.s3.ssl.enabled=false
    hive.s3select-pushdown.enabled=true

  hive.properties: |
    connector.name=hive-hadoop2
    hive.metastore.uri=thrift://hive:9083
    hive.allow-drop-table=true
    hive.s3.aws-access-key= miniobucketuserid
    hive.s3.aws-secret-key= miniobucketuserpassword
    hive.s3.endpoint=http://minio:9000
    hive.s3.path-style-access=true
    hive.s3.ssl.enabled=false

  cassandra.properties: |
    connector.name=cassandra
    cassandra.contact-points=cassandra-data-r1-0,cassandra-
data-r1-1,cassandra-data-r1-2

  mysql.properties: |
    connector.name=mysql
    connection-url=jdbc:mysql://mysql:3306
```

```
    connection-user= root
    connection-password= mysqlrootpassword
coordinatorConfigs: {}
workerConfigs: {}
environmentVariables: {}
coordinatorResources: {}
workerResources: {}
coordinatorNodeSelector: {}
workerNodeSelector: {}
coordinatorTolerations: []
workerTolerations: {}
coordinatorAffinity: {}
workerAffinity: {}
```

Next, clone the Presto Helm chart repository:

```
$ git clone git@github.com:apk8s/presto-chart.git
```

Note   The GitHub repository apk8s/presto-chart[34] is forked
from wiwdata/presto-chart and contains minor updates required
for compatibility with Kubernetes 1.16+. Refer to the upstream
repository for future releases or compatibility with older versions of
Kubernetes.

Create a new Presto cluster by applying the preceding Helm chart
clone, along with custom configuration from values.yml:

---

[34]https://github.com/apk8s/presto-chart

```
$ helm upgrade --install presto-data \
  --namespace data \
  --values values.yml \
  ./presto-chart/presto
```

Once Helm completes the install process, the Kubernetes cluster contains two Presto worker nodes and one Presto coordinator.

Finally, add a Kubernetes Ingress configuration backed by the new presto-data:80 service generated by the Helm chart. The following Ingress uses the secret sysop-basic-auth set up in the "Data Namespace" section of Chapter 5 to add simple Basic Auth security. Create a file named 50-ingress.yml from Listing 8-14.

Listing 8-14. Presto Ingress

```
apiVersion: networking.k8s.io/v1beta1
kind: Ingress
metadata:
  name: presto
  namespace: data
  annotations:
    cert-manager.io/cluster-issuer: letsencrypt-production
    nginx.ingress.kubernetes.io/auth-type: basic
    nginx.ingress.kubernetes.io/auth-secret: sysop-basic-auth
    nginx.ingress.kubernetes.io/auth-realm: "Authentication
Required"
spec:
  rules:
    - host: presto.data.dev5.apk8s.dev
      http:
        paths:
          - backend:
              serviceName: presto-data
```

```
            servicePort: 80
        path: /
  tls:
    - hosts:
        - presto.data.dev5.apk8s.dev
      secretName: presto-data-production-tls
```

Apply the Presto Ingress configuration:

```
$ kubectl apply -f 50-ingress.yml
```

The next section demonstrates connecting to Presto from within a
Jupyter Notebook using the presto-python-client library.

Query

This section demonstrates interaction with Presto using a Python-based
Jupyter Notebook running within the Kubernetes cluster (see Chapter 6).

Start a new Python 3 Notebook from the JupyterLab environment, add
and execute the following code in individual cells. Starting with the first
cell, use pip to install the presto-python-client library:

```
!pip install presto-python-client==0.7.0
```

Import the prestodb (from the package presto-python-client), os,
and pandas Python libraries; create a new Presto database connection
object and cursor used to execute commands as shown in Figure 8-7.
Executing the command SHOW CATALOGS reveals the four data sources,
cassandra, hive, mysql, and obj configured in the previous section.
The system catalog contains Presto internal configuration and
operational data.

```
[1]:  import prestodb
      import os
      import pandas as pd
```

```
[2]:  conn=prestodb.dbapi.connect(
          host='presto-data.data',
          port=80,
          user=os.environ['HOSTNAME'],
      )
      cur = conn.cursor()
```

```
[3]:  cur.execute('SHOW CATALOGS')
      rows = cur.fetchall()
      rows
```

```
[3]:  [['cassandra'], ['hive'], ['mysql'], ['obj'], ['system']]
```

Figure 8-7. *Jupyter Notebook executing show catalogs Presto command*

Query the system catalog for a list of Presto nodes as shown in Figure 8-8. Loading the results of a select statement into a Pandas[35] DataFrame[36] along with the column names provides a user interface for managing and displaying the result set. This method becomes especially useful when performing analytics and Data Science activities. Pandas is often a central component in Python data libraries and contains many powerful features for data transformation and mathematical operations.

---

[35]https://pandas.pydata.org/

[36]https://pandas.pydata.org/pandas-docs/stable/reference/frame.html

```
[4]:  cur.execute('SELECT * FROM system.runtime.nodes')
      rows = cur.fetchall()

      df = pd.DataFrame(
          rows,
          columns=[d[0] for d in cur.description]
      )

      df.loc[:, 'http_uri':'state']
```

[4]:		http_uri	node_version	coordinator	state
	0	http://10.32.160.14:8080	0.217	False	active
	1	http://10.32.128.13:8080	0.217	False	active
	2	http://10.32.160.13:8080	0.217	True	active

Figure 8-8. *Retrieving a list of Presto nodes*

Describe the donors schema configured with Apache Hive in the previous section as shown in Figure 8-9. Hive and Presto completely abstract the location and underlying data structure of the donors data set, generated and uploaded earlier in this chapter as a series of one thousand CSV files to the exports bucket.

```
[5]:  cur.execute('DESCRIBE hive.exports.donors')
      rows = cur.fetchall()
      df = pd.DataFrame(
          rows,
          columns=[d[0] for d in cur.description]
      )
      df
```

[5]:		Column	Type	Extra	Comment
	0	email	varchar		
	1	name	varchar		
	2	blood_type	varchar		
	3	birthday	date		
	4	state	varchar		

Figure 8-9. *Describing tables in Presto*

330

Figure 8-10 depicts an SQL select statement utilizing Presto to scan all one thousand CSV files for records where the values of the state column beginning with "New" and grouping the records by state and blood_type with a count of all records for each group.

Presto provides a mature, well-documented, and full-featured SQL interface along with dozens of functions and operators. Utilizing Presto for initial data analysis, application of mathematical functions and operators, aggregation, and more removes operational complexity from applications by leveraging Presto's distributed execution engine for these intensive tasks, especially on massive volumes of data.

```
[6]: cur.execute("""
     SELECT d.state, d.blood_type, count(1) as total
     FROM hive.exports.donors AS d
     WHERE d.state LIKE 'New%'
     GROUP BY (d.state, d.blood_type)
     """)
     rows = cur.fetchall()
     df = pd.DataFrame(
         rows,
         columns=[d[0] for d in cur.description]
     )

     df = df.sort_values(by=['state','blood_type'])
     df.loc[df['state'] == 'New Jersey']
```

	state	blood_type	total
24	New Jersey	A+	2310
15	New Jersey	A-	2289
28	New Jersey	AB+	2444
31	New Jersey	AB-	2299
26	New Jersey	B+	2362
23	New Jersey	B-	2297
22	New Jersey	O+	2444
27	New Jersey	O-	2363

Figure 8-10. *SQL select statement in Presto*

Joining diverse data sets is a fundamental feature of Presto and the central concept of Data Warehouses. As an exercise for the reader, create or import data into Apache Cassandra or MySQL that correlates to the sample donor data used earlier. A typical SQL join may resemble Figure 8-11; in this example, a Cassandra table named appointment exists in the Keyspace lab, representing appointment data.

Figure 8-11: Example using Presto to SQL join Hive and Cassandra data sets.

```
[9]:  %%time
      cur.execute("""
      SELECT d.name, d.email, d.state, a.completed_on
      FROM
          hive.default.donors AS d,
          cassandra.lab.appointment as a
      WHERE a.email = d.email
      AND a.completed_on > date '2019-09-30'
      AND d.state LIKE 'New%'
      """)
      rows = cur.fetchall()
      df = pd.DataFrame(
          rows,
          columns=['Name','Email', 'State', 'DateTime']
      )
      df
```

```
CPU times: user 37.1 ms, sys: 2.22 ms, total: 39.3 ms
Wall time: 2.31 s
```

[9]:		Name	Email	State	DateTime
	0	Renee Wang	zmartin@example.net	New York	2019-12-19 16:43:00.000
	1	Renee Wang	zmartin@example.net	New York	2019-09-30 02:07:00.000
	2	Emma Perez	amorris@example.org	New York	2019-12-25 10:30:00.000
	3	Christian Anthony	rhoward@example.net	New Jersey	2019-11-23 22:28:00.000
	4	Christian Anthony	rhoward@example.net	New Jersey	2019-10-04 04:39:00.000
	5	Sheila Willis	rhoward@example.net	New Mexico	2019-11-23 22:28:00.000
	6	Sheila Willis	rhoward@example.net	New Mexico	2019-10-04 04:39:00.000

Figure 8-11. SQL join statement in Presto

Joining and performing operations on large data sets across a variety of data sources creates elaborate execution plans. Presto provides an intuitive web-based user interface for exploring, monitoring, and debugging queries. An Ingress configuration, defined in the previous section, exposes the Presto UI at `https://presto.data.dev5.apk8s.dev` as depicted in Figure 8-12.

***Figure 8-12.** SQL join statement in Presto*

Monitoring and observability are critical, for both Big Data and web-scale data operations. The Presto web user interface supports drill-downs into each query providing query details including resource utilization, timeline, error information, stages, and tasks related to the execution. Additionally, Presto provides a Live Plan, as shown in Figure 8-13 depicting the execution flow between stages in real time through a network diagram.

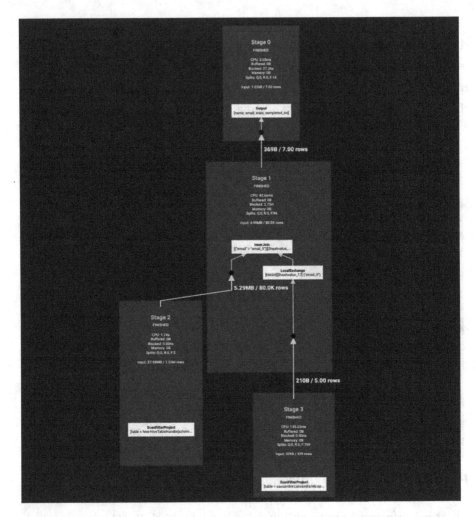

Figure 8-13. *SQL join statement in Presto*

Presto is a comprehensive solution for building a modern Data Warehouse within Kubernetes; its support for a range of data sources fits the growing needs of IoT and Machine Learning, providing the ability to retrieve, coalesce, correlate, transform, and analyze limitless quantities and structures of data.

Summary

This chapter, along with Chapter 6, demonstrated a small-scale representation of Data Lake and Data Warehouse concepts constructed atop Kubernetes. Technologies such as Apache Hive and Presto help organizations struggling with siloed data management operations; running these solutions on Kubernetes further reduces the logical and conceptual proximity of these applications by unifying the underlying data and control planes.

This chapter covered the installation of a MySQL cluster representing a massively popular RDBMS, Apache Cassandra as Big Data key/value store, and Hive exposing limitless structured and semi-structured data objects. While there are a large number of specialized applications for a range of data-centric problem domains (from Machine Learning to IoT), this book covers a general yet comprehensive set of data (and event) management solutions. If following along from previous chapters, Listing 8-15 represents a high-level snapshot of the current organization of Kubernetes-based data platform components up to this point.

Now with the ability to store and retrieve near-limitless volumes and forms of data, the next chapter extends this Kubernetes-based data platform by expanding the capabilities for data collection, routing, transformation, and processing.

Listing 8-15. Organization of Kubernetes-based data platform components

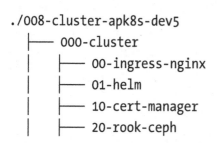

```
./008-cluster-apk8s-dev5
├── 000-cluster
│   ├── 00-ingress-nginx
│   ├── 01-helm
│   ├── 10-cert-manager
│   ├── 20-rook-ceph
```

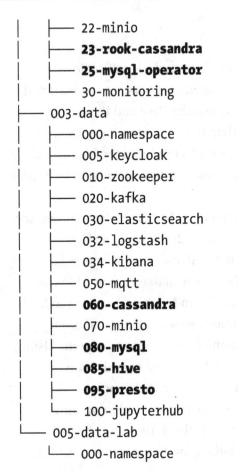

```
│      ├── 22-minio
│      ├── 23-rook-cassandra
│      ├── 25-mysql-operator
│      └── 30-monitoring
├── 003-data
│      ├── 000-namespace
│      ├── 005-keycloak
│      ├── 010-zookeeper
│      ├── 020-kafka
│      ├── 030-elasticsearch
│      ├── 032-logstash
│      ├── 034-kibana
│      ├── 050-mqtt
│      ├── 060-cassandra
│      ├── 070-minio
│      ├── 080-mysql
│      ├── 085-hive
│      ├── 095-presto
│      └── 100-jupyterhub
└── 005-data-lab
       └── 000-namespace
```

CHAPTER 9

Routing and Transformation

Previous chapters covered the construction of databases, Data Lakes, and Data Warehouses, the foundational elements of a data platform, all from within Kubernetes, demonstrating a robust distributed services platform. This chapter focuses on the collection, extraction, movement, and processing of data, rounding out the majority of functionality required for any data-centric application. The ability to efficiently **extract, transform, and load** data from one diverse system into another is essential in harnessing the explosive growth of data from consumer and industrial IoT, social media, and digital transformation occurring in many organizations. The ability to quickly construct routes that move, transform, and process data is vital in leveraging the ever-advancing, data-driven trends such as Machine Learning based AI, technologies particularly hungry for large quantities of processed data. An effective data platform provides all the generalized mechanisms needed to **extract, transform, and load** data across data management systems and offers an application layer for supporting specialized processing and custom business logic.

This chapter extends the Kubernetes-based data platform built up from previous chapters with ETL/ELT (extract, transform, load) and FaaS (functions as a service, also known as Serverless) functionality. Techniques and technologies focused on ETL have been maturing for many years. Data engineers can now combine ETL with Serverless platforms, quickly developing, integrating, and deploying directly into the data pipeline.

ETL and Data Processing

This chapter introduces two new technologies into Kubernetes: Apache NiFi and OpenFaaS, demonstrating a purely open source method of extracting, loading, transforming, and processing data without the need for domain-specific languages and complicated configuration files. Apache NiFi brings hundreds of prebuilt data "processors" for the extraction and loading of data to and from nearly any standard network protocol or API implementation, along with the ability to transform it to almost any desired form. OpenFaaS is a vendor-neutral approach to the concept of Serverless/FaaS (functions as a services); in this case, FaaS allows for the limitless extensibility of the ETL pipeline through custom, highly focused code, developed in any language.

Figure 9-1 depicts an ETL, data processing, and visualization demonstration developed throughout this chapter. The end goal is to visualize the range of sentiment expressed over some time on a specific set of Twitter messages. The following sections install OpenFaaS and deploy a prepacked sentiment analysis Function. Later sections introduce Apache NiFi and configure directed graphs of data routing and transformation from Twitter to Kafka and out of Kafka to the OpenFaaS sentiment analysis Function, finally recording the results in Elasticsearch, exposed for analysis by a Jupyter Notebook. While none of these technologies requires Kubernetes, this demonstration aims to illuminate the advantages of a unified control plane, networking, monitoring, and the extensibility of its container-based application platform capabilities.

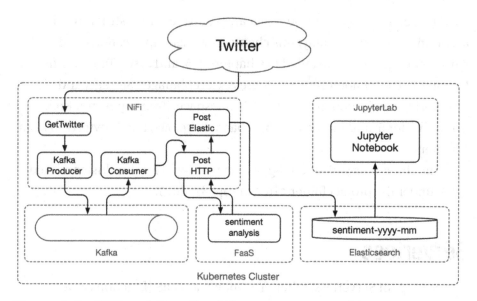

Figure 9-1. *NiFi and OpenFaaS demonstration architecture*

Some technologies in this book, namely, databases, may sacrifice a degree of performance when running over abstracted infrastructure; however, some applications will find this an acceptable trade-off for the reduction of technical debt incurred when managing many systems with thoroughly distinctive dependencies. Depending on the size of the organization or budgetary concerns of the project, it may not be feasible to employ infrastructure expertise for each enterprise-focused technology such as Apache NiFi, Kafka, and Elasticsearch. This book hopes to demonstrate these technologies on a scale nearly any project may utilize by leveraging Kubernetes, from a startup proof of concept to a web-scale social network.

Development Environment

The following exercises continue to utilize the inexpensive Hetzner cluster mentioned in Chapter 6, including one CX21 (2 vCPU/8G RAM/40G SSD) for the Kubernetes master node and four CX41 (4 vCPU/16G RAM/160G

SSD) instances for worker nodes, yet any equivalent infrastructure will accommodate. Additionally, this chapter leverages applications and cluster configurations installed in Chapters 3, 5, and 6; see Table 7-1 from Chapter 7. This chapter requires Ingress, Cert Manager, Storage, and Monitoring configured in Chapter 3; Namespace, Zookeeper, and Kafka from Chapter 5; and Elasticsearch, Kibana, Keycloak, and JupyterHub from Chapter 6.

This chapter organizes configuration manifests for the cluster named dev5, under the project folder `cluster-apk8s-dev5`.

Serverless

The concept of Serverless, otherwise known as FaaS (functions as a service), has continued to mature and fill the need for the streamlined deployment of small units of functional code. The difference between a monolithic application, a microservice, and a (Serverless) Function resides in the implementation, operational infrastructure, and context of the broader architecture. For example, many microservice and function-based architectures still rely on monolithic databases. The term Serverless implies that the developer should require little or no concern over the server-side implementation. Serverless, or FaaS (functions as a service), aims to abstract away nearly all aspects of integration, deployment, and runtime operations, leaving functional business logic as the only responsibility of the developer.

Cloud vendors market the central appeal of Serverless technology, the ability to allow developers to focus solely on business logic, abstracting and managing infrastructure, operating systems, and runtime and application layers. The major cloud vendors' offerings include Amazon's

AWS Lambda,[1] Microsoft's Azure Functions,[2] Google Cloud Functions,[3] and IBM Cloud Functions.[4] These products can significantly reduce time to market and technical debt for many organizations, albeit at the cost of vendor lock-in. Organizations already invested in Kubernetes, however, can take advantage of the growing number of open source, vendor-neutral Serverless platforms such as Apache OpenWhisk,[5] Kubeless,[6] and OpenFaaS.[7] Knative[8] is a popular choice for those looking to develop a custom Serverless platform.

This chapter demonstrates OpenFaaS for use in an example ETL application and how Serverless/functions as a service can make an excellent addition to any data platform.

OpenFaaS

OpenFaaS is a stable, well-maintained, Serverless application platform used by a growing number of organizations. OpenFaaS runs nearly anywhere, yet integrates well with Kubernetes, supporting languages such as Go, Java, Python, PHP, Rust, Perl, C#, and Ruby, along with application platforms including Express.js, Django, and ASP.NET Core. OpenFaaS supports custom-built containers for wrapping powerful binaries such as FFmpeg[9] and ImageMagick.[10]

---

[1]https://aws.amazon.com/lambda/
[2]https://azure.microsoft.com/en-us/services/functions/
[3]https://cloud.google.com/functions/docs/
[4]www.ibm.com/cloud/functions
[5]https://openwhisk.apache.org/
[6]https://kubeless.io/
[7]www.openfaas.com/
[8]https://knative.dev/
[9]https://ffmpeg.org/
[10]https://imagemagick.org/

The management of containerized workloads is Kubernetes's central capability; however, a platform such as OpenFaaS provides a formal tooling and operations framework for the development, cataloging, integration, deployment, scaling, and monitoring of workloads expressed as Functions.

Serverless/functions as a service are a natural fit for ETL and data processing pipelines, as demonstrated later in this chapter.

Install OpenFaaS

Update Helm with the OpenFaaS repository:

```
$ helm repo add openfaas \
        https://openfaas.github.io/faas-netes/
$ helm repo update
```

Next, use Helm to install the OpenFaaS gateway into the data Namespace with the argument --namespace data. The OpenFaaS gateway can set Functions to run in an alternate Namespace, but for this example, use the data Namespace by setting functionNamespace=data. OpenFaaS is capable of utilizing Kubernetes Node Ports and load balancers;[11] however, this example uses Ingress to expose the deployed Functions by setting exposeServices=false and ingress.enabled=true. Lastly, set the option generateBasicAuth=true to protect the Ingress exposed gateway user interface with Basic Authentication:

```
$ helm upgrade apk8s-data-openfaas -install \
        openfaas/openfaas \
        --namespace data \
        --set functionNamespace=data \
        --set exposeServices=false \
        --set ingress.enabled=true \
        --set generateBasicAuth=true
```

---

[11]https://kubernetes.io/docs/concepts/services-networking/service/
#publishing-services-service-types

Create the directory cluster-apk8s-dev5/003-data/120-openfaas. Within the new 120-openfaas directory, create a file named 50-ingress. yml from Listing 9-1.

Listing 9-1. OpenFaaS Ingress

```
apiVersion: networking.k8s.io/v1beta1
kind: Ingress
metadata:
  name: faas
  namespace: data
  annotations:
    cert-manager.io/cluster-issuer: letsencrypt-production
spec:
  rules:
    - host: faas.data.dev5.apk8s.dev
      http:
        paths:
          - backend:
              serviceName: gateway
              servicePort: 8080
            path: /
  tls:
    - hosts:
        - faas.data.dev5.apk8s.dev
      secretName: faas-data-production-tls
```

Apply the OpenFaaS Ingress configuration:

```
$ kubectl apply -f 50-ingress.yml
```

After successfully applying Ingress, retrieve the Basic Authentication credentials generated by the OpenFaaS Helm installation with the following command:

```
$ echo $(kubectl -n data get secret basic-auth -o jsonpath="{.
data.basic-auth-password}" | base64 --decode)
```

The previous command returns the Basic Auth password used to log in to the OpenFaaS UI portal; the username is admin. Browse to the ingress URL, in this example (see Figure 9-2):

```
https://faas.data.dev5.apk8s.dev.
```

Figure 9-2. *OpenFaaS UI portal*

The OpenFaaS UI portal is a convenient web-based, visual interface for installing and managing Functions. However, the CLI utility faas-cli is often the preferred method of interacting with OpenFaaS, capable of supporting all aspects of developing, testing, deploying, and administering and automating functions as a service. Install the OpenFaaS CLI on a local workstation:

```
$ curl -sLSf https://cli.openfaas.com | sudo sh
```

Execute the OpenFaaS CLI for a top-level list of commands:

```
$ faas-cli
```

While this book recommends the CLI utility for regular use, the following section uses the web-based interface as a simple visual demonstration of installing and interacting with an OpenFaaS Function.

Install Sentiment Analysis

Sentiment Analysis,[12] otherwise known as emotion recognition[13] or opinion mining,[14] is a form of natural language processing (NLP). NLP applies linguistics, artificial intelligence, and information engineering to natural (human) languages. This section deploys a prebuilt OpenFaaS Function container,[15] implementing the Python library TextBlob[16] to perform Sentiment Analysis on one or more sentences of raw text. This chapter later uses the deployed Sentiment Analysis Function to analyze a real-time stream of Twitter messages tagged with keywords related to COVID-19.

Browse to the OpenFaaS UI portal set up in the previous section (https://faas.data.dev5.apk8s.dev) and click the DEPLOY NEW FUNCTION button in the center of the screen. Next, use the Search for

---

[12]Gupta, Shashank. "Sentiment Analysis: Concept, Analysis and Applications." Medium, January 19, 2018. https://towardsdatascience.com/sentiment-analysis-concept-analysis-and-applications-6c94d6f58c17.

[13]Kołakowska, Agata, Agnieszka Landowska, Mariusz Szwoch, Wioleta Szwoch, and Michał Wróbel. "Emotion Recognition and Its Applications." Advances in Intelligent Systems and Computing 300 (July 1, 2014): 51–62. https://doi.org/10.1007/978-3-319-08491-6_5.

[14]Analytics Vidhya. "A NLP Approach to Mining Online Reviews Using Topic Modeling," October 16, 2018. www.analyticsvidhya.com/blog/2018/10/mining-online-reviews-topic-modeling-lda/.

[15]https://github.com/openfaas/faas/tree/master/sample-functions/SentimentAnalysis

[16]https://textblob.readthedocs.io/en/dev/

Function feature and search for the term SentimentAnalysis as shown in Figure 9-3, select the Function SentimentAnalysis, and click DEPLOY on the bottom left of the dialog.

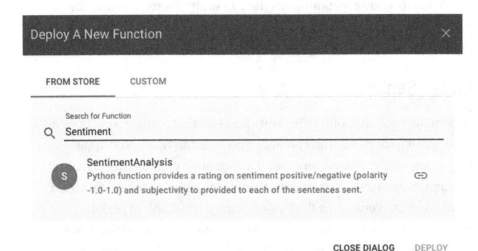

Figure 9-3. *OpenFaaS Deploy the prebuilt Sentiment Analysis Function*

After deploying the OpenFaaS Sentiment Analysis Function, select it from the left-hand navigation. The UI portal displays the Status, Replicas, Invocation count, image, and URL for the Function in the upper section of the page (see Figure 9-4). The URL is the publicly exposed endpoint. The OpenFaaS gateway does not protect function endpoints by default;[17] security is the responsibility of the Function itself. OpenFaaS documentation walks through developing custom Function authentication by implementing HMAC security using Kubernetes Secrets.[18]

---

[17]https://docs.openfaas.com/reference/authentication/#for-functions
[18]https://github.com/openfaas/workshop/blob/master/lab11.md

The OpenFaaS UI portal provides a convenient web form for testing the deployed Function under the Invoke function section shown in Figure 9-4. Alternatively, invoke the Sentiment Analysis Function using `faas-cli` utility installed in the previous section:

```
$ echo "Kubernetes is easy" | faas-cli invoke \
    sentimentanalysis -g https://faas.data.dev5.apk8s.dev/
```

sentimentanalysis

Status	Replicas	Invocation count
Ready	1	53246

Image
functions/sentimentanalysis:latest

URL
https://faas.data.dev5.apk8s.dev/function/sentimentanal:

Invoke function

```
    INVOKE
```

◉ Text ○ JSON ○ Download
Request body
Kubernetes is great

Response status
200

Round-trip (s)
0.638

Response body
```
{
   "polarity": 0.8,
   "sentence_count": 1,
   "subjectivity": 0.75
}
```

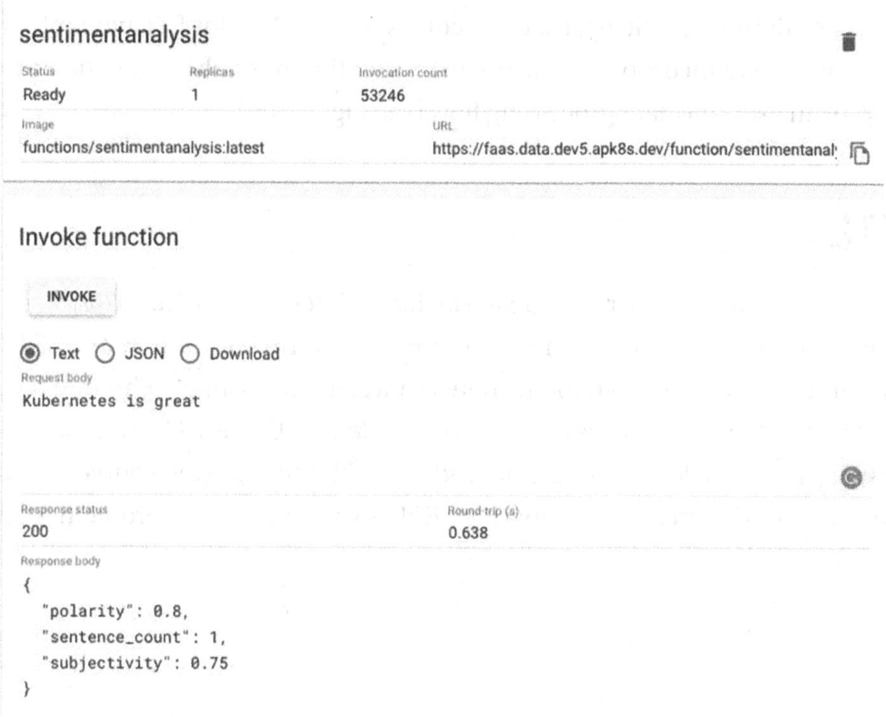

Figure 9-4. *Testing the Sentiment Analysis Function with the OpenFaaS UI portal*

Finally, test public access to the new Function with cURL:

```
$ curl -X POST -d "People are kind" \
https://faas.data.dev5.apk8s.dev/function/sentimentanalysis
```

Example output:

```
{"polarity": 0.6, "sentence_count": 1, "subjectivity": 0.9}
```

The OpenFaaS Sentiment Analysis Function is an excellent example of a focused, self-contained bit of processing logic deployed and managed by OpenFaaS atop Kubernetes. The OpenFaaS documentation contains a well-written set of tutorials on building, testing, and implementing Functions.[19] Functions are a great way to extend the data platform developed in this book continuously. The next section covers Apache NiFi for ETL types of operations and incorporates the use of the Sentiment Analysis Function as part of an example data processing flow (see Figure 9-5).

ETL

The practice of ETL (extract, transform, load) dates back to the 1970s.[20] The need to pull data from one source and transform it for use by another is a timeless problem, and today there is a wealth of existing techniques and technologies to address it. Pentaho,[21] Talend,[22] CloverETL,[23] and JasperETL[24] are a few commercial products with limited open source, community-driven options. However, ETL is such a common problem

---

[19]https://github.com/openfaas/workshop

[20]Health Catalyst. "Healthcare Information Systems: Past, Present, Future," May 20, 2014. www.healthcatalyst.com/insights/healthcare-information-systems-past-present-future.

[21]https://wiki.pentaho.com/

[22]www.talend.com/products/talend-open-studio

[23]www.cloverdx.com/

[24]https://community.jaspersoft.com/project/jaspersoft-etl

that new approaches and generalized solutions such as the open source (vendor-neutral) Apache NiFi have been gaining popularity for ease of use and a simplistic, intuitive approach to data collection, routing, and transformation.

Apache NiFi

Apache NiFi is the data ingestion front-end of choice for the data-centric platform described in this book. "Apache NiFi supports powerful and scalable directed graphs of data routing, transformation, and system mediation logic."[25]

NiFi ships with nearly 300 unique data processors usable for the collection, transformation, processing, and modeling of data from sources as diverse as Twitter, SMTP, HDFS, Redis, UDP, HBase, and HTTP API endpoints.[26]

At the time of this book's publication, there is little official documentation and support for running NiFi within Kubernetes. However, the NiFi maintainers are aware of the rapid growth in demand for first-class Kubernetes support, and readers should expect significant contributions to this effort in the coming years.

The following sections install a multi-node Apache NiFi cluster in Kubernetes and demonstrate a flow of data extraction from Twitter with transformation, processing, and utilizing OpenFaaS, Kafka, and Elasticsearch, as shown in Figure 9-5.

---

[25]https://nifi.apache.org/
[26]https://nifi.apache.org/docs.html

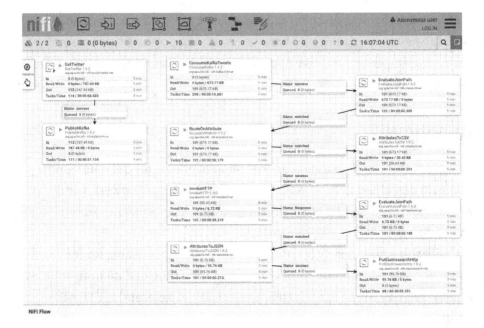

NiFi Flow

Figure 9-5. *Apache NiFi flow overview*

Install Apache NiFi

This section installs Apache NiFi with three Kubernetes resources consisting of a Headless Service, StatefulSet, and Ingress. Review the "Development Environment" section earlier in this chapter for requirements, including Ingress Nginx, Ceph storage, Cert Manager, and Apache Zookeeper.

Although this book avoids Helm installations at times, in favor of a more verbose representation of concepts through hand-crafted manifests, readers should also consider the Apache NiFi Helm chart by Cetic.[27]

---

[27]https://github.com/cetic/helm-nifi

Create the directory `cluster-apk8s-dev5/003-data/060-nifi`. Within the new `060-nifi` directory, create a file named `10-service-headless.yml` from Listing 9-2. The StatefulSet defined in the following calls for two replicas of the Pod `nifi` running an apache/nifi:1.9.2 container. Each NiFi instance in the cluster requires some custom configuration on boot. Rather than allow the standard startup script to run, the `command:` section invokes Bash and pipes in a script to customize a few properties based on the hostname Kubernetes assigns to the Pod.

Listing 9-2. NiFi Headless Service

```
apiVersion: v1
kind: Service
metadata:
  name: nifi
  namespace: data
  labels:
    app: nifi
  annotations:
    service.alpha.kubernetes.io/tolerate-unready-endpoints:
    "true"
spec:
  type: ClusterIP
    clusterIP: None
  selector:
    app: nifi
  ports:
  - port: 8080
    name: http
  - port: 6007
    name: cluster
```

Apply the NiFi Headless Service configuration:

```
$ kubectl apply -f 10-service-headless.yml
```

Next, create a StatefulSet configuration for NiFi in a file named 40-statefulset.yml from Listing 9-3.

Listing 9-3. NiFi StatefulSet

```
apiVersion: apps/v1
kind: StatefulSet
metadata:
  name: nifi
  namespace: data
  labels:
    app: nifi
spec:
  replicas: 2
  revisionHistoryLimit: 1
  selector:
    matchLabels:
      app: nifi
  serviceName: nifi
  template:
    metadata:
      labels:
        app: nifi
    spec:
      affinity:
        podAntiAffinity:
          requiredDuringSchedulingIgnoredDuringExecution:
            - labelSelector:
```

```yaml
          matchExpressions:
            - key: "app"
              operator: In
              values:
                - "nifi"
        topologyKey: "kubernetes.io/hostname"
containers:
  - name: nifi
    imagePullPolicy: IfNotPresent
    image: apache/nifi:1.9.2
    command:
      - bash
      - -ce
      - |
        FQDN=$(hostname -f)
        PROP_FILE=${NIFI_HOME}/conf/nifi.properties

        p_repl () {
          echo "setting ${1}=${2}"
          sed -i -e "s|^$1=.*$|$1=$2|" ${PROP_FILE}
        }
        p_repl nifi.remote.input.host ${FQDN}
        p_repl nifi.cluster.is.node true
        p_repl nifi.cluster.node.protocol.port 6007
        p_repl nifi.cluster.node.address ${FQDN}
        p_repl nifi.cluster.protocol.is.secure false
        p_repl nifi.security.user.authorizer managed-
        authorizer
        p_repl nifi.web.http.host ${FQDN}
        p_repl nifi.web.http.port 8080
        p_repl nifi.zookeeper.connect.string ${NIFI_
        ZOOKEEPER_CONNECT_STRING}
```

```
          p_repl nifi.cluster.flow.election.max.wait.time
          "1 mins"

          tail -F "${NIFI_HOME}/logs/nifi-app.log" & exec
          bin/nifi.sh run
        env:
          - name: NIFI_ZOOKEEPER_CONNECT_STRING
            value: "zookeeper-headless:2181"
        ports:
          - containerPort: 8080
            name: http
            protocol: TCP
          - containerPort: 6007
            name: cluster
            protocol: TCP
```

Apply the NiFi StatefulSet configuration:

```
$ kubectl apply -f 40-statefulset.yml
```

Lastly, create an Ingress configuration for NiFi in a file named
50-ingress.yml from Listing 9-4. Apache NiFi supports authentication;[28]
however, this requires it to run in SSL mode and needs additional
component configuration to manage certificates and Ingress. In keeping
this demonstration concise, the Ingress configuration secures NiFi with
Basic Auth credentials stored in the Kubernetes Secret sysop-basic-auth.

---

[28]https://nifi.apache.org/docs/nifi-docs/html/administration-guide.
  html#user_authentication

Listing 9-4. NiFi Ingress

```
apiVersion: extensions/v1beta1
kind: Ingress
metadata:
  name: nifi
  namespace: data
  annotations:
    cert-manager.io/cluster-issuer: letsencrypt-production
    nginx.ingress.kubernetes.io/auth-type: basic
    nginx.ingress.kubernetes.io/auth-secret: sysop-basic-auth
    nginx.ingress.kubernetes.io/auth-realm: "Authentication
    Required"
spec:
  rules:
    - host: nifi.data.dev3.apk8s.dev
      http:
        paths:
          - backend:
              serviceName: nifi
              servicePort: 8080
            path: /
  tls:
    - hosts:
      - nifi.data.dev3.apk8s.dev
      secretName: data-production-tls
```

Apply the NiFi Ingress configuration:

```
$ kubectl apply -f 50-ingress.yml
```

Verify the new NiFi cluster is up and running by browsing to https://
nifi.data.dev3.apk8s.dev/nifi, open the Global Menu in the upper-left
corner of the user interface, and select the item Cluster. Review the list of
running nodes as shown in Figure 9-6.

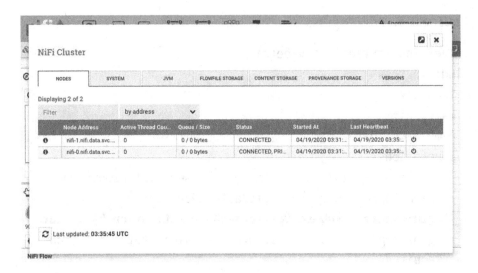

Figure 9-6. *Apache NiFi cluster status*

The following section demonstrates an example of an ETL/ELT data pipeline utilizing OpenFaaS installed earlier in this chapter, along with Apache Kafka, Elasticsearch, and JupyterLab introduced in previous chapters.

Example ETL Data Pipeline

Traditional examples of ETL (extract, transform, load) operations would likely demonstrate the extraction of data collected and stored in Big Data systems such as HDFS or any variety of commercial and open source data lakes and legacy or modern enterprise data management systems. Although the following example demonstrates the extraction of data from Twitter, it should be easy to appreciate the flexibility of NiFi's wide range of prebuilt data processors and apply these same essential abilities to nearly any variety of ETL challenges.

This example requires OpenFaaS and the SentimentAnalysis Function installed earlier in this chapter; Apache Kafka, configured in Chapter 5; and Elasticsearch, Kibana, Keycloak, and JupyterHub, introduced in Chapter 6.

The following example ETL data pipeline extracts messages from Twitter with the NiFi Twitter processor and publishes them to Apache Kafka topic. Subsequently, a Kafka processor consumes messages in the topic, preparing and sending them to the OpenFaaS SentimentAnalysis Function, finally storing the results in an Elasticsearch index for analysis within a JupyterLab environment. This example demonstrates the ease in which Kubernetes manages all the required workloads in a distributed, highly available, monitored, and unified control plane (see Figures 9-1 and 9-5).

NiFi Template

Apache NiFi provides detailed documentation for users, administrators, and developers looking to extend its capabilities.[29] Covering all the capabilities of Apache NiFi would alone fill many chapters if not the entire book; therefore, to get a quick demonstration of its use, along with utilizing the components configured and installed in this book, a prebuilt template is available at `https://github.com/apk8s/nifi-demo`.

Clone the `apk8s/nifi-demo` repository:

```
git clone git@github.com:apk8s/nifi-demo.git
```

After browsing to the running NiFi cluster at `https://nifi.data.dev3.apk8s.dev/nifi`, click the template upload button shown in the Operate Palette on the left-hand side of the screen (see Figure 9-7). When prompted, upload the file `Twitter_Sentiment.xml` found in the `templates` directory of the `apk8s/nifi-demo` repository.

---

[29]`https://nifi.apache.org/docs.html`

Figure 9-7. *Apache NiFi upload template*

After uploading the template, drag the template icon (three connected boxes) from the Components Toolbar (top navigation), into the canvas (grid) as shown in Figure 9-8. Before completing, the template component prompts the user with a list of available templates; choose "Twitter Sentiment v2" and click the add button.

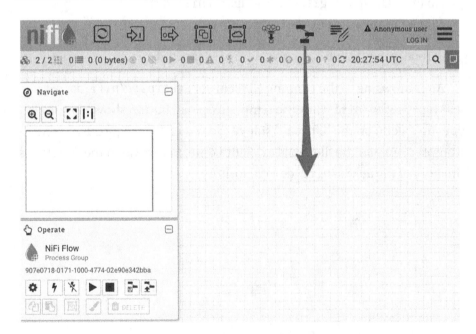

Figure 9-8. *Apache NiFi add template*

After adding the template, the canvas now contains ten NiFi processors, as shown earlier in Figure 9-5. The processors provided by the template are preconfigured to utilize components installed in previous chapters, such as Apache Kafka and Elasticsearch. Double-click any processor and select the Properties tab to view its configuration.

Before activating the new dataflow, the processor *GetTwitter* requires a Consumer Key, Consumer Secret, Access Token, and Access Token Secret provided by Twitter. Generate these values by creating a Twitter account, visiting the portal, and then selecting Apps from the drop-down navigation.[30] On the Apps page for Twitter developers,[31] click the Create an app button and complete the required steps. Once Twitter approves the new app, retrieve the tokens, keys, and secrets shown in Figure 9-9.

---

[30] https://developer.twitter.com/en
[31] https://developer.twitter.com/en/apps

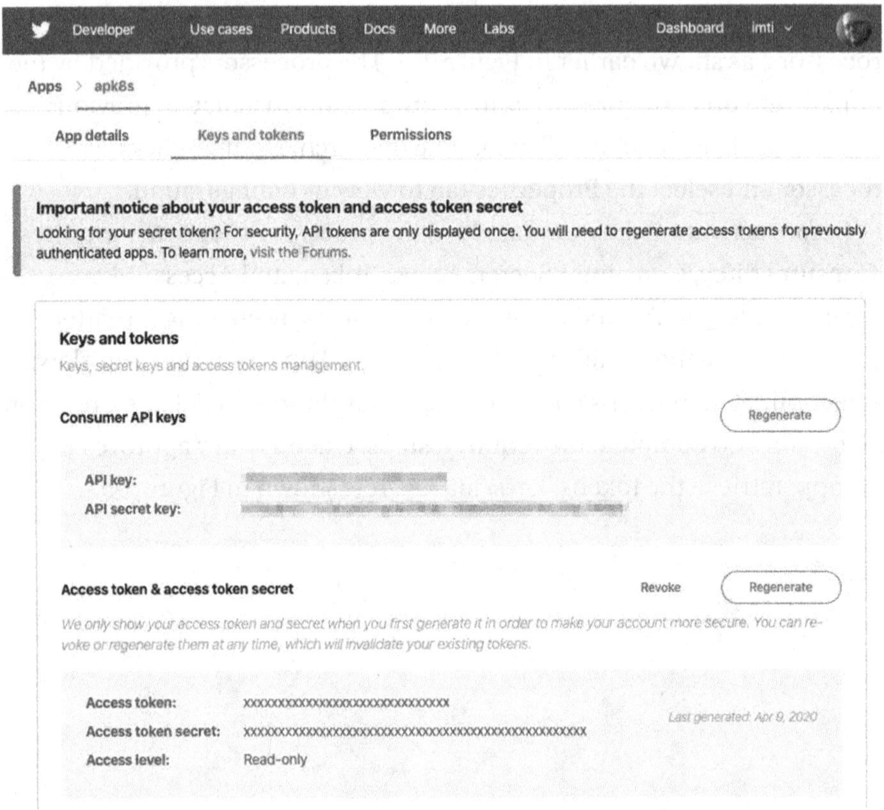

Figure 9-9. *Apache NiFi Twitter keys and tokens*

Populate the values required by the *GetTwitter* processor shown in Figure 9-10.

Property		Value	
Twitter Endpoint	❷	**Filter Endpoint**	
Consumer Key	❷	Sensitive value set	
Consumer Secret	❷	Sensitive value set	
Access Token	❷	Sensitive value set	
Access Token Secret	❷	Sensitive value set	
Languages	❷	en	
Terms to Filter On	❷	covid19, covid-19	
IDs to Follow	❷	No value set	
Locations to Filter On	❷	No value set	

Processor Details

SETTINGS   SCHEDULING   PROPERTIES   COMMENTS

Required field

Figure 9-10. *Configure the Apache NiFi GetTwitter processor*

The new dataflow is ready to run. However, Elasticsearch is the final endpoint and requires an index template to store the data fields suitably. The next section adds an index template to Elasticsearch.

Prepare Elasticsearch

The NiFi processor PutElasticsearchHttp provided by the template puts the final processed data into an Elasticsearch index, matching the pattern sentiment-${now():format('yyyy-MM')}, creating a new index for each month of the year. PutElasticsearchHttp receives and puts JSON data assembled by the previous processors. This JSON data structure contains text, numeric, and date values. Elasticsearch can detect and automatically set data types, but it's not perfect and easily confused by varied date formats. Elasticsearch is naturally unable to determine if values such as the number zero are an integer or a float. Enforcing proper indexing is accomplished by providing Elasticsearch with an index template.[32]

---

[32]www.elastic.co/guide/en/elasticsearch/reference/current/indices-templates.html

Index templates consist of a JSON-based configuration, defining how one or more fields should be indexed. The following commands port-forward Elasticsearch and post an index template matching the data types resulting from the processed data.

Open a terminal and port-forward Elasticsearch:

```
$ kubectl port-forward elasticsearch-0 9200:9200 -n data
```

Open another terminal and post the index template by issuing the command in Listing 9-5.

Listing 9-5. HTTP post an Elasticsearch index template

```
cat <<EOF | curl -X POST \
-H "Content-Type: application/json" \
-d @- http://localhost:9200/_template/all
{
  "index_patterns": ["sentiment-*"],
  "settings": {
    "number_of_shards": 1
  },
  "mappings": {
    "_source": {
      "enabled": true
    },
    "properties": {
      "polarity": {
        "type": "float"
      },
      "subjectivity": {
        "type": "float"
      },
```

```
    "sentence_count": {
      "type": "integer"
    },
    "Content-Length": {
      "type": "integer"
    },
    "X-Start-Time": {
      "type": "date",
      "format": "epoch_millis"
    },
    "X-Duration-Seconds": {
      "type": "float"
    },
    "twitter.created_at": {
      "type": "date",
      "format": "EEE MMM dd HH:mm:ss Z yyyy",
      "null_value": ""
    },
    "Date": {
      "type": "date",
      "format": "EEE, dd MMM yyyy HH:mm:ss z"
    }
  }
}
}
EOF
```` ` `

Elasticsearch is now able to properly index processed data from the dataflow defined by the NiFi template loaded in the previous section. The following section starts up the dataflow and queries the resulting processed data.

Dataflow

The example ETL data pipeline loaded as a template earlier in this chapter extracts data from Twitter and publishes it to an Apache Kafka topic. Another set of processors consumes data from the Kafka topic, obtains the text of the Twitter message, and sends it to the OpenFaaS Sentiment Analysis function. A final set of processors combines the results of Sentiment Analysis along with fields from the original data and posts the results as JSON to Elasticsearch for indexing.

Twitter produces a high-velocity, endless flow of semi-structured data representing a typical data processing scenario. The use of Apache Kafka in this example is not necessary and only used to demonstrate additional NiFi processors. However, the use of Kafka allows external systems the opportunity to act on its data event stream, providing more opportunity for expanding the pipeline.

To start the new dataflow, click anywhere on the NiFi canvas (grid) and start all data processors by clicking the play button provided by the Operate Palette.

After a few minutes, open a terminal and port-forward Elasticsearch:

```
$ kubectl port-forward elasticsearch-0 9200:9200 -n data
```

Open another terminal and post an Elasticsearch query by issuing the command in Listing 9-6. The following query aggregates the last hour of the polarity metric from Sentiment Analysis into histogram buckets at every 0.5 interval from -1 to 1. Elasticsearch supports a robust set of aggregation capabilities.[33]

---

[33]www.elastic.co/guide/en/elasticsearch/reference/current/search-aggregations.html

Listing 9-6. HTTP post an Elasticsearch Sentiment Analysis query

```
cat <<EOF | curl -X POST \
-H "Content-Type: application/json" \
-d @- http://localhost:9200/sentiment-*/_search
{
  "size": 0,
  "aggs": {
    "polarity": {
      "histogram" : {
          "field" : "polarity",
          "interval" : 0.5,
          "extended_bounds" : {
              "min" : -1,
              "max" : 1
          }
      }
    }
  },
  "query": {
      "range": {
          "Date": {
              "gt": "now-1h"
          }
      }
  }
}
EOF
```

The example results (see Listing 9-7) show there were ten times more negative Twitter posts ("doc_count": 40) regarding COVID-19 than positive ("doc_count": 4) in the last hour.

Listing 9-7. Example aggregation output from Elasticsearch Sentiment Analysis query

```
{
  "took": 5,
  "timed_out": false,
  "_shards": {
    "total": 1,
    "successful": 1,
    "skipped": 0,
    "failed": 0
  },
  "hits": {
    "total": {
      "value": 2276,
      "relation": "eq"
    },
    "max_score": null,
    "hits": []
  },
  "aggregations": {
    "polarity": {
      "buckets": [
        {
          "key": -1,
          "doc_count": 40
        },
```

```
{
    "key": -0.5,
    "doc_count": 404
},
{
    "key": 0,
    "doc_count": 1718
},
{
    "key": 0.5,
    "doc_count": 110
},
{
    "key": 1,
    "doc_count": 4
}
]
}
}
}
```

The example ETL dataflow attempts to demonstrate a small set of the many features provided by Apache NiFi, along with Kubernetes's ability to provide an ideal platform for the near-seamless interconnectivity of data management, storage, and processing systems. The platform in this book demonstrates Kubernetes's handling of widely diverse applications, from large monoliths such as NiFi, Elasticsearch, and Kafka to Serverless Functions, wrapped in containers, deployed, monitored, and managed across multiple servers with a unified network and control plane.

The next section leverages a JupyterLab environment, demonstrating the ability for real-time experimentation and interaction with platform data.

Analysis and Programmatic Control

JupyterHub, installed and configured in Chapter 6, provides JupyterLab environments, facilitating the operation of one or more Jupyter Notebooks running directly in the cluster. The following two exercises demonstrate both the simple query and visualization of data indexed in Elasticsearch and the ability to develop NiFi dataflows programmatically.

Analysis and Visualization

This example uses a Python-based Jupyter Notebook provided by JupyterHub (see Chapter 6). As data flow into Elasticsearch, it is immediately indexed and searchable by all its fields. The example returns up to 10,000 records from Elasticsearch indexes starting with sentiment- and the Date field value is within the last hour.

Open a new Python-based Jupyter Notebook and add each of the following code blocks to individual cells.

Install the Elasticsearch package version 7.6.0 by adding the following command to the first cell:

```
!pip install elasticsearch==7.6.0
```

Import elasticsearch, pandas, and matplotlib:

```
from elasticsearch import Elasticsearch
import pandas as pd
from matplotlib import pyplot
```

Create an Elasticsearch client connected to the elasticsearch service running in the Kubernetes Namespace data:

```
es = Elasticsearch(["elasticsearch.data"])
```

Use the Elasticsearch client's search function to query the index pattern sentiment-*, and store the results in the variable response:

```
response = es.search(
    index="sentiment-*",
    body={
        "size": 10000,
        "query": {
            "range": {
                "Date": {
                    "gt": "now-1h"
                }
            }
        },
        "_source": [
            "Date",
            "polarity",
            "subjectivity" ],
    }
)
```

Map and transpose the response from Elasticsearch into Pandas DataFrame:

```
df = pd.concat(map(pd.DataFrame.from_dict,
                   response['hits']['hits']),
               axis=1)['_source'].T
```

Convert the Date column to a Python Datetime data type:

```
datefmt = '%a, %d %b %Y %H:%M:%S GMT'
df['Date'] = pd.to_datetime(df['Date'], format=datefmt)
```

Assign the Date field to the DataFrame index and convert all numeric values to floats:

```
df = df.set_index(['Date'])
df = df.astype(float)
```

Print the first five records (as shown in Figure 9-11):

```
df.head()
```

	polarity	subjectivity
Date		
2020-04-20 21:41:25	-0.500000	1.000000
2020-04-20 21:41:26	0.171212	0.507576
2020-04-20 21:41:27	0.000000	0.000000
2020-04-20 21:41:28	0.112500	0.412500
2020-04-20 21:41:29	0.000000	0.000000

Figure 9-11. Sample Sentiment Analysis DataFrame rows

Finally, plot sentiment by calling the plot function of the DataFrame, assigning polarity to the y axis (see Figure 9-12):

```
df.plot(y=["polarity"], figsize=(13,5))
```

```
[9]: df.plot(y=["polarity"], figsize=(10,5))
```

```
[9]: <matplotlib.axes._subplots.AxesSubplot at 0x7f504409c978>
```

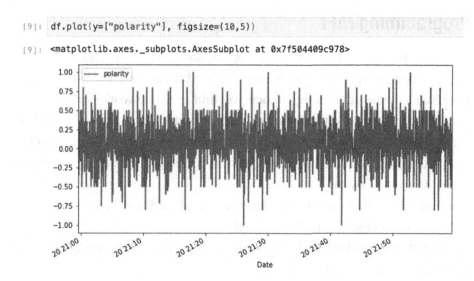

Figure 9-12. *Sentiment Analysis DataFrame plot*

The previous example is a rudimentary sample of data analysis and visualization. A data scientist or analyst's first step may include similar tasks to form a cursory understanding of the available data. Data Science activities such as Machine Learning typically require sets of immutable/ fixed data to facilitate reproducible experiments. The ability to connect in-cluster Jupyter Notebooks with MinIO object storage (installed in Chapter 7), along with event queues, data management, and ETL systems, provides many opportunities for efficiently building and sharing these valuable data sets.

The Kubernetes-backed JupyterLab environment provides a suitable platform for interactive programmatic control over cluster resources with internally exposed APIs, such as Apache NiFi; the next section covers a quick example of this.

Programming NiFi

Apache NiFi supports extension through custom controllers and processors written in Java.[34] However, NiFi's robust set of standard processors means that many projects will find a set that works for a surprising number of circumstances. Another extension of NiFi's capability is through the API,[35] facilitating automation and monitoring. This section contains a brief example of creating a NiFi process group and populating it with a single processor.

Open a new Python-based Jupyter Notebook and add each of the following code blocks to individual cells.

Install the NiPyApi[36] Python package version 1.14.3 by adding the following command to the first cell:

```
!pip install nipyapi==0.14.3
```

Import the package:

```
import nipyapi
```

Configure the NiFi client with the API endpoint, in this case the Kubernetes Service nifi in the data Namespace:

```
api_url = "http://nifi.data:8080/nifi-api"
nipyapi.utils.set_endpoint(api_url)
```

---

[34]https://medium.com/hashmapinc/creating-custom-processors-and-controllers-in-apache-nifi-e14148740ea

[35]https://nifi.apache.org/docs/nifi-docs/rest-api/index.html

[36]https://github.com/Chaffelson/nipyapi

Test the client connection by retrieving information on the first node in the cluster; Figure 9-13 depicts example output:

```
nodes = nipyapi.system.get_cluster().cluster.nodes
nodes[0]
```

```
[4]: nodes = nipyapi.system.get_cluster().cluster.nodes
     nodes[0]

[4]: {'active_thread_count': 0,
      'address': 'nifi-0.nifi.data.svc.cluster.local',
      'api_port': 8080,
      'connection_requested': None,
      'events': [{'category': 'INFO',
                  'message': 'Received first heartbeat from connecting node. Node '
                             'connected.',
                  'timestamp': '04/19/2020 03:32:20 UTC'},
                 {'category': 'INFO',
                  'message': 'Connection requested from existing node. Setting '
                             'status to connecting.',
                  'timestamp': '04/19/2020 03:32:20 UTC'}],
      'heartbeat': '04/21/2020 03:02:44 UTC',
      'node_id': 'fa833f50-442d-464c-8aab-16fd8e412daa',
      'node_start_time': '04/19/2020 03:31:15 UTC',
      'queued': '0 / 0 bytes',
      'roles': ['Primary Node', 'Cluster Coordinator'],
      'status': 'CONNECTED'}
```

Figure 9-13. *NiFi Python client node output*

Create a NiFi Process Group[37] and place it on the canvas (above the processors added earlier in this chapter):

```
pgOid = nipyapi.canvas.get_process_group(
    nipyapi.canvas.get_root_pg_id(),
    'id'
)
```

---

[37]https://nifi.apache.org/docs/nifi-docs/html/user-guide.
  html#process_group_anatomy

```
pg0 = nipyapi.canvas.create_process_group(
    pg0id,
    "apk8s_process_group_0",
    location=(800.0, 200.0)
)
```

After executing the cell with the code in the preceding example, visit the NiFi web interface and note the new apk8s_process_group_0 process group above the processors added earlier as shown in Figure 9-14. Double-clicking the new process group reveals a blank canvas.

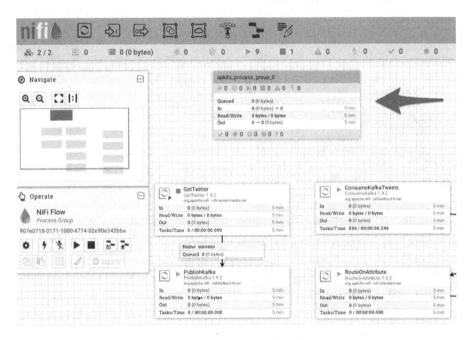

Figure 9-14. *NiFi Process Group added by the Python API client*

Create a GenerateFlowFile[38] processor in the new NiFi Process Group created previously and place it on the canvas:

```
gf = nipyapi.canvas.get_processor_type('GenerateFlowFile')

p0 = nipyapi.canvas.create_processor(
    parent_pg=pg0,
    processor=gf,
    location=(250.0, 0.0),
    name="apk8s_processor_0",
    config=nipyapi.nifi.ProcessorConfigDTO(
        scheduling_period='1s',
        auto_terminated_relationships=['success']
    )
)
```

After executing the cell with the code in the preceding example, visit the NiFi web interface, double-click the new process group, and view the newly created GenerateFlowFile as shown in Figure 9-15.

---

[38]https://nifi.apache.org/docs/nifi-docs/components/org.apache.nifi/
nifi-standard-nar/1.11.4/org.apache.nifi.processors.standard.
GenerateFlowFile/index.html

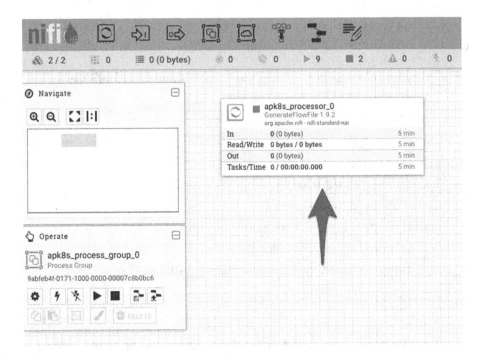

Figure 9-15. *NiFi Processor added by Python API client*

This section automates the creation of a NiFi Process Group along with a NiFi GenerateFlowFile Processor. This example demonstrates a granular method of dataflow development. The NiFi API and NiPyApi Python package also support the installation and configuration of templates, allowing developers to design and save a variety of complete dataflows as templates, such as the Twitter Sentiment v2 (added earlier in the chapter), making them available for programmatic configuration, deployment, and monitoring.

Summary

This chapter installed the Serverless platform OpenFaaS and the data routing and transformation platform Apache NiFi (see Listing 9-8), demonstrating interconnectivity with other data management components installed from previous chapters, specifically Apache Kafka, Elasticsearch, and JupyterLab. This chapter showed the extraction, transformation, loading, processing, and analysis of Twitter messages all without the need for custom code, yet provides many ways to extend with code, from writing custom (Serverless) Functions for OpenFaaS or interacting with Elasticsearch, Kafka, and NiFi interactively through Python in JupyterLab.

This book aims to demonstrate the ease in which a data platform may be quickly assembled, managed, and monitored atop Kubernetes. The level of integration with Kubernetes is wide ranging. Software such as OpenFaaS and JupyterHub utilizes the Kubernetes API themselves for deploying and scaling Pods, while others like NiFi operate with no awareness of Kubernetes.

The Kubernetes data platform developed in this book runs on a small-scale, resource-constrained, four-node development cluster, costing only a few dollars a day. Yet, this small cluster covers many fundamental data handling concepts, including data events, indexing, processing, databases, data lakes, data warehouses, distributed query execution, modern ETL operations, and data science environments. These capabilities are essential for organizations expected to collect, process, and analyze a variety of data. IoT and machine learning are examples of concepts with heavy demands on data management ranging from the collection of high-velocity real-time unstructured and semi-structured data to processed, normalized, well-structured data catalogs for training and refining machine learning models.

Listing 9-8. Organization of Kubernetes-based data platform components

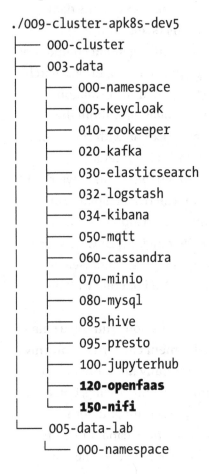

```
./009-cluster-apk8s-dev5
├── 000-cluster
├── 003-data
│   ├── 000-namespace
│   ├── 005-keycloak
│   ├── 010-zookeeper
│   ├── 020-kafka
│   ├── 030-elasticsearch
│   ├── 032-logstash
│   ├── 034-kibana
│   ├── 050-mqtt
│   ├── 060-cassandra
│   ├── 070-minio
│   ├── 080-mysql
│   ├── 085-hive
│   ├── 095-presto
│   ├── 100-jupyterhub
│   ├── 120-openfaas
│   └── 150-nifi
└── 005-data-lab
    └── 000-namespace
```

CHAPTER 10

Platforming Blockchain

Blockchain is a concept enabling the ability to maintain a decentralized and trustless database of transactions. The Bitcoin network, released in 2009,[1] popularized blockchain technology by implementing a method for generating and trading cryptocurrency over a shared public ledger. Although Bitcoin has remained the most popular form of cryptocurrency,[2] new blockchain technologies have risen to expand the capabilities beyond currency exchange.

This book focuses on Ethereum, one of the most successful alternatives to Bitcoin. Although Bitcoin has some ability for Smart Contracts, Ethereum natively supports the storage and execution of distributed applications compiled from Solidity, its DSL (domain-specific language) for Smart Contracts.

---

[1] Marr, Bernard. "A Short History Of Bitcoin And Crypto Currency Everyone Should Read." Forbes. Accessed May 12, 2020. www.forbes.com/sites/bernardmarr/2017/12/06/a-short-history-of-bitcoin-and-crypto-currency-everyone-should-read/.

[2] Baccardax, Martin. "Bitcoin Tops $10,000 Ahead of Halving Event; Tudor-Jones Backs 'Fastest Horse' in Inflation Race." TheStreet. Accessed May 12, 2020. www.thestreet.com/investing/bitcoin-tops-10000-ahead-of-halving-tudor-jones-gives-ok.

© Craig Johnston 2020
C. Johnston, *Advanced Platform Development with Kubernetes*,
https://doi.org/10.1007/978-1-4842-5611-4_10

There are a growing number of business-focused blockchain technologies available, including Hyperledger Fabric,[3] Corda,[4] and Quorum.[5] These blockchain applications focus directly on permissioned or private blockchain networks and are an excellent choice for some organizations. However, Ethereum[6] supports private and permissioned blockchains along with its enormously successful public network.[7] Developing Solidity-based[8] applications means portability to any Ethereum implementation: public, private, or permissioned. Permissioned Ethereum networks are discussed later in this chapter.

This book implements a closed, private Ethereum network suitable for experimentation and development. A private centralized Ethereum network has little production application since a single party controls the consensus of nodes. Development environments such as the Truffle Suite offer excellent turnkey solutions for individual developers; however, operating a private Ethereum network aids in both the understanding of the public network along with providing a controlled, multi-tenant development environment.

Private Blockchain Platform

This chapter focuses on building a private Ethereum Blockchain network operating similarly to the global public Ethereum network. Running Ethereum nodes within Kubernetes, whether public, private, or protected,

---

[3]www.hyperledger.org/projects/fabric

[4]www.corda.net/

[5]www.goquorum.com/

[6]https://ethereum.org/

[7]Live Bitcoin News. "Ernst & Young: Ethereum Can Do A Lot for Businesses," April 27, 2020. www.livebitcoinnews.com/ernst-young-ethereum-can-do-a-lot-for-businesses/.

[8]https://github.com/ethereum/solidity

provides all the advantages of this elegant application platform, including unified networking and control plane, fault tolerance and self-healing, declarative configuration, monitoring, and the transparent distribution of workloads scaled across a vast number of servers.

Figure 10-1 represents a high-level goal of this chapter, platforming Ethereum nodes and interacting with them, both through application development by Serverless functions (with OpenFaaS) and experimentation and development with Jupyter Notebooks provided by the multi-tenant JupyterHub. Kubernetes facilitates the mixing of these diverse applications and opens many opportunities for assembling exotic platforms supporting novel technologies.

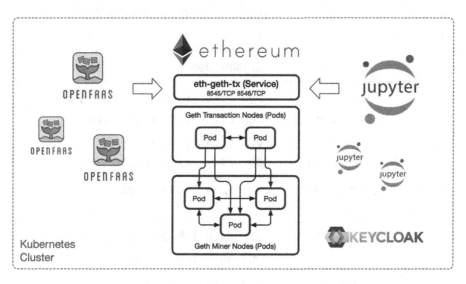

Figure 10-1. *Blockchain network development platform*

Figure 10-1 represents Serverless, Blockchain, and Data Science environments brought together in the context of a data platform.

Development Environment

The following Blockchain development platform utilizes an inexpensive Hetzner cluster first mentioned in Chapter 6, including one CX21 (2 vCPU/8G RAM/40G SSD) for the Kubernetes master node and four CX41 (4 vCPU/16G RAM/160G SSD) instances for worker nodes. Any equivalent infrastructure will accommodate the following exercise.

This chapter creates a new Kubernetes cluster called eth and leverages applications and cluster configurations installed in Chapters 3, 5, and 6 (as described in Table 10-1). This chapter organizes all configuration manifests under the folder cluster-apk8s-eth.

Table 10-1. *Key applications and configurations assembled from previous chapters*

	Resources	Organization
Chapter 3	Ingress	000-cluster/00-ingress-nginx
	Cert Manager	000-cluster/10-cert-manager
	Storage	000-cluster/20-rook-ceph
	Monitoring	000-cluster/30-monitoring
Chapter 5	Namespace	003-data/000-namespace
Chapter 6	Keycloak	003-data/005-keycloak
	JupyterHub	005-data-lab/000-namespace
		003-data/100-jupyterhub
Chapter 9	OpenFaaS	003-data/120-openfaas

Private Ethereum Network

The following sections assemble an Ethereum Blockchain development cluster (see Figure 10-2), mimicking the general operation of a public Ethereum network. The essential components are the same for public, private, or permissioned systems.

Miner nodes (also known as Full Nodes) are the central component of an Ethereum network. Ethereum nodes may be any application implementing the Ethereum protocol. This chapter uses Geth,[9] developed in Go as one of the original three implementations of the Ethereum protocol. Geth provides a stand-alone binary along with an open source library suitable for building custom applications/nodes implementing the Ethereum protocol. This chapter uses Geth binaries wrapped in containers (ethereum/client-go) representing three types of nodes: Bootnodes (a separate binary in the Geth package), Miners, and Transaction nodes.

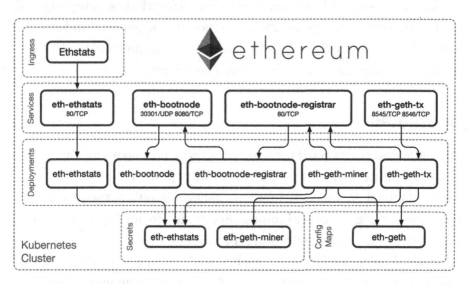

Figure 10-2. *Private Ethereum network*

Ethereum is a peer-to-peer network of Nodes and uses established Bootnodes[10] to connect new nodes to the network. Bootnodes[11] do not mine or submit transactions; they are only responsible for initial

---

[9]https://geth.ethereum.org/

[10]https://github.com/ethereum/go-ethereum/blob/master/params/
  bootnodes.go

[11]https://geth.ethereum.org/docs/interface/peer-to-peer

peer discovery. Geth ships with a list of main network and test network Bootnode addresses; however, the private Ethereum network in this chapter requires Geth to use local Bootnodes. This chapter uses a Bootnode Registrar Service to provide the address of the local Bootnodes.

Transaction nodes are optional; any node, including Miners, may submit presigned transactions for inclusion into the Blockchain. Miner nodes use attached Ethereum accounts[12] to sign their transactions; allowing remote connections to these nodes provides anyone with access to submit transactions signed by the miner. Transaction nodes can only send transactions signed by the end user since there is no private account attached.

Finally, Geth provides the ability to report its current state and metrics to an API endpoint. This chapter utilizes the Ethstats project[13] to collect node metrics and present them on a web dashboard.

Bootnodes

Ethereum Bootnodes assist the bootstrapping of new nodes into an Ethereum network by providing an initial set of peers. Bootnodes are a subset of the Ethereum client implementation and only participate in the network node discovery protocol. Bootnodes do not implement any higher-level Ethereum application protocols.

The following configurations set up an eth-bootnode Service. A DNS request to this headless service returns the internal hostnames of any Pods matching the selector app: eth-bootnode. This service comes in handy for generating a registry for Bootnodes, as developed in the next section.

Create the directory cluster-apk8s-eth/003-data/200-eth/10-bootnode. Within the new 10-bootnode directory, create a file named 10-service.yml from Listing 10-1.

---

[12]https://blockgeeks.com/how-to-create-an-ethereum-account/
[13]https://github.com/cubedro/eth-netstats

Listing 10-1. Bootnode Service

```
apiVersion: v1
kind: Service
metadata:
  name: eth-bootnode
  namespace: data
  labels:
    app: eth-bootnode
spec:
  selector:
    app: eth-bootnode
  clusterIP: None
  ports:
    - name: discovery
      port: 30301
      protocol: UDP
    - name: http
      port: 8080
```

Apply the Ethereum Bootnode Service configuration:

```
$ kubectl apply -f 10-service.yml
```

Next, create a Deployment for the Ethereum Bootnodes in a file named 30-deployment.yml from Listing 10-2. The following Bootnode Deployment consists of two containers and one container for initialization. The initialization container generates a key and stores it in the Volume Mount data shared with the other containers in the Pod. The key is used by the Bootnode to create its enode identifier (an Ethereum node's unique ID).

The first of the two containers is the Ethereum Bootnode, which mounts the key generated in the initialization container and communicates on port 30301/UDP. The second container, named bootnode-server, executes a small shell script echoing the full Ethereum address of the Bootnode over port 8080 using netcat.[14] The full address consists of the enode identifier, IP address, and port. The Bootnode Registrar in the following section uses the headless service (configured in the previous section) to discover Bootnode Pods and then retrieves each of their Ethereum network addresses via HTTP port 8080, served by the bootnode-server container.

Listing 10-2. Bootnode Deployment

```
apiVersion: apps/v1
kind: Deployment
metadata:
  name: eth-bootnode
  namespace: data
  labels:
    app: eth-bootnode
spec:
  replicas: 2
  revisionHistoryLimit: 1
  selector:
    matchLabels:
      app: eth-bootnode
  template:
    metadata:
      labels:
        app: eth-bootnode
    spec:
      volumes:
        - name: data
          emptyDir: {}
```

---

[14]https://en.wikipedia.org/wiki/Netcat

```
initContainers:
  - name: genkey
    image: ethereum/client-go:alltools-v1.9.13
    imagePullPolicy: IfNotPresent
    command: ["/bin/sh"]
    args:
      - "-c"
      - "bootnode --genkey=/etc/bootnode/node.key"
    volumeMounts:
      - name: data
        mountPath: /etc/bootnode
containers:
  - name: bootnode
    image: ethereum/client-go:alltools-v1.9.13
    imagePullPolicy: IfNotPresent
    resources:
      limits:
        cpu: ".5"
      requests:
        cpu: "0.25"
    command: ["/bin/sh"]
    args:
      - "-c"
      - "bootnode --nodekey=/etc/bootnode/
      node.key --verbosity=4"
    volumeMounts:
      - name: data
        mountPath: /etc/bootnode
    ports:
      - name: discovery
        containerPort: 30301
```

```
          protocol: UDP
    - name: bootnode-server
      image: ethereum/client-go:alltools-v1.9.13
      imagePullPolicy: IfNotPresent
      command: ["/bin/sh"]
      args:
        - "-c"
        - "while [ 1 ]; do echo -e \"HTTP/1.1 200 OK\n\
        nenode://$(bootnode -writeaddress --nodekey=/etc/
        bootnode/node.key)@$(POD_IP):30301\" | nc -l -v -p
        8080 || break; done;"
      volumeMounts:
        - name: data
          mountPath: /etc/bootnode
      env:
        - name: POD_IP
          valueFrom:
            fieldRef:
              fieldPath: status.podIP
      ports:
        - containerPort: 8080
```

The cluster now contains two Ethereum Bootnodes; however, new Ethereum nodes require the full enode address (enode://ENODE_IDENTIFIER@POD_IP:30301) in order to use them. As discussed previously, the Kubernetes headless Service eth-bootnode provides the hostnames of the individual nodes, while the container bootnode-server reports its enode address over HTTP on port 8080. The Bootnode Registrar, defined in the following section, combines these two actions.

Bootnode Registrar

The Bootnode Registrar is a small Golang application for looking up the DNS entries exposed by the eth-bootnode headless Service, querying each Pod for its enode address, and returning a comma-separated string through a simple HTTP request. Later sections configure each Geth node with this Bootnode Registrar's string of enode addresses.

Note   Jason Poon[15] wrote the Bootnode Registrar application,[16] along with the Kubernetes Ethereum Helm chart.[17] Concepts and inspiration for this chapter come from these projects and the Microsoft Developer blog post *Building a Private Ethereum Consortium*.[18]

Create the directory cluster-apk8s-eth/003-data/200-eth/20-bootnode-reg. Within the new 20-bootnode-reg directory, create a file named 10-service.yml from Listing 10-3.

Listing 10-3. Bootnode Registrar Service

```
apiVersion: v1
kind: Service
metadata:
  name: eth-bootnode-registrar
  namespace: data
  labels:
    app: eth-bootnode-registrar
```

---

[15]https://devblogs.microsoft.com/cse/author/jason-poon/
[16]https://github.com/jpoon/bootnode-registrar
[17]https://github.com/helm/charts/tree/master/stable/ethereum
[18]https://devblogs.microsoft.com/cse/2018/06/01/
  creating-private-ethereum-consortium-kubernetes/

```
spec:
  selector:
    app: eth-bootnode-registrar
  type: ClusterIP
  ports:
    - port: 80
      targetPort: 9898
```

Apply the Ethereum Bootnode Regis.trar Service configuration:

```
$ kubectl apply -f 10-service.yml
```

Next, create a Deployment for the Ethereum Bootnode Registrar in a file named 30-deployment.yml from Listing 10-4.

Listing 10-4. Bootnode Deployment

```
apiVersion: apps/v1
kind: Deployment
metadata:
  name: eth-bootnode-registrar
  namespace: data
  labels:
    app: eth-bootnode-registrar
spec:
  replicas: 1
  revisionHistoryLimit: 1
  selector:
    matchLabels:
      app: eth-bootnode-registrar
  template:
    metadata:
      labels:
        app: eth-bootnode-registrar
```

```
spec:
  containers:
    - name: bootnode-registrar
      image: jpoon/bootnode-registrar:v1.0.0
      imagePullPolicy: IfNotPresent
      env:
        - name: BOOTNODE_SERVICE
          value: "eth-bootnode.data.svc.cluster.local"
      ports:
        - containerPort: 9898
```

The Kubernetes cluster now contains a Bootnode Registrar Service. Later on, Geth miner and transaction node deployments call this Service on initialization to provide a list of Ethereum Bootnode addresses.

Ethstats

Geth nodes emit metrics when configured with an Ethstats endpoint. The Ethstats web dashboard[19] configured in this section ingests Ethereum metrics and presents them on an attractive web interface[20] (as shown in Figure 10-3). This section sets an Ethstats Service, Deployment, and Secret used later in the command-line arguments supplied to Geth nodes.

---

[19]https://github.com/cubedro/eth-netstats
[20]https://imti.co/ethereum-ethstats/

Figure 10-3. *Ethereum network statistics from ethstats.net*

Create the directory `cluster-apk8s-eth/003-data/200-eth/30-ethstats`. Within the new `30-ethstats` directory, create a file named `10-service.yml` from Listing 10-5.

Listing 10-5. Ethstats Service

```
apiVersion: v1
kind: Service
metadata:
  name: eth-ethstats
  namespace: data
  labels:
    app: eth-ethstats
spec:
  selector:
    app: eth-ethstats
```

```
type: ClusterIP
ports:
  - port: 8080
    targetPort: http
```

Apply the Ethstats Service configuration:

```
$ kubectl apply -f 10-service.yml
```

Next, create a Secret for Ethstats in a file named 15-secret.yml from Listing 10-6.

Listing 10-6. Ethstats Secret

```
apiVersion: v1
kind: Secret
metadata:
  name: eth-ethstats
  namespace: data
  labels:
    app: eth-ethstats
type: Opaque
stringData:
  WS_SECRET: "uGYQ7lj55FqFxdyIwsv1"
```

Apply the Ethstats Service configuration:

```
$ kubectl apply -f 15-secret.yml
```

Next, create a Deployment for Ethstats in a file named 30-deployment.yml from Listing 10-7.

Listing 10-7. Ethstats Deployment

```
apiVersion: apps/v1
kind: Deployment
metadata:
  name: eth-ethstats
  namespace: data
  labels:
    app: eth-ethstats
spec:
  replicas: 1
  revisionHistoryLimit: 1
  selector:
    matchLabels:
      app: eth-ethstats
  template:
    metadata:
      labels:
        app: eth-ethstats
    spec:
      containers:
        - name: ethstats
          image: ethereumex/eth-stats-dashboard:v0.0.1
          imagePullPolicy: IfNotPresent
          ports:
            - name: http
              containerPort: 3000
          env:
            - name: WS_SECRET
              valueFrom:
                secretKeyRef:
                  name: eth-ethstats
                  key: WS_SECRET
```

Apply the Ethstats Deployment configuration:

```
$ kubectl apply -f 30-deployment.yml
```

Next, create an Ingress configuration for Ethstats in a file named 50-ingress.yml from Listing 10-8.

Listing 10-8. Ethstats Ingress

```
apiVersion: networking.k8s.io/v1beta1
kind: Ingress
metadata:
  name: eth-ethstats
  namespace: data
  labels:
    app: eth-ethstats
  annotations:
    cert-manager.io/cluster-issuer: letsencrypt-production
spec:
  rules:
    - host: stats.data.eth.apk8s.dev
      http:
        paths:
          - backend:
              serviceName: eth-ethstats
              servicePort: 8080
            path: /
  tls:
    - hosts:
        - stats.data.eth.apk8s.dev
      secretName: eth-ethstats-production-tls
```

Apply the Ethstats Ingress configuration:

```
$ kubectl apply -f 50-ingress.yml
```

Finally, visit `https://stats.data.eth.apk8s.dev` in a web browser. There should be no data until Geth nodes begin reporting as configured in the following sections.

Geth Miners

This book does not explore the details of the Ethereum protocol. However, this section and the next install two types of Ethereum nodes supported by Geth: miner nodes[21] and transaction nodes. All nodes on an Ethereum network communicate peer-to-peer, sharing network topology, blockchain state, and transactions. Miner nodes work to create new blocks on the Blockchain consisting of any pending transactions.[22]

Create the directory `cluster-apk8s-eth/003-data/200-eth/40-miner`. Within the new `40-miner` directory, create a file named `15-secret.yml` from Listing 10-9. Geth miners require an Ethereum account for use in signing transactions and receiving mining rewards. An initialization container, later defined in each Geth Deployment, creates an Ethereum account with the password specified in the Secret defined in Listing 10-9.

Listing 10-9. Geth Secret

```
apiVersion: v1
kind: Secret
metadata:
  name: eth-geth-miner
  namespace: data
```

---

[21]`https://github.com/ethereum/go-ethereum/wiki/Mining`
[22]`https://geth.ethereum.org/docs/interface/mining`

```
labels:
  app: eth-geth-miner
type: Opaque
stringData:
  accountsecret: "strongpassword"
```

Apply the Geth Secret configuration:

```
$ kubectl apply -f 15-secret.yml
```

Install Geth on a local workstation following the online install documentation.[23] Geth provides installers for all major operating systems and most package management systems. For example, Macs with Homebrew may issue the command:

```
$ brew install geth.
```

Create two or more Ethereum accounts. The Ethereum Genesis file defined in the following ConfigMap instructs the new Blockchain to pre-fund these accounts (in the first block) with a specified amount of Ether (Ethereum cryptocurrency) available for use within the private network.

```
$ geth account new
```

After creating multiple accounts with the geth account new command, copy and save the "Public address of the key:" from the output. Next, create a ConfigMap for Geth in a file named 20-configmap.yml from Listing 10-10. Update the alloc section of the genesis.json with the newly created accounts.

The genesis.json file defined within the ConfigMap in Listing 10-10 configures the first block of an Ethereum Blockchain. Any node wishing to join the private network must first initialize against this Ethereum

---

[23]https://geth.ethereum.org/downloads/

Genesis file.[24] Both miner and transaction nodes described in the following are configured to mount the genesis.json file defined as a key in the ConfigMap (Listing 10-10).

Listing 10-10. Geth ConfigMap

```
apiVersion: v1
kind: ConfigMap
metadata:
  name: eth-geth
  namespace: data
  labels:
    app: eth-geth
data:
  networkid: "27587"
  genesis.json: |-
    {
        "config": {
            "chainId": 27587,
            "homesteadBlock": 0,
            "eip150Block": 0,
            "eip155Block": 0,
            "eip158Block": 0
        },
        "difficulty": "0x400",
        "gasLimit": "0x8000000",
        "nonce"    : "0x0000000000000000",
```

---

[24]Ting, 李婷婷 Lee Ting. "Beginners Guide to Ethereum (3) — Explain the Genesis File and Use It to Customize Your Blockchain." Medium, November 23, 2018. https://medium.com/taipei-ethereum-meetup/beginners-guide-to-ethereum-3-explain-the-genesis-file-and-use-it-to-customize-your-blockchain-552eb6265145.

```
"alloc": {
  "0xFa4087D3688a289c9C92e773a7b46cb9CCf80353": {
  "balance": "10000000000000000000" },
  "0x8ab8F3fc6c660d3f0B22490050C843cafd2c0AAC": {
  "balance": "20000000000000000000" }
  }
}
```

Apply the Geth ConfigMap configuration:

```
$ kubectl apply -f 20-configmap.yml
```

Next, create a Deployment configuration for Geth in a file named 30-deployment.yml from Listing 10-11. The Geth miner Deployment in Listing 10-11 establishes a data volume mounted by all containers along with a config volume previously applied from the ConfigMap in Listing 10-10.

The first initialization container init-genesis runs the Geth init command against the Genesis file mounted from the ConfigMap and creates a new Ethereum Blockchain database in the shared data volume mounted as /root/.ethereum.

The second initialization container create-account creates a unique Ethereum account for the Geth miner using a password defined in the Secret eth-geth-miner applied earlier from Listing 10-9. Geth stores the new Ethereum account in /root/.ethereum, mounted as the shared data volume.

The final initialization container get-bootnodes runs a small shell script attempting to retrieve the list of Bootnodes with a curl call to the Bootnode Registrar configured earlier in this chapter. If successful, the output of the curl call writes the returned (comma-separated) list of bootnodes to the file /geth/bootnodes mounted in the shared volume data.

After initialization, Pods defined in the eth-geth-miner Deployment start the geth-miner container and mount the shared volume data (/root/.ethereum), where the initialization containers initialized the

Blockchain database, created an Ethereum account, and stored a file with a list of Bootnode addresses. The geth-miner container executes geth with the following arguments: **--bootnodes** defines the initial set of bootnodes to find peers. **--mine** instructs geth to operate as a miner attempting to create blocks. **--minerthreads** sets the number of parallel mining threads. **--nousb** disables checks for USB hardware wallets. **--miner.etherbase** takes an index pointing to an Ethereum account used to collect mining rewards; in this case, the initialization container create-account generated the first (and only) account (index zero). **--networkid** instructs geth to connect to a particular network, in this case as defined in the eth-geth ConfigMap. **--ethstats** accepts an endpoint capable of receiving metrics from geth; in this case, the Ethstats Dashboard configured in the previous section. Finally, **--verbosity** sets the depth of logging to output.

Listing 10-11. Geth Deployment

```
apiVersion: apps/v1
kind: Deployment
metadata:
  name: eth-geth-miner
  namespace: data
  labels:
    app: eth-geth-miner
spec:
  replicas: 3
  revisionHistoryLimit: 1
  selector:
    matchLabels:
      app: eth-geth-miner
```

```
template:
  metadata:
    labels:
      app: eth-geth-miner
  spec:
    volumes:
      - name: data
        emptyDir: {}
      - name: config
        configMap:
          name: eth-geth
    initContainers:
      - name: init-genesis
        image: ethereum/client-go:v1.9.13
        imagePullPolicy: IfNotPresent
        args:
          - "init"
          - "/var/geth/genesis.json"
        volumeMounts:
          - name: data
            mountPath: /root/.ethereum
          - name: config
            mountPath: /var/geth
      - name: create-account
        image: ethereum/client-go:v1.9.13
        imagePullPolicy: IfNotPresent
        command: ["/bin/sh"]
        args:
          - "-c"
          - "printf '$(ACCOUNT_SECRET)\n$(ACCOUNT_SECRET)\n'
            | geth account new"
```

```
  env:
    - name: ACCOUNT_SECRET
      valueFrom:
        secretKeyRef:
          name: eth-geth-miner
          key: accountsecret
  volumeMounts:
    - name: data
      mountPath: /root/.ethereum
- name: get-bootnodes
  image: ethereum/client-go:v1.9.13
  imagePullPolicy: IfNotPresent
  command: ["/bin/sh"]
  args:
    - "-c"
    - |-
      apk add --no-cache curl;
      CNT=0;
      echo "retrieving bootnodes from $BOOTNODE_
      REGISTRAR_SVC"
      while [ $CNT -le 90 ]
      do
        curl -m 5 -s $BOOTNODE_REGISTRAR_SVC | xargs
        echo -n >> /geth/bootnodes;
        if [ -s /geth/bootnodes ]
        then
          cat /geth/bootnodes;
          exit 0;
        fi;

        echo "no bootnodes found. retrying $CNT...";
        sleep 2 || break;
```

```
          CNT=$((CNT+1));
        done;
        echo "WARNING. unable to find bootnodes.";
        exit 0;
      env:
        - name: BOOTNODE_REGISTRAR_SVC
          value: eth-bootnode-registrar
      volumeMounts:
        - name: data
          mountPath: /geth
  containers:
    - name: geth-miner
      image: ethereum/client-go:v1.9.13
      imagePullPolicy: IfNotPresent
      command: ["/bin/sh"]
      args:
        - "-c"
        - "geth --bootnodes=\"`cat /root/.ethereum/
        bootnodes`\" --mine --minerthreads=1
        --nousb --miner.etherbase=0 --networkid=$
        {NETWORK_ID} --ethstats=${HOSTNAME}:${ETHSTATS_
        SECRET}@${ETHSTATS_SVC} --verbosity=3"
      env:
        - name: ETHSTATS_SVC
          value: eth-ethstats:8080
        - name: ETHSTATS_SECRET
          valueFrom:
            secretKeyRef:
              name: eth-ethstats
              key: WS_SECRET
        - name: NETWORK_ID
```

```
              valueFrom:
                configMapKeyRef:
                  name: eth-geth
                  key: networkid
          ports:
            - name: discovery-udp
              containerPort: 30303
              protocol: UDP
            - name: discovery-tcp
              containerPort: 30303
          volumeMounts:
            - name: data
              mountPath: /root/.ethereum
          resources:
            limits:
              cpu: "400m"
            requests:
              cpu: "400m"
```

Apply the Geth Deployment configuration:

```
$ kubectl apply -f 30-deployment.yml
```

After applying the eth-geth-miner Deployment and the three replica Pods have initialized, the miners begin generating a DAG (directed acyclic graph) represented as one or more gigabytes of data used in Ethereum's PoW (proof-of-work) protocol. On this highly constrained development cluster, expect these processes to take anywhere from 20 minutes to an hour. Once the geth miners complete DAG generation, mining commences, and the Blockchain begins to grow as miners add blocks.

The new mining pool adds blocks to the chain about every 15–30 seconds, depending on CPU resources and the Ethereum PoW difficulty level calibrated by the network. Although initially set low in the Genesis file defined earlier at 0x400, the Ethereum network calibrates difficulty based on the time difference between blocks added to the chain.

The initial set of miners continues to build the Blockchain indefinitely, whether or not there are transactions to include with each block. The next section added nodes specifically purposed for interacting with the private Ethereum blockchain, including submitting transactions.

Geth Transaction Nodes

This section configures Geth nodes with an RPC (Remote Procedure Call) management API enabled. The following transaction nodes implement the full Ethereum protocol without mining enabled, therefore not requiring an Ethereum account. Transaction nodes may only submit transactions presigned by an external Ethereum account, making them a suitable gateway for external communication with the Blockchain. Later on, this chapter demonstrates interactivity with the Blockchain through Jupyter Notebooks and Serverless Functions.

Create the directory cluster-apk8s-eth/003-data/200-eth/50-tx. Within the new 50-tx directory, create a file named 10-service.yml from Listing 10-12.

Listing 10-12. Geth transaction node Service

```
apiVersion: v1
kind: Service
metadata:
  name: eth-geth-tx
  namespace: data
  labels:
    app: eth-geth-tx
```

```
spec:
  selector:
    app: eth-geth-tx
  type: ClusterIP
  ports:
    - name: rpc
      port: 8545
    - name: ws
      port: 8546
```

Apply the Geth transaction node Service configuration:

```
$ kubectl apply -f 10-service.yml
```

Next, create a Deployment configuration for Geth transaction nodes in a file named 30-deployment.yml from Listing 10-13.

The eth-geth-tx Deployment is nearly identical to the eth-geth-miner configured in the previous section, with a few key differences. The Geth eth-geth-tx Deployment does not initialize an Ethereum account and does not set the --mine, --minerthreads, and --miner.etherbase command-line options. The new command-line options for (transaction mode) geth include the following: **--rpc** enables the HTTP-RPC[25] server, supporting remote connections on port 8548; **--rpcaddr** sets HTTP-RPC server listening interface, in this case, all of them (IP 0.0.0.0); **--rpcapi** sets APIs to enable over HTTP-RPC interface, in this case, eth, net, and web3;[26] **--rpcvhosts** sets a list of domains allowed to connect (enforced by the server); and **--rpccorsdomain** sets the (enforced by web browsers) allowable domains for cross-origin requests.

---

[25]https://github.com/ethereum/wiki/wiki/JSON-RPC
[26]https://github.com/ethereum/go-ethereum/wiki/Management-APIs

Listing 10-13. Geth transaction node Deployment

```
apiVersion: apps/v1
kind: Deployment
metadata:
  name: eth-geth-tx
  namespace: data
  labels:
    app: eth-geth-tx
spec:
  replicas: 2
  selector:
    matchLabels:
      app: eth-geth-tx
  template:
    metadata:
      labels:
        app: eth-geth-tx
    spec:
      volumes:
        - name: data
          emptyDir: {}
        - name: config
          configMap:
            name: eth-geth
      initContainers:
        - name: init-genesis
          image: ethereum/client-go:v1.9.13
          imagePullPolicy: IfNotPresent
          args:
            - "init"
            - "/var/geth/genesis.json"
```

```yaml
        volumeMounts:
          - name: data
            mountPath: /root/.ethereum
          - name: config
            mountPath: /var/geth
      - name: get-bootnodes
        image: ethereum/client-go:v1.9.13
        imagePullPolicy: IfNotPresent
        command: ["/bin/sh"]
        args:
          - "-c"
          - |-
            apk add --no-cache curl;
            COUNT=0;
            echo "calling $BOOTNODE_REGISTRAR_SVC"
            while [ $COUNT -le 100 ]
            do
              curl -m 5 -s $BOOTNODE_REGISTRAR_SVC | xargs
              echo -n >> /geth/bootnodes;
              if [ -s /geth/bootnodes ]
              then
                cat /geth/bootnodes;
                exit 0;
              fi;

              echo "Attempt $COUNT. No bootnodes found...";
              sleep 2 || break;
              COUNT=$((COUNT+1));
            done;
            echo "ERROR: Unable to find bootnodes.";
            exit 0;
```

```
    env:
      - name: BOOTNODE_REGISTRAR_SVC
        value: eth-bootnode-registrar
    volumeMounts:
      - name: data
        mountPath: /geth
containers:
  - name: geth-tx
    image: ethereum/client-go:v1.9.13
    imagePullPolicy: IfNotPresent
    command: ["/bin/sh"]
    args:
      - "-c"
      - "geth --nousb --bootnodes=`cat /root/.
      ethereum/bootnodes` --rpc --rpcaddr='0.0.0.0'
      --rpcapi=eth,net,web3 --rpcvhosts='*'
      --rpccorsdomain='*' --ws --networkid=${NETWORK_
      ID} --ethstats=${HOSTNAME}:${ETHSTATS_
      SECRET}@${ETHSTATS_SVC} --verbosity=2"
    env:
      - name: ETHSTATS_SVC
        value: eth-ethstats:8080
      - name: ETHSTATS_SECRET
        valueFrom:
          secretKeyRef:
            name: eth-ethstats
            key: WS_SECRET
      - name: NETWORK_ID
        valueFrom:
          configMapKeyRef:
            name: eth-geth
            key: networkid
```

```
ports:
  - name: rpc
    containerPort: 8545
  - name: ws
    containerPort: 8546
  - name: discovery-udp
    containerPort: 30303
    protocol: UDP
  - name: discovery-tcp
    containerPort: 30303
volumeMounts:
  - name: data
    mountPath: /root/.ethereum
```

Apply the Geth transaction node Deployment configuration:

```
$ kubectl apply -f 30-deployment.yml
```

At this stage, there should now be five nodes reporting into the Ethstats Dashboard configured earlier (see Figure 10-4), consisting of three miners and two transaction nodes.

Figure 10-4. *Ethstats Private Ethereum nodes reporting*

This network is a highly constrained, miniature replica of the public Ethereum network. Private Blockchain networks such as this are useful for building and deploying experimental nodes, smart contract[27] development, and connecting any aspect of the Blockchain operations into the more extensive data and application platform developed throughout this book. Consider the following section on private networks before opening this network up to third-party nodes.

Private Networks

Extending this network as is, through remote nodes operated by external organizations, would have limited value. PoW-based Blockchains rarely make sense on a small scale. Any organization able to provide more than 50% of the network's mining hash rate could validate an otherwise invalid transaction, known as the 51% attack.[28] Organizations looking to participate with a select set of other organizations can adapt the concepts in this chapter to Ethereum's new Clique consensus protocol supported by Geth. Clique-configured nodes do not mine for PoW and instead use PoA (proof of authority[29]).

Converting this network to use Clique involves creating a new Genesis Block with an initial list of nodes permitted to sign blocks. See Ethereum's well-documented guide for instructions on converting this network to the Clique consensus protocol.[30]

---

[27]https://coinsutra.com/smart-contracts/

[28]www.investopedia.com/terms/1/51-attack.asp

[29]https://blockonomi.com/proof-of-authority/

[30]https://geth.ethereum.org/docs/interface/private-network

Blockchain Interaction

Interacting with a Blockchain is performed by communicating with a node. Full Ethereum nodes (miner nodes in the context of this book) manage a complete copy of the Blockchain and communicate transactions and state with other nodes (peers) on the network. Geth provides an HTTP-RPC API providing external access. Two of the five nodes configured earlier in this chapter, known as transaction nodes, provide HTTP-RPC access exposed by the Service eth-geth-tx.

Geth Attach

Geth offers an interactive console[31] for interacting with its API. One of the easiest ways to experiment with the API involves using geth to attach to another local instance of geth. The following example executes geth on one of the three miner nodes and interacts with the running miner:

```
$ kubectl exec -it -n data eth-geth-miner-789dd75565-gk25b --
geth attach
```

Example geth console output:

```
Welcome to the Geth JavaScript console!

instance: Geth/v1.9.13-stable-cbc4ac26/linux-amd64/go1.14.2
coinbase: 0x284f99f929b49da9d85b2a3dbf606ed38eec393e
at block: 1134 (Fri May 08 2020 06:19:03 GMT+0000 (UTC))
 datadir: /root/.ethereum
 modules: admin:1.0 debug:1.0 eth:1.0 ethash:1.0 miner:1.0
net:1.0 personal:1.0 rpc:1.0 txpool:1.0 web3:1.0

> eth.blockNumber
1159
```

---

[31]https://github.com/ethereum/go-ethereum/wiki/JavaScript-Console

Communicate with geth from a local workstation by port-forwarding the eth-geth-tx Service, set up earlier in this chapter, and attach a local geth to the forwarded Service.

```
$ kubectl port-forward svc/eth-geth-tx 8545 -n data
Forwarding from 127.0.0.1:8545 -> 8545
Forwarding from [::1]:8545 -> 8545
```

Open an additional terminal on the local workstation and attach geth:

```
$ geth attach http://localhost:8545
```

Geth's interactive JavaScript console is a great way to explore the API. However, Ethereum provides a variety of mature client libraries for building applications that interact with the Ethereum Blockchain. The following sections examine Ethereum's Web3 Python library, both through an interactive Python environment provided by a Jupyter Notebook and the development of a small function in the Serverless platform OpenFaaS, returning information on the latest block in the chain.

Jupyter Environment

The experimentation and development of software against complex and sophisticated cloud architectures often presents unique challenges in connecting developers and analysts to services. Many, if not most, applications in a cloud-based architecture communicate system to system with other applications with no explicit method for external access. Port-forwarding is a typical method for accessing internal services within a Kubernetes cluster from a local workstation; however, web-based IDEs may function as an extension of the platform itself.

Jupyter Notebooks are a browser-based (or web-based) IDE required to run the following examples within the Kubernetes cluster. Chapter 6 describes the configuration of JupyterHub (along with Keycloak) for use as a multi-tenant provisioner of JupyterLab environments managing one or more Jupyter Notebooks. Create a new Python 3 Jupyter Notebook from within the cluster; copy and execute the following code examples within individual cells.

Import the Python libraries web3,[32] json, and time:

```
import web3, json, time
import pandas as pd
from IPython.display import clear_output
from web3.contract import ConciseContract
from web3 import Web3
from web3.auto.gethdev import w3
```

Connect to the Geth transaction node:

```
rpc_ep = "http://eth-geth-tx.data:8545"
web3 = Web3(Web3.HTTPProvider(rpc_ep))

if web3.isConnected():
    print(f"Connected: {rpc_ep}")
    print(f"Peers: {web3.net.peerCount}")
    print(f"Chain ID: {web3.net.version}")
    print(f"Last block: {web3.eth.blockNumber}")
else:
    print("Not connected")
```

Example output:

```
Connected: http://eth-geth-tx.data:8545
Peers: 4
Chain ID: 27587
Last block: 5549
```

---

[32]https://github.com/ethereum/web3.py

Check the eth balance of the accounts pre-funded in the Genesis block defined earlier in this chapter:

```
account_1 = "0xFa4087D3688a289c9C92e773a7b46cb9CCf80353"
account_2 = "0x8ab8F3fc6c660d3f0B22490050C843cafd2c0AAC"

a1_bal = web3.eth.getBalance(account_1)
a2_bal = web3.eth.getBalance(account_2)

print(f"Account 1: {web3.fromWei(a1_bal, 'ether')} ether")
print(f"Account 2: {web3.fromWei(a2_bal, 'ether')} ether")
```

Example output:

```
Account 1: 100 ether
Account 2: 200 ether
```

Add the following code to create a transaction, transferring one ether to account_2:

```
nonce = web3.eth.getTransactionCount(account_1)
print(f"Account 1 nonce: {nonce}")

tx = {
    'nonce': nonce,
    'to': account_2,
    'value': web3.toWei(1, 'ether'),
    'gas': 2000000,
    'gasPrice': web3.toWei('50', 'gwei'),
}

tx
```

Example output:

```
{'nonce': 15,
 'to': '0x8ab8F3fc6c660d3f0B22490050C843cafd2c0AAC',
 'value': 1000000000000000000,
 'gas': 2000000,
 'gasPrice': 50000000000}
```

Warning   Do not use the Ethereum accounts generated in this chapter for any transactions on the public/main Ethereum network. The examples in this book do not provide adequate security for protecting these accounts.

The private key file and password are required to sign the transaction as account_1. Within the JupyterLab environment, create a text file named pass1.txt and populate it with the password used to create account_1 earlier in this chapter, the first pre-funded account used in the alloc section of the genesis.json configuration. Additionally, upload the secret key file generated from the geth account new command (performed earlier in this chapter to create the pre-funded Ethereum accounts). Name the secret key account1.json (see Figure 10-5).

Figure 10-5. *Ethereum account private key and password*

Load the private key and password for account_1 and sign the transaction created earlier:

```
with open('pass1.txt', 'r') as pass_file:
    kf1_pass = pass_file.read().replace('\n', '')

with open("account1.json") as kf1_file:
    enc_key = kf1_file.read();

p_1 = w3.eth.account.decrypt(enc_key, kf1_pass)
signed_tx = web3.eth.account.signTransaction(tx, p_1)
signed_tx
```

Example output:

```
AttributeDict({'rawTransaction': HexBytes('0xf86d0f850ba43b74
00831e8480948ab8f3fc6c660d3f0b22490050c843cafd2c0aac880de0b6b3
a7640000801ca0917ae987a8c808cf01221dad4571fd0b1b8f5429d13c469
c72bc13647e9c1744a068507c8542ccdebb96e534d13a140ddcbdaedbfa3b
a82dcbf86d4b196cc41b1f'),
```

```
'hash': HexBytes('0x9de62dc620274e2c9dba2194d90c245a933af8468
ace5f2d38e802da09c06769'),
'r': 65802530150742945852115878650256413649726940478651153584
824595116007827969860,
's': 47182743427096773798449059805443774712403275692049277894
020390344384483433247,
'v': 28}
```

Send the signed transaction to the transaction node and retrieve the resulting hash. This hash is the unique identifier for the transaction on the Ethereum Blockchain:

```
signed_tx = signed_tx.rawTransaction
tx_hash = web3.eth.sendRawTransaction(signed_tx)
web3.toHex(tx_hash)
```

Example output:

```
'0x9de62dc620274e2c9dba2194d90c245a933af8468ace5f2d38e802d
a09c06769'
```

After a node receives the transaction, it propagates to all nodes for validation and inclusion into the pending transaction pool, ready to be mined with the next block.[33] The following code queries the connected transaction node every second until the transaction returns with a block number:

```
%%time
blockNumber = None
check = 0
```

---

[33]Murthy, Mahesh. "Life Cycle of an Ethereum Transaction." Medium, April 18, 2018. https://medium.com/blockchannel/life-cycle-of-an-ethereum-transaction-e5c66bae0f6e.

```
while type(blockNumber) is not int:
    check += 1
    tx = web3.eth.getTransaction(tx_hash)
    blockNumber = tx.blockNumber
    clear_output(wait=True)

    print(f"Check #{check}\n")
    if type(blockNumber) is not int:
        time.sleep(1)

tx
```

Example output:

```
Check #12

CPU times: user 129 ms, sys: 904 µs, total: 130 ms
Wall time: 11.1 s
AttributeDict({'blockHash': HexBytes('0x676a24aa8117b51958031a2
863b17f91ed3356276036a9de7c596124a6234986'),
 'blockNumber': 8050,
 'from': '0xFa4087D3688a289c9C92e773a7b46cb9CCf80353',
 'gas': 2000000,
 'gasPrice': 50000000000,
 'hash': HexBytes('0xa3f02c685ff05b13b164afcbe11d2aa83d2dab3ff9
72ee7008cc931282587cee'),
 'input': '0x',
 'nonce': 16,
 'to': '0x8ab8F3fc6c660d3f0B22490050C843cafd2c0AAC',
 'transactionIndex': 0,
 'value': 1000000000000000000,
 'v': 28,
```

```
'r': HexBytes('0x89d052927901e8a7a727ebfb7709d4f9b99362c0f0001
f62f37300ed17cb7414'),
's': HexBytes('0x3ea3b4f5f8e4c10e4f30cc5b8a7ff0a833d8714f20744
c289dee86006af420c8')})
```

The transaction is now complete and its record immutably stored on the private blockchain. The network attempts to create a new block every 10 to 15 seconds[34] by adjusting the required difficulty;[35] however, this resource-constrained network with only three miners may fluctuate considerably. The final code block in the exercise queries the transaction node for the last 100 blocks and plots the time delta between block timestamps:

```
df = pd.DataFrame(columns=['timestamp'])
for i in range (0,100):
    block = web3.eth.getBlock(tx.blockNumber - i)
    df.loc[i] = [block.timestamp]

df['delta'] = df.timestamp.diff().shift(-1) * -1

df.reset_index().plot(x='index', y="delta", figsize=(12,5))
```

See Figure 10-6 for example output from the block timestamp delta plot.

---

[34]https://etherscan.io/chart/blocktime

[35]Siriwardena, Prabath. "The Mystery Behind Block Time." Medium, July 8, 2018. https://medium.facilelogin.com/the-mystery-behind-block-time-63351e35603a.

[12]: <matplotlib.axes._subplots.AxesSubplot at 0x7fe6e615c0f0>

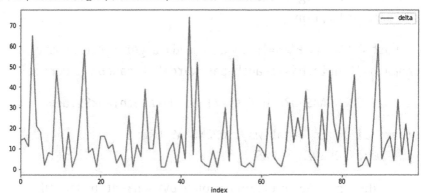

Figure 10-6. *Plot of block timestamp deltas*

This section demonstrated programmatic interactivity with a private blockchain network from within the Kubernetes cluster. Operating one or more Ethereum nodes in a Kubernetes cluster opens up numerous opportunities to extend and leverage Blockchain concepts through streamlined interconnectivity with existing and custom applications. The final section deploys a Serverless function, creating a public API for accessing Blockchain data.

Serverless/OpenFaaS

This book introduced the Serverless platform OpenFaaS in Chapter 9 and installed the prebuilt function Sentiment Analysis. This section builds and deploys a custom function for exposing a public API into the private blockchain network. See Chapter 9 for installation instructions using Helm. The following exercise uses the ingress URL `https://faas.data.eth.apk8s.dev`.

Log in and configure the faas-cli to use the new eth Blockchain cluster on a local workstation:

```
$ export OPENFAAS_PASS=$(kubectl -n data get secret basic-auth -o
jsonpath="{.data.basic-auth-password}" | base64 --decode)

$ export OPENFAAS_URL=https://faas.data.eth.apk8s.dev

$ faas-cli login --gateway=$OPENFAAS_URL \
--password=$OPENFAAS_PASS
```

Pull the OpenFaaS function template python3-http-debian:

```
$ faas-cli template store pull python3-http-debian
```

Create the directory cluster-apk8s-eth/003-data/200-eth/ functions. Within the new functions directory, create a new OpenFaaS function named last-block using the python3-http-debian template:

```
$ faas-cli new last-block --lang python3-http-debian
```

The faas-cli command created the folder last-block and yaml file last-block.yml. If necessary, install Python 3 on the local workstation. Change directory to the last-block and create a Python virtual environment. This helps in generating a requirements.txt later used to configure the OpenFaaS function with the required Python packages. Finally, activate the virtual environment:

```
$ cd last-block
$ python3 -m venv venv
$ source ./venv/bin/activate
```

Install the Python packages hexbytes and web3:

```
$ pip install hexbytes==0.2.0 web3==5.9.0
```

pip will install the hexbytes and web3 and all the dependent packages into the virtual environment. The new virtual environment contains only the packages required to run the function. Use pip to create a list of required packages in the requirements.txt file:

```
$ pip freeze > requirements.txt
```

Create the function by replacing the contents in handler.py with Listing 10-14.

Listing 10-14. OpenFaaS function for returning details on the last block in the Blockchain

```
#!/usr/bin/env python3
""" handler.py
OpenFaaS Blockchain function returning the last block
in the chain.
"""

import os
import json
import hexbytes
from web3 import Web3

def handle(event, context):
    """

    handle a request to the function
    """
    ep_url = "http://eth-geth-tx:8545"
    ep = os.getenv('GETH_RPC_ENDPOINT', ep_url)

    w3 = Web3(Web3.HTTPProvider(ep))
    latest_block = w3.eth.getBlock('latest')
    lbd = latest_block.__dict__
```

```python
    return {
        "statusCode": 200,
        "body": json.loads(
            json.dumps(lbd, cls=CustomEncoder)
        )
    }

class CustomEncoder(json.JSONEncoder):
    """

    CustomEncoder decodes HexBytes
    in Geth response dict.
    """

    def default(self, o):
        if isinstance(o, hexbytes.main.HexBytes):
            return o.hex()

        return json.JSONEncoder.default(self, o)

if __name__ == '__main__':
    """

    Run code from command line for testing.
    Mock event and context.
    """

    print(handle(event={}, context={}))
```

Test the new function on a local workstation by port-forwarding the eth-geth-tx service in one terminal and executing the Python script handler.py in another. Open a separate terminal and port-forward eth-geth-tx:

```
$ kubectl port-forward svc/eth-geth-tx 8545:8545 -n data
```

Execute the Python script handler.py from the current (virtual environment enabled) terminal:

```
$ export GETH_RPC_ENDPOINT=http://localhost:8545
$ python3 ./handler.py
```

Example output:

```
{'statusCode': 200, 'body': {'difficulty': 471861, 'extraData':
'0xd88301090d846765746888676f312e31342e32856c696e6e7578',
'gasLimit': 8000000, 'gasUsed': 0, 'hash': '0x8b4ebaca1d3606630
c872cba9ccf4a968c43af24e02800b0a182ef89b149f08b', 'logsBloom':
'0x00000000000000000000000', 'miner': '0x284F99f929B49Da9D85b2a3
dbF606Ed38EeC393E', 'mixHash': '0xd92b8eaa4a7f103f9c76bf7bf9b13
b90271fed7f1f25c72f81e429f2108755bc', 'nonce': '0x1f110a5f5dc6
9827', 'number': 9107, 'parentHash': '0xd40382cd4c2e75cc919d11
318672820aab10854951ee4ee137a08d97e84aa4c7', 'receiptsRoot':
'0x56e81f171bcc55a6ff8345e692c0f86e5b48e01b996cadc001622fb5e36
3b421', 'sha3Uncles': '0x1dcc4de8dec75d7aab85b567b6ccd41ad3124
51b948a7413f0a142fd40d49347', 'size': 538, 'stateRoot':
'0xbe54d463bf9ffeda68975ff839eec7ecabd42c2f88cfc75372765891f4
3b1f18', 'timestamp': 1589012313, 'totalDifficulty': 3333037812,
'transactions': [], 'transactionsRoot': '0x56e81f171bcc55a6ff8
345e692c0f86e5b48e01b996cadc001622fb5e363b421', 'uncles': []}}
```

Next, build, push, and deploy the function. The OpenFaaS CLI uses Docker to build and push a container image of the Function to the repository configured automatically in last-block.yml; see OpenFaaS configuration options[36] to customize the defaults. If using the default configuration, install Docker on the local workstation and sign up for a free Docker Hub[37] account:

```
$ faas-cli build --build-arg ADDITIONAL_PACKAGE=gcc -f ./last-block.yml
```

```
$ faas-cli push -f ./last-block.yml
$ faas-cli deploy -f ./last-block.yml
```

Example output:

```
Deploying: last-block.
```

```
Deployed. 202 Accepted.
URL: https://faas.data.eth.apk8s.dev/function/last-block
```

Finally, use a web browser or curl to access the new public last-block function:

```
$ curl https://faas.data.eth.apk8s.dev/function/last-block
```

Example output (truncated):

{"difficulty":474599,"extraData":"0xd88301090d846765746888676f
312e31342e32856c696e7578","gasLimit":8000000,"gasUsed":0,"hash
":"0x8154d9edf431821a239fbb72bc2636304e254663b11cddc6987095d39
1f35248","logsBloom":"0x000...","miner":"0xcc7ADDFC03cb5ec2E3894
583895C1bE385625c62","mixHash":"0xd20bf313f1834ec333d7d5cb2870
b42487b462ee322aeccdd699fc017f86be51","nonce":"0x1a11af75e7ff4
68f","number":11694,"parentHash":"0x930d5f7340997cc1f0cd4be6e2
2aefe02c136c2e93b38ce75eff1815455f730d","receiptsRoot":"0x56e8

---

[36]https://docs.openfaas.com/reference/yaml/
[37]https://hub.docker.com/

1f171bcc55a6ff8345e692c0f86e5b48e01b996cadc001622fb5e363b421",
"sha3Uncles":"0x1dcc4de8dec75d7aab85b567b6ccd41ad312451b948a74
13f0a142fd40d49347","size":538,"stateRoot":"0x51a5a7bb73dd5bd6
ebb3a96606e115033e6b3bdcdb4a326b5a6c67718969f6cc","timestamp":
1589048551,"totalDifficulty":4550348128,"transactions":[],
"transactionsRoot":"0x56e81f171bcc55a6ff8345e692c0f86e5b48e0
1b996cadc001622fb5e363b421","uncles":[]}

The last-block function represents a minimal and straightforward demonstration of application development atop Kubernetes and OpenFaaS. OpenFaaS manages, monitors, and scales Functions. Kubernetes glues together technologies as diverse as Serverless, Blockchain, and web-based IDEs (integrated development environments).

Summary

This chapter installed an Ethereum Blockchain network consisting of two Bootnodes, a Bootnode Registrar, an Ethstats Dashboard, three miner nodes, and two transaction nodes (see Listing 10-15), all running across a three-node Kubernetes cluster. Adapting the Ethereum Blockchain network in this chapter to support a protected public network involves exposing bootnodes and miners for external third-party access and moving from the Ethereum standard proof-of-work consensus protocol to the new Clique, proof of authority. The configuration of a shared production Blockchain network is dependent on business goals and requirements, and it is therefore beyond the scope of this book. However, the demonstrated Kubernetes implementation applies to many flavors of Blockchain and Serverless platforms.

Implementing Blockchain technology within Kubernetes may seem counterintuitive at first; it is an example where the technology itself does not require any of the functionality provided by Kubernetes. However,

Kubernetes is not presented here as a solution to running Blockchain, or even Serverless technology. This book presents Kubernetes as a standardized, unified platform for extending data management, Serverless, data science, and Blockchain platforms, supported by unified storage, network, and control plane, implemented by declarative configuration.

The next and final chapter in this book covers the management of data science and Machine Learning workloads across cloud and on-premises infrastructure.

Listing 10-15. Chapter 10 organization of Kubernetes-based Blockchain platform components

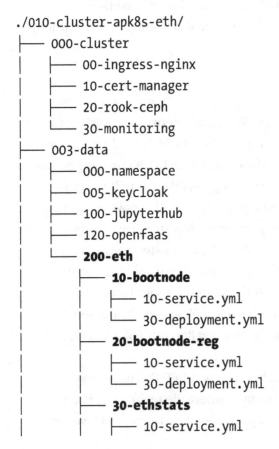

```
./010-cluster-apk8s-eth/
├── 000-cluster
│   ├── 00-ingress-nginx
│   ├── 10-cert-manager
│   ├── 20-rook-ceph
│   └── 30-monitoring
├── 003-data
│   ├── 000-namespace
│   ├── 005-keycloak
│   ├── 100-jupyterhub
│   ├── 120-openfaas
│   └── 200-eth
│       ├── 10-bootnode
│       │   ├── 10-service.yml
│       │   └── 30-deployment.yml
│       ├── 20-bootnode-reg
│       │   ├── 10-service.yml
│       │   └── 30-deployment.yml
│       ├── 30-ethstats
│       │   ├── 10-service.yml
```

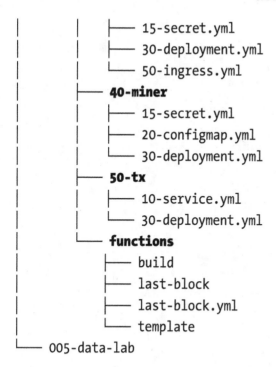

```
|         |      ├──── 15-secret.yml
|         |      ├──── 30-deployment.yml
|         |      └──── 50-ingress.yml
|         ├──── 40-miner
|         |      ├──── 15-secret.yml
|         |      ├──── 20-configmap.yml
|         |      └──── 30-deployment.yml
|         ├──── 50-tx
|         |      ├──── 10-service.yml
|         |      └──── 30-deployment.yml
|         └──── functions
|                ├──── build
|                ├──── last-block
|                ├──── last-block.yml
|                └──── template
└──── 005-data-lab
```

CHAPTER 11

Platforming AIML

Platforming AI/ML (Artificial Intelligence/Machine Learning) in the context of this book involves implementing all the components necessary to develop and deploy artificial intelligence based on Machine Learning leveraging Kubernetes. This chapter uses specific technologies to illustrate broad concepts, from distributing and managing data collection applications on IoT devices and ETL operations to building and training Machine Learning models with on-premises GPUs, and deploying inference-based artificial intelligence into a distributed cloud environment.

Data Science frameworks such as TensorFlow, Keras, scikit-Learn, and PyTorch simplify the development and training of machine learning models. These frameworks lower the barrier of entry to the concepts of Artificial Intelligence through Machine Learning. These modern data science frameworks facilitate rapid experimentation and development. Kubernetes complements this ecosystem by simplifying the complex problems of managing and connecting applications responsible for collecting, storing, distributing, processing, and analyzing data and workloads that process it, making Kubernetes well suited as the foundation for an end-to-end Machine Learning platform.

The AIML life cycle begins with raw data and ends with valuable inferences made on that data. There are numerous books on nearly every stage of this process; this Kubernetes-centric book can only scratch the surface in a single chapter, yet aims to demonstrate concepts useful in constructing custom AIML platforms building from previous chapters (see Figure 11-1).

© Craig Johnston 2020
C. Johnston, *Advanced Platform Development with Kubernetes*,
https://doi.org/10.1007/978-1-4842-5611-4_11

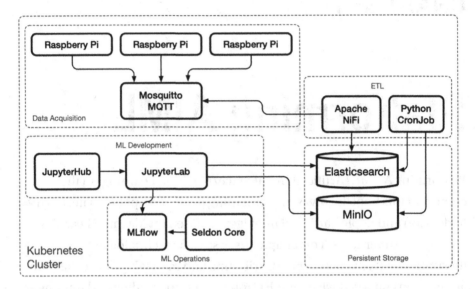

Figure 11-1. *Demonstration of end-to-end AIML platform*

Data

A significant portion of this book covers data management applications:
Chapters 5 through 9 cover data pipelines, data indexing and analytics,
data lakes, data warehouses, and data transformation. This chapter adds
raw data acquisition to the cluster. It demonstrates the capabilities of
Kubernetes in reducing the conceptual distance between the collection
of raw data and access to packaged data sets suitable for Data Science
activities, including the development of Machine Learning–based artificial
intelligence.

Hybrid Infrastructure

The application of Machine Learning–based artificial intelligence (AIML)
extends well beyond packaged data sets and the latest algorithms. Full
AIML life cycles often involve data acquisition, ETL, processing, and data

432

routing to and from inference-/prediction-based workloads across various locations and infrastructure.

Figure 11-2 depicts an infrastructure familiar to many organizations, including on-premises facilities containing sensor devices, offices with servers and workstations, and multiregional presence in multiple public clouds.

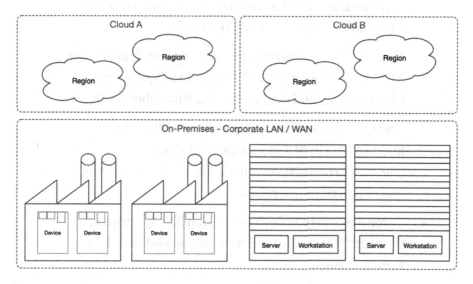

Figure 11-2. *Corporate infrastructure example*

Kubernetes provides a platform capable of supporting the entire end-to-end life cycle of AIML-driven initiatives, from the raw data collected by devices and their sensors to the deployment and management of highly scalable distributed inference workloads. The following sections implement a representative sampling of the broad scope of infrastructure shown in Figure 11-2.

Development Environment

The exercises in this chapter utilize the following scaled-back demonstration infrastructure shown in Figure 11-3. To follow along with the examples in this chapter, use the following or equivalent resources:

- One Droplet from Digital Ocean providing 2 CPUs, 2 GB memory, 60 GB of disk storage, running Ubuntu 18.04, and deployed in the NYC3 region

- Three CX31 cloud servers from Hetzner, each providing 2 CPUs, 2 GB memory, 80 GB of disk storage, running Ubuntu 18.04, and deployed in the Nuremberg region

- One physical workstation providing 4 CPUs, 16 GB memory, 80 GB of disk storage, 1 NVIDIA GPU (GeForce GTX 1070, or better), running Ubuntu 18.04, and deployed on-premises

- Three Raspberry Pi devices (version 3 or 4), running Raspberry Pi OS Lite (32-bit) minimal, and based on Debian Buster[1]

---

[1] www.raspberrypi.org/downloads/raspberry-pi-os/

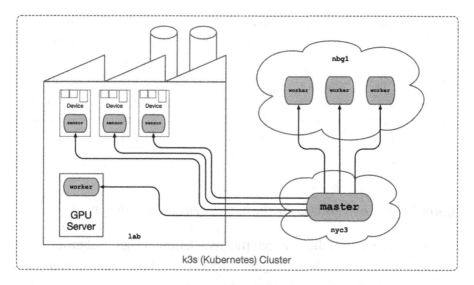

Figure 11-3. *Corporate infrastructure example*

The hybrid cluster in this chapter is intentionally complicated for its scale; however, this complexity demonstrates Kubernetes's flexibility in a wide range of infrastructure challenges.

DNS

This chapter uses Cloudflare[2] to manage the following DNS A entries (see Figure 11-4) for a new development cluster called hc1: *.hc1 points to the three IP addresses assigned to the Hetzner cloud instances used as worker nodes. master.hc1 points to a Digital Ocean Droplet created for the Kubernetes master node. nbg1-n1.hc1, nbg1-n2.hc1, and nbg1-n3.hc1 are optional entries pointed to each worker node. Finally, lab-gpu.hc1 points to an on-premises Internet router; if this router has a dynamic IP address (common for home Internet service), use a dynamic DNS service.[3]

---

[2]www.cloudflare.com/

[3]www.ionos.com/digitalguide/server/tools/free-dynamic-dns-providers-
an-overview/

Type	Name	Content	TTL	Proxy status
A	*.hc1	.36	Auto	☁ DNS only
A	*.hc1	.70	Auto	☁ DNS only
A	*.hc1	.123	Auto	☁ DNS only
A	lab-gpu.hc1	.214	Auto	☁ DNS only
A	master.hc1	.220	Auto	☁ DNS only
A	nbg1-n1.hc1	.36	Auto	☁ DNS only
A	nbg1-n2.hc1	.70	Auto	☁ DNS only
A	nbg1-n3.hc1	.123	Auto	☁ DNS only

Figure 11-4. DNS entries for the hc1 development cluster

The next section walks through the installation of eight Kubernetes nodes using k3s across three regions, on-premises devices and servers, and public clouds in New York and Nuremberg.

k3s Hybrid Cloud

This chapter uses k3s to demonstrate a fully functional Kubernetes cluster across a wide range of hardware. k3s is a lightweight certified Kubernetes distribution, well suited for hybrid infrastructure with support ranging from cloud compute resources to IoT devices.

The following sections create an eight-node Kubernetes cluster consisting of three Raspberry Pi devices used for sensor data collection, one GPU workstation for machine learning, three public cloud nodes for distributed workloads, and one public cloud node in a master role.

The three Raspberry Pi devices represent any IoT device responsible for collecting sensor data and transmitting it to an MQTT broker. Later, it is stored in Elasticsearch and MinIO object storage running on the worker nodes. The GPU server trains Machine Learning models from collected data and deploys the trained models to the cloud nodes for inference/prediction workloads. A single Kubernetes cluster manages all workloads and communication across this small yet global cluster.

Kilo VPN

Extra attention to security is required when operating a Pod network across multiple public networks. Any communication over the open Internet must be encrypted, and a VPN is one of the ways to ensure this. Previous chapters used private networks to communicate across nodes; private networking is a standard feature provided by every major cloud vendor. However, these private networks are typically limited to the vendor and, in some cases, limited by region.

WireGuard (first introduced in Chapter 3) is a high-performance VPN capable of providing an efficient encrypted tunnel for Pod communication across public networks. Yet, configuring and managing routing and tunneling between public network interfaces to and from nodes on each region is a complicated and tedious task.

The Kilo[4] project uses WireGuard to create an encrypted layer-3[5] network overlay. Kilo manages the IP routing along with the WireGuard public/private key pairs for each node in the Kubernetes cluster. Kilo supports full-cluster and region-based node-to-node encryption. Full-cluster encryption may add unnecessary overhead between nodes already communicating in a private network. Therefore, the following examples use a region-based Kilo network, creating VPN tunnels only between regions, as shown in Figure 11-5.

---

[4]https://github.com/squat/kilo
[5]www.infoblox.com/glossary/layer-3-of-the-osi-model-network-layer/

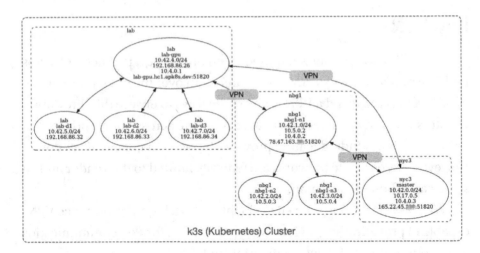

Figure 11-5. *Hybrid Kubernetes cluster with topology-aware VPN tunnels*

Figure 11-6 depicts the network interfaces used by each node for both internal and external communication to each of the other nodes in the cluster.

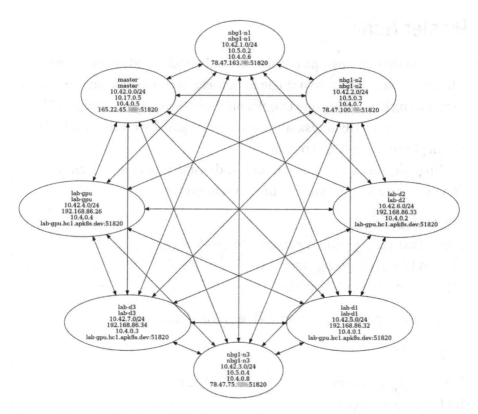

Figure 11-6. *Kilo VPN full-cluster network connections*

The complex hybrid cluster depicted in this section gives a brief overview of the network topology created with each node over the next few sections. Refer back to these diagrams after each node is installed for reference. This network demonstrates Kubernetes support for a wide range of networked environments and solves challenges common to many organizations: the need to standardize and unify diverse development and production environments.

Master Node

As a means to demonstrate a scaled-down hybrid-cloud network, the following example installs a single Kubernetes master node on Digital Ocean using k3s. Create one Droplet on Digital Ocean, providing 2 CPUs, 2 GB memory, 60 GB of disk storage, and configured with Ubuntu 18.04, and deploy it to the NYC3 region.

Upgrade packages on the Droplet and install WireGuard (later used by Kilo to create a VPN tunnel) on the new Droplet:

```
$ apt upgrade -y
$ apt install -y apt-transport-https \
ca-certificates gnupg-agent \
software-properties-common

$ add-apt-repository -y ppa:wireguard/wireguard

$ apt update

$ apt -o Dpkg::Options::=--force-confnew \
install -y wireguard
```

Next, create a shared secret for the cluster and store the generated value in a safe place. Additional nodes use the shared secret for acceptance into the k3s cluster by the master node:

```
$ export K3S_CLUSTER_SECRET=$(head -c48 /dev/urandom | base64)

# copy the echoed secret
$ echo $K3S_CLUSTER_SECRET
```

Install k3s without the default Flannel Pod network; Kilo, installed later in this chapter, will handle the layer-3 networking:

```
$ curl -sfL https://get.k3s.io | \
sh -s - server --no-flannel
```

k3s supports both single- and multi-node operation; this chapter builds an eight-node cluster with a dedicated master. Taint the master node to prevent the scheduling of regular workloads:

```
$ kubectl taint node master dedicated=master:NoSchedule
```

Kilo creates VPN tunnels between regions using the name label `topology.kubernetes.io/region`; label the `master` node with its region, in this example, `nyc3`:

```
$ kubectl label node master \
topology.kubernetes.io/region=nyc3
```

Next, copy the k3s kubectl configuration file located at `/etc/rancher/k3s/k3s.yaml` to root home:

```
$ cp /etc/rancher/k3s/k3s.yaml ~
```

Create a DNS entry for the `master` node, in this case, `master.hc1.apk8s.dev,` and update the copied `~/k3s.yml` file with the new public DNS. Edit the file manually or use `sed` for quick replace:

```
$ sed -i "s/127.0.0.1/master.hc1.apk8s.dev/" k3s.yaml
$ sed -i "s/default/apk8s-hc1/" k3s.yaml
```

Finally, copy the modified `k3s.yaml` onto a local workstation with kubectl installed. From a local workstation, use secure copy:

```
$ scp root@master.hc1.apk8s.dev:~/k3s.yaml ~/.kube/apk8s-hc1
```

Use the new kubectl configuration file to query the master node:

```
$ export KUBECONFIG=~/.kube/apk8s-hc1
$ kubectl describe node master
```

This section installed a single master node on Digital Ocean's public cloud in the nyc3 region. The next section creates three worker nodes on the Hetzner public cloud in the Nuremberg region.

Worker Nodes

This section continues the development of a hybrid-cloud network, attaching three worker nodes to the master node created in the previous section. Start three CX31 (2 CPUs, 2 GB memory, 80 GB of disk storage) cloud servers on Hetzner, running Ubuntu 18.04, and deployed in the Nuremberg region. Name the new instances nbg1-n1, nbg1-n2, and nbg1-n3.

To avoid the cost and complexity of a load balancer on the demo cluster, create a wildcard DNS A record *.hc1.apk8s.dev for each of the new instances' IP addresses. All ingress rules for the subdomain hc1.apk8s.dev now route to one of the three Hetzner instances.

Log in to each new cloud server instance, and upgrade and install required packages along with WireGuard on each instance:

```
$ apt upgrade -y
$ apt install -y apt-transport-https \
ca-certificates gnupg-agent \
software-properties-common

# Install kernel headers (missing on Hetzner instances)
$ apt install -y linux-headers-$(uname -r)

# Ceph block device kernel module (for Ceph support)
$ modprobe rbd

$ add-apt-repository -y ppa:wireguard/wireguard

$ apt update

$ apt -o Dpkg::Options::=--force-confnew \
install -y wireguard
```

Next, install k3s on each new Hetzner instance. Begin by populating the environment variables K3S_CLUSTER_SECRET, the cluster secret generated on the master node in the previous section, and K3S_URL, the master node address, in this case `master.hc1.apk8s.dev`. Pipe the k3s installer script to sh along with the command-line argument agent (run as nonworker) and a network topology label:

```
$ export K3S_CLUSTER_SECRET="<PASTE VALUE>"
$ export K3S_URL="https://master.hc1.apk8s.dev:6443"

$ curl -sfL https://get.k3s.io | \
sh -s - agent --no-flannel \
--node-label=\"topology.kubernetes.io/region=nbg1\"
```

The `hc1.apk8s.dev` cluster now consists of four nodes, one master node at Digital Ocean and three worker nodes at Hetzner. On a local workstation with the kubectl configuration file copy and modified in the previous section, list the four nodes:

```
$ export KUBECONFIG=~/.kube/apk8s-hc1
$ kubectl get nodes -o wide
```

`kubectl` lists four nodes in the cluster. The cluster lacks a Pod network and will therefore report a `NotReady` status for each node. This chapter installs the Kilo Pod network after configuring all eight nodes. The following section begins work on the third and final region of the hybrid-cluster, the `lab`.

On-premises

The term on-premises can mean any specific physical location outside a data center or cloud presence. This section continues the build-out of a hybrid Kubernetes cluster with a final region called `lab`. The new lab region may be one or more physical locations on a single corporate WAN or LAN. The following demonstration configures a single bare-metal server with an NVIDIA GPU for processing Machine Learning workloads, along with three Raspberry Pi devices used to collect data from onboard sensors.

GPU

The following example GPU server uses a generic motherboard, Intel CPU, 120 GB SSD drive, and 16 GB of memory, and an NVIDIA GeForce 1070 (Gaming) GPU.[6] NVIDIA does not license drivers for GeForce 1070 GPUs for use in data centers. However, these cards are inexpensive and suitable for small-scale on-premises experimentation and testing. Organizations looking to utilize NVIDIA hardware for production should carefully examine NVIDIA's licensing terms. Refer to NVIDIA's line of Cloud and data center hardware for production-scale machine learning.[7]

NVIDIA GPU models typically offered by public clouds include the K80, P100, and V100.

GPU/CUDA

NVIDIA GPUs are popular for Machine Learning projects due to the broad support for CUDA[8] across major frameworks and software libraries. CUDA (Compute Unified Device Architecture) is NVIDIA's proprietary API and is only supported by NVIDIA GPUs. CUDA's open alternative is OpenCL[9] supported on both NVIDIA and AMD GPUs. However, there is limited support for open OpenCL in the data science ecosystem and no support by the most popular frameworks, TensorFlow and PyTorch, as of 2020.[10]

---

[6]www.nvidia.com/en-in/geforce/products/10series/geforce-gtx-1070/

[7]www.nvidia.com/en-us/data-center/

[8]https://developer.nvidia.com/cuda-zone

[9]www.khronos.org/opencl/

[10]Dimolarov, Nikolay. "On the State of Deep Learning Outside of CUDA's Walled Garden." Blog. Towards Data Science, June 4, 2019. https://towardsdatascience.com/on-the-state-of-deep-learning-outside-of-cudas-walled-garden-d88c8bbb4342.

Install Ubuntu

The following example created a fresh install of Ubuntu 18.04.4 for a new or repurposed desktop workstation with an NVIDIA GeForce 1070 GPU.

Download Ubuntu 18.04.4 LTS (Bionic Beaver) 64-bit PC (AMD64) server install image[11] and create a bootable USB thumb drive.[12] This example uses an MSI motherboard, where holding down F11 on boot launches the Boot Menu; consult the manual for other manufacturers. Boot the workstation from the new thumb drive and follow the standard installation instructions.

Install WireGuard for Kilo support and rbd kernel module for Ceph support:

```
$ sudo su
$ apt update && apt upgrade -y
$ apt install -y apt-transport-https \
ca-certificates gnupg-agent \
software-properties-common

$ apt install -y linux-headers-$(uname -r)

# Ceph block device kernel module (for Ceph support)
$ modprobe rbd

$ add-apt-repository -y ppa:wireguard/wireguard

$ apt update

$ apt -o Dpkg::Options::=--force-confnew \
install -y wireguard
```

---

[11]http://releases.ubuntu.com/18.04.4/
[12]https://help.ubuntu.com/community/Installation/FromUSBStick

Assign a static IP address or reserve a DHCP assigned address and forward port 5180 (used for the WireGuard VPN tunnel) from the public IP address on an Internet-facing router. Finally, create a DNS A record named lab-gpu.hc1.apk8s.dev pointing to the public IP of the on-premises Internet router. Use a dynamic DNS service[13] if this address is likely to change. Kilo is configured later in this chapter to route external Pod network traffic to and from any other on-premises nodes through this node.

NVIDIA GPU Support

The previous section installed Ubuntu 18.04.4 on a workstation on-premises called lab-gpu. The following exercise installs NVIDIA GPU drivers along with the nvidia-container-runtime plug-in for containerd,[14] the default container runtime for k3s.

Execute all the following commands as the root user:

$ sudo su

Update apt, upgrade existing packages, and install common Ubuntu driver packages:

$ apt update && apt upgrade -y
$ apt install ubuntu-drivers-common

Enable the Intelligent Platform Management Interface kernel module:

$ modprobe ipmi_devintf

Add the proprietary GPU driver repository to apt:

$ add-apt-repository -y ppa:graphics-drivers

---

[13]https://en.wikipedia.org/wiki/Dynamic_DNS
[14]https://containerd.io/

Add NVIDIA's GPG key to apt:

```
$ curl -s -L \
  https://nvidia.github.io/nvidia-docker/gpgkey \
  | sudo apt-key add -
```

Add NVIDIA's driver repositories to apt:

```
$ curl -s -L https://nvidia.github.io/nvidia-container-runtime/
ubuntu18.04/nvidia-container-runtime.list | tee /etc/apt/
sources.list.d/nvidia-container-runtime.list
```

Install NVIDIA packages:

```
$ apt-get install -y nvidia-driver-440
$ apt-get install -y nvidia-container-runtime
$ apt-get install -y nvidia-modprobe nvidia-smi
```

Load NVIDIA kernel modules:

```
$ /sbin/modprobe nvidia
$ /sbin/modprobe nvidia-uvm
```

After booting the workstation, ensure the nvidia-smi command returns results similar to those shown in Figure 11-7:

```
$ reboot
```

```
$ nvidia-smi
```

```
+---------------------------------------------------------------------------+
| NVIDIA-SMI 440.82         Driver Version: 440.82       CUDA Version: 10.2  |
|-------------------------------+----------------------+----------------------+
| GPU  Name        Persistence-M| Bus-Id        Disp.A | Volatile Uncorr. ECC |
| Fan  Temp  Perf  Pwr:Usage/Cap|         Memory-Usage | GPU-Util  Compute M. |
|===============================+======================+======================|
|   0  GeForce GTX 1070     Off | 00000000:03:00.0 Off |                  N/A |
| 25%   36C    P0    30W / 151W |     0MiB /  8119MiB  |      0%      Default |
+-------------------------------+----------------------+----------------------+

+---------------------------------------------------------------------------+
| Processes:                                                    GPU Memory  |
|  GPU       PID   Type   Process name                          Usage       |
|===========================================================================|
|  No running processes found                                               |
+---------------------------------------------------------------------------+
```

***Figure 11-7.** nvidia-smi output*

The newly installed workstation now supports an NVIDIA GPU as recognized by the operating system and the NVIDIA System Management Interface. The next section adds NVIDIA runtime support for containerd.

k3s with NVIDIA Runtime

NVIDIA provides extensive documentation on configuring Docker[15] for supporting their GPUs, along with a Container Toolkit. Although k3s supports Docker, containerd[16] is its default container runtime. containerd is a component of Docker without the Docker Engine and utilities. This section installs k3s and configures containerd with the nvidia-container-runtime.[17]

Begin by setting the following environment variables: set K3S_ CLUSTER_SECRET to the secret generated when installing the master node; set K3S_URL as the URL of the master node; and set INSTALL_K3S_SKIP_ START to true to prevent k3s from starting automatically:

---

[15]https://github.com/NVIDIA/nvidia-docker

[16]https://computingforgeeks.com/docker-vs-cri-o-vs-containerd/

[17]https://dev.to/mweibel/add-nvidia-gpu-support-to-k3s-with-containerd-4j17

```
$ sudo su
$ export K3S_CLUSTER_SECRET="<PASTE VALUE>"
$ export K3S_URL="https://master.hc1.apk8s.dev:6443"
$ export INSTALL_K3S_SKIP_START=true
```

Use the k3s default installer with parameters and arguments similar to those set previously on worker nodes; however, this GPU workstation is part of the new on-premises region named lab:

```
$ curl -sfL https://get.k3s.io | \
sh -s - agent --no-flannel \
--node-label=\"topology.kubernetes.io/region=lab\"
```

Run the following commands to create or overwrite the config.toml in the directory /var/lib/rancher/k3s/agent/etc/containerd/; this new configuration instructs containerd to load nvidia-container-runtime plug-in and its required runtime type io.containerd.runtime.v1.linux:

```
$ mkdir -p /var/lib/rancher/k3s/agent/etc/containerd/
$ cat <<"EOF" > \
/var/lib/rancher/k3s/agent/etc/containerd/config.toml
[plugins.opt]
  path = "/var/lib/rancher/k3s/agent/containerd"

[plugins.cri]
  stream_server_address = "127.0.0.1"
  stream_server_port = "10010"
  sandbox_image = "docker.io/rancher/pause:3.1"

[plugins.cri.containerd.runtimes.runc]
  runtime_type = "io.containerd.runtime.v1.linux"

[plugins.linux]
  runtime = "nvidia-container-runtime"
EOF
```

Finally, start k3s:

```
$ systemctl start k3s
```

The new hc1 Kubernetes hybrid cluster now contains five nodes across three regions: nyc3 at Digital Ocean, nbg1 at Hetzner, and now lab on-premises. The next section extends the on-premises region with three Raspberry Pi devices.

IoT / Raspberry Pi

Over the last ten chapters, this book has demonstrated various uses for Kubernetes in distributed workloads, networking, data processing, and data management. Machine Learning–based Artificial Intelligence begins with the collection of raw data, and for many projects, devices (also known as IoT) collect this data. This section brings IoT into the cluster, specifically the popular Raspberry Pi. Raspberry Pi devices make excellent platforms for development and prototyping, and a growing number of projects are using them in production.[18] Raspberry PI devices use an ARM-based[19] CPU typical for nearly all mobile phones and a growing number of IoT devices.[20] As ARM CPUs have grown in popularity,[21] many projects are cross-compiled and maintain version executes on x86 and ARM-based systems, including Kubernetes.

The hybrid cluster (hc1) developed in this chapter uses k3s. k3s is a lightweight yet certified Kubernetes distribution with support for ARM and able to run on resource-limited devices. This section demonstrates the

---

[18]Piltch, Avram, and 2020. "Raspberry Pi to Power Ventilators as Demand for Boards Surges." Tom's Hardware. Accessed June 26, 2020. www.tomshardware.com/news/raspberry-pi-ventilators.

[19]www.arm.com/products/silicon-ip-cpu

[20]www.embedded.com/dev-boards-help-speed-iot-design/

[21]https://bgr.com/2020/04/23/arm-based-mac-release-date-apple-processor-2021/

use of Kubernetes as an IoT management platform by providing workload scheduling and management, self-healing, networking, and monitoring for multiple devices, and unified with on-premises workstations and multiple public cloud instances (shown in Figure 11-3).

Raspberry Pi OS

Install[22] three Raspberry Pi devices (version 3 or 4) with **Raspberry Pi OS Lite (32-bit) minimal based on Debian Buster**.[23] Name the devices lab-d1, lab-d2, and lab-d3. The number of devices is optional for the examples in this chapter. These devices represent IoT data collection sensors within a facility and are attached to a local network (LAN) with access to the Internet (see Figure 11-5). Each device requires a private static IP address or a DHCP reservation.

WireGuard

Kilo (installed later in this chapter) provides an encrypted Pod network for secure communication over the public Internet. Kilo uses WireGuard on each node to manage VPN tunnels.

Log in to each Raspberry Pi and install the required packages, beginning with updating apt packages and upgrading to the latest versions:

```
$ sudo su
$ apt-get update && apt-get upgrade
```

Install kernel headers:

```
$ apt-get install raspberrypi-kernel-headers
```

---

[22]www.raspberrypi.org/downloads/

[23]https://downloads.raspberrypi.org/raspios_lite_armhf_latest

Next, install WireGuard. WireGuard is available for Raspberry Pi OS through the Debian "unstable" distribution repository (containing the latest packages):

```
$ wget -O - https://ftp-master.debian.org/keys/archive-key-
$(lsb_release -sr).asc | sudo apt-key add -

$ printf 'Package: *\nPin: release a=unstable\nPin-Priority:
150\n' | tee --append /etc/apt/preferences.d/limit-unstable

$ echo "deb http://deb.debian.org/debian/ unstable main" |
tee --append /etc/apt/sources.list.d/unstable.list

$ apt-get update
$ apt install -y dirmngr wireguard-dkms
$ apt -o Dpkg::Options::=--force-confnew \
install -y wireguard
```

There are a few good tutorials for installing WireGuard Raspberry Pi if any issues arise with the preceding method.[24,25,26]

k3s on Raspberry Pi

Finally, install k3s on each Raspberry Pi. Start by setting the K3S_CLUSTER_ SECRET with the value generated when installing the master node and set the K3S_URL to the master node (on Digital Ocean):

```
$ sudo su
$ export K3S_CLUSTER_SECRET="<PASTE VALUE>"
$ export K3S_URL="https://master.hc1.apk8s.dev:6443"
```

---

[24]https://engineerworkshop.com/blog/how-to-set-up-wireguard-on-a-raspberry-pi/

[25]https://github.com/adrianmihalko/raspberrypiwireguard

[26]https://sigmdel.ca/michel/ha/wireguard/wireguard_02_en.html#buster

Install k3s using the default installer with options similar to the previous nodes. Set the region topology to lab, assuming these devices are in the same facility or local network as the GPU workstation installed earlier. Add the parameter --node-taint set to dedicated=pi:NoSchedule. Nodes with a NoSchedule taint inform the Kubernetes scheduler only to allow Pods with specific tolerations:

```
$ curl -sfL https://get.k3s.io | \
sh -s - agent --no-flannel \
--node-label=\"topology.kubernetes.io/region=lab\" \
--node-taint="dedicated=pi:NoSchedule"
```

There are now eight nodes that make up the new hc1 hybrid cluster: one master node at Digital Ocean named master within the region nyc3; three worker nodes on Hetzner called nbg1-n1, nbg1-n2, and nbg1-n3 within the region nbg1; and four nodes on-premises called lab-gpu, lab-d1, lab-d2, and lab-d3 within the lab region. See Figure 11-5 for an overview of the network topology.

The next section sets roles for the nodes for assistance in scheduling.

Node Roles

A Kubernetes node role is a simple label starting with node-role. kubernetes.io/<role>. The Pod scheduler is designed by Kubernetes to find the best location for Pod. Pods are ephemeral; they may fail or be drained from a node and rescheduled to another at any time. However, there are times when specialized workloads necessitate additional scheduling requirements. In the case of the hc1 cluster defined in this chapter, three nodes have the unique role of sensor. Role labels may be any value reflective of their operational characteristic.

The master node already possesses the label master. Label the remaining nodes as follows:

```
$ kubectl label node nbg1-n1 kubernetes.io/role=worker
$ kubectl label node nbg1-n2 kubernetes.io/role=worker
$ kubectl label node nbg1-n3 kubernetes.io/role=worker
$ kubectl label node lab-gpu kubernetes.io/role=worker

$ kubectl label node lab-d1 kubernetes.io/role=sensor
$ kubectl label node lab-d2 kubernetes.io/role=sensor
$ kubectl label node lab-d3 kubernetes.io/role=sensor
```

Issue the command kubectl get nodes from a local workstation and observe output similar to Figure 11-8. The nodes now report their intended Roles.

NAME	STATUS	ROLES	AGE	VERSION
lab-d1	NotReady	sensor	11m	v1.18.2+k3s1
lab-d2	NotReady	sensor	11m	v1.18.2+k3s1
lab-d3	NotReady	sensor	11m	v1.18.2+k3s1
master	NotReady	master	48m	v1.18.2+k3s1
lab-gpu	NotReady	worker	23m	v1.18.2+k3s1
nbg1-n3	NotReady	worker	41m	v1.18.2+k3s1
nbg1-n1	NotReady	worker	41m	v1.18.2+k3s1
nbg1-n2	NotReady	worker	41m	v1.18.2+k3s1

Figure 11-8. *node Roles*

Node status continue to report as NotReady as there is not yet a Pod network for them to communicate over. The following section completes the hc1 cluster set up by installing the Kilo Pod network.

Install Kilo

The "k3s Hybrid Cloud" section of this chapter began with a detailed explanation of Kilo and its role in using WireGuard to create VPN tunnels, providing secure, encrypted communication between Pods across a cluster spanning three regions over the public Internet. Installing Kilo is the last step in setting up the k3s Hybrid Cloud.

At least one node in each region must have an externally accessible endpoint.[27] The cloud instances on Digital Ocean and Hetzner already have public IP addresses. When setting up the GPU workstation, the domain lab-gpu.hc1.apk8s.dev resolves to the on-premises Internet router and forwards the port 51820 to the GPU workstation on its private LAN IP. The three Raspberry Pi devices have private LAN IP addresses and are not accessible from the Internet. The following annotations instruct Kilo to form VPN tunnels from the GPU workstation to the Raspberry Pi devices:

```
$ kubectl annotate node lab-d1 \
kilo.squat.ai/force-endpoint="lab-gpu.hc1.apk8s.dev:51820"
$ kubectl annotate node lab-d2 \
kilo.squat.ai/force-endpoint="lab-gpu.hc1.apk8s.dev:51820"
$ kubectl annotate node lab-d3 \
kilo.squat.ai/force-endpoint="lab-gpu.hc1.apk8s.dev:51820"
```

Next, Kilo requires access to the kubectl config for each node in the cluster to communicate with the master node. The kilo-k3s.yaml applied requires the kubectl config /etc/rancher/k3s/k3s.yaml on each node. The master node k3s install generated the file /etc/rancher/k3s/k3s.yaml. Download, modify, and distribute this file to the same path on all worker and sensor nodes (it does not need modification on the master node):

---

[27]https://github.com/squat/kilo/blob/master/docs/topology.md

```
$ ssh root@master.hc1.apk8s.dev \
sed "s/127.0.0.1/master.hc1.apk8s.dev/" \ /etc/rancher/k3s/k3s.
yaml >k3s.yaml
```

Copy the modified k3s.yaml to /etc/rancher/k3s/k3s.yaml on each node.

Finally, install Kilo by applying the kilo-k3s.yaml configuration manifest:

```
$ kubectl apply -f \
https://raw.githubusercontent.com/squat/kilo/master/manifests/
kilo-k3s.yaml
```

A Kilo agent is now running on each node, as shown in Figure 11-9. Once Kilo has completed the VPN setup, each node reports as Ready, and the new hc1 hybrid cluster is ready for use.

```
~ $ export KUBECONFIG=~/.kube/apk8s-hc1
~ $ kubectl get pods -n kube-system -l app.kubernetes.io/name=kilo -o wide
NAME          READY   STATUS    RESTARTS   AGE   IP              NODE       NOMINATED NODE   READINESS GATES
kilo-q88l7    1/1     Running   0          32d   165.22.45.220   master     <none>           <none>
kilo-ff2lh    1/1     Running   0          32d   78.47.100.70    nbg1-n2    <none>           <none>
kilo-k2jkb    1/1     Running   0          32d   78.47.163.36    nbg1-n1    <none>           <none>
kilo-qkzh8    1/1     Running   0          32d   78.47.75.123    nbg1-n3    <none>           <none>
kilo-7zsj5    1/1     Running   1          32d   192.168.86.34   lab-d3     <none>           <none>
kilo-j7p6p    1/1     Running   1          32d   192.168.86.33   lab-d2     <none>           <none>
kilo-7h5rm    1/1     Running   1          32d   192.168.86.26   lab-gpu    <none>           <none>
kilo-ndckv    1/1     Running   3          29d   192.168.86.32   lab-d1     <none>           <none>
~ $ █
```

Figure 11-9.   Kilo agent Pod on each cluster

The new hc1 hybrid cluster, as depicted at the beginning of this section in Figure 11-3 and Figure 11-5, is ready for applications. The following section reviews a sampling of applications used to demonstrate end-to-end Machine Learning–based artificial intelligence platforms, from raw data collection to inference workloads operating entirely on Kubernetes.

Platform Applications

This chapter created a new Kubernetes cluster called hc1. The remaining examples leverage applications and cluster configurations installed in Chapters 3, 5, 6, 7, and 9 (as described in Table 11-1). This chapter organizes all configuration manifests under the folder cluster-apk8s-hc1.

Table 11-1. *Required configuration and applications from previous chapters*

	Resources	Directory Organization
Chapter 3	Ingress	000-cluster/00-ingress-nginx
	Cert Manager	000-cluster/10-cert-manager
	Storage	000-cluster/20-rook-ceph
	Monitoring	000-cluster/30-monitoring
Chapter 5	Namespace	003-data/000-namespace
	Mosquitto	003-data/050-mqtt
	Zookeeper	003-data/010-zookeeper
Chapter 6	Keycloak	003-data/005-keycloak
	JupyterHub	005-data-lab/000-namespace
	Elasticsearch	003-data/100-jupyterhub
	Kibana	003-data/030-elasticsearch
		003-data/034-kibana
Chapter 7	MinIO	000-cluster/22-minio
		003-data/070-minio
Chapter 9	NiFi	003-data/060-nifi

The following sections use applications covered in previous chapters: Mosquitto (MQTT) to communicate sensor data from Raspberry Pi devices (IoT); Apache NiFi to listen to MQTT events, transforming and loading data (ETL) into Elasticsearch; JupyterHub for working with data and developing and training AI models with Machine Learning (AIML) on a GPU node; and MinIO for storing Machine Learning models and artifacts.

The chapter uses the following ingress domains: `nifi.hc1.apk8s.dev` for Apache Nifi, `hub.hc1.apk8s.dev` for JupyterHub, `kib.hc1.apk8s.dev` for Kibana, `iam.hc1.apk8s.dev` for Keycloak, and `minio.hc1.apk8s.dev` for MinIO.

The next section begins collecting raw data from the Raspberry Pi IoT nodes on the cluster.

Data Collection

The following sections use a Kubernetes `DaemonSet` object to deploy and manage data collection workloads on Raspberry Pi (IoT) devices and a `CronJob` object to deploy ETL workloads performing data aggregation.

MQTT IoT Client

Many IoT applications follow a traditional model of platform-specific software development. Developers write code for a specific device and support one or more protocols for communication with the device, whether it be collecting sensor data or starting a pot of coffee. However, along with Kubernetes, containerization opens up novel approaches to IoT application development, deployment, networking, monitoring, and control.

The following example deploys a shell script within a Kubernetes ConfigMap. A DaemonSet deploys a slim Debian Buster container[28] (with a command-line MQTT client) on a selected set of (`sensor`) nodes and executes the shell script mounted from the ConfigMap.

---

[28]`https://hub.docker.com/_/debian/`

Create the directory cluster-apk8s-hc1/020-data/220-smon. Within the new 220-smon directory, create a file named 20-configmap.yml from Listing 11-1.

Listing 11-1. Signal monitor script ConfigMap

```
apiVersion: v1
kind: ConfigMap
metadata:
  name: smon
  namespace: data
  labels:
    app: smon
data:
  collect.sh: |-
    for (( ; ; ))
    do
      load=$(cat /proc/loadavg | cut -d\  -f 1)
      temp=$(cat /sensor/temp)
      mosquitto_pub \
        -h mqtt.data \
        -i $DEVICE \
        -t sensor/$DEVICE \
        -m "{\"device\":\"$DEVICE\",\"temp\":$temp,
            \"load\":$load}"
      echo "device: $DEVICE, temp: $temp, load: $load"
    sleep 15
    done
```

Apply the ConfigMap:

```
$ kubectl apply -f 20-configmap.yml
```

Next, create a DaemonSet for the signal monitor in a file named
40-daemonset.yml from Listing 11-2. The shell script defined in the
ConfigMap reads internal sensor data (CPU load and temperature) from
a Raspberry Pi; developers may follow a similar design for extracting
external sensor data or controlling attached devices. The DaemonSet uses
a combination of nodeSelector and tolerations, instructing Kubernetes
to schedule this container on all Raspberry Pi sensor devices.

Listing 11-2. Signal monitor DaemonSet deployment

```
apiVersion: apps/v1
kind: DaemonSet
metadata:
  name: smon
  namespace: data
  labels:
    app: smon
    component: sensor
spec:
  selector:
    matchLabels:
      name: smon
  template:
    metadata:
      labels:
        name: smon
        component: sensor
    spec:
      nodeSelector:
        kubernetes.io/role: sensor
      tolerations:
        - key: dedicated
```

```yaml
      value: pi
      effect: NoSchedule
containers:
  - name: smon
    image: apk8s/mosquitto-clients:1.5.7_1
    command: ["/bin/bash",
              "/scripts/collect.sh"]
    env:
      - name: DEVICE
        valueFrom:
          fieldRef:
            fieldPath: spec.nodeName
    securityContext:
      privileged: true
    volumeMounts:
      - name: scripts
        mountPath: /scripts
      - name: sensor
        mountPath: /sensor
    resources:
      limits:
        memory: 200Mi
      requests:
        cpu: 50m
        memory: 200Mi
volumes:
  - name: sensor
    hostPath:
      path: /sys/class/thermal/thermal_zone0/
  - name: scripts
    configMap:
      name: smon
```

Apply the DaemonSet:

```
$ kubectl apply -f 40-daemonset.yml
```

The DaemonSet uses the image apk8s/mosquitto-clients:1.5.7_1 that generated the Dockerfile in Listing 11-3.

Listing 11-3. MQTT Client Dockerfile

```
FROM debian:buster-slim

RUN apt-get update \
 && apt-get install -y mosquitto-clients curl \
 && apt-get clean
```

The three Raspberry Pi devices now report their CPU load and temperature every 15 seconds to the MQTT broker running in the cluster under the topic /sensor/DEVICE_NAME. The next section uses Apache NiFi to create a directed data processing graph, listening to all messages published in the /sensor topic, processing the data, and loading it as time series data into Elasticsearch for indexing an analysis.

ETL

The previous section implemented a DaemonSet executing a shell script responsible for scraping metrics from Raspberry Pi devices every 15 seconds. The previous shell script publishes its results as JSON into the MQTT topic /sensor/DEVICE_NAME. The following sections use Apache Nifi to extract the MQTT messages, transform them, and load them into Elasticsearch for indexing and a Python script with a Kubernetes CronJob to create CSV objects from ranges of collected data for long-term object storage.

Apache NiFi

Chapter 9 introduced Apache NiFi for use in data routing and transformation; review Chapter 9 for installation instructions and an overview of concepts. The following example uses the NiFi processors *ConsumeMQTT*, *JoltTransformJSON*, and *PutElasticsearchHttp* as depicted in Figure 11-10.

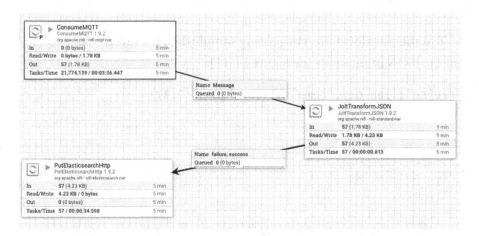

Figure 11-10. *NiFi MQTT transformation and Elasticsearch loading*

Create a *ConsumeMQTT* processor and set the properties Broker URI to `tcp://mqtt:1883`, Topic Filter to `sensor/+`, and Max Queue Size to 1000.

Use the advanced button to configure the processor with the Jolt transformation language from Listing 11-4.

Listing 11-4. Jolt transformation

```
[
  {
    "operation": "default",
    "spec": {
      "collected": "${now():toNumber()}"
    }
  },
```

```
{
    "operation": "modify-overwrite-beta",
    "spec": {
      "collected": "=toLong"
    }
  }
]
```

Test the transformation by pasting sample data retrieved from MQTT into the JSON input field (see Figure 11-11):

```
{"device":"lab-d1","temp":51540, "load":0.37}
```

Figure 11-11. *NiFi Jolt transformation specification*

Finally, add a *PutElasticsearchHttp* processor and connect the output from the *JoltTransformJSON* processor. Configure *PutElasticsearchHttp* with the properties Elasticsearch URL set to `http://elasticsearch:9200`, Index set to `sensor-${now():format('yyyy-MM')}`, and Type to _doc.

The previous steps created a small ETL pipeline with Apache Nifi, extracting from MQTT, and transforming messages by augmenting JSON data with an additional field and loading each transformed message into Elasticsearch as time-series data for indexing and analysis.

Python CronJob

Data Science and specifically Machine Learning research need static data sets for experimentation and training. Reproducible results for refining and sharing research typically require the ability to couple source code with data used in its development. While time-series data stored in Elasticsearch is unlikely to change, sharing database access with internal and external teams presents additional challenges. Creating CSV snapshots of indexed data and loading them onto distributed object storage provides a compelling option for storing and sharing persistent, long-term data across teams and projects.

This section demonstrates the use of a Kubernetes CronJob for ETL activities. The following examples extract the last hour of indexed data from Elasticsearch (see Chapter 6), serializing the data as a CSV file and loading it into MinIO (see Chapter 7) distributed object storage.

Begin by creating a Python script that extracts the last hour of sensor data from Elasticsearch, converts it to a CSV, and loads it into MinIO. Add the new Python script as a value in a Kubernetes ConfigMap. Create the directory `cluster-apk8s-hc1/020-data/500-jobs`. Within the new `500-jobs` directory, create a file named `01-configmap-hrdump.yml` from Listing 11-5.

Listing 11-5. ConfigMap with Python data dump script

```yaml
apiVersion: v1
kind: ConfigMap
metadata:
  name: hrdump
  namespace: data
  labels:
    app: hrdump
data:
  hrdump.py: |-
    import requests
    import pandas as pd
    import boto3
    import datetime
    import os

    d = datetime.datetime.now()
    idx = f"sensor-{d.year}-{d.month:02d}"

    query = {
      "size": 10000,
      "query": {
        "range" : {
          "collected" : {
              "gte" : "now-1h"
          }
        }
      }
    }
```

```python
r = requests.post(
    f'http://elasticsearch.data:9200/{idx}/_search',
    json=query
)

df = pd.DataFrame()

for rec in r.json()['hits']['hits']:
    df = df.append(rec['_source'], ignore_index=True)

csv_data = df.to_csv(index_label="idx")

s3 = boto3.client('s3',
    endpoint_url='http://minio-internal-service.data:9000',
    aws_access_key_id=os.environ['ACCESS_KEY_ID'],
    aws_secret_access_key=os.environ['ACCESS_KEY'],
    region_name='')

try:
    s3.create_bucket(Bucket='sensor-hourly')
except s3.exceptions.BucketAlreadyOwnedByYou:
    print("Bucket Exists")
except:
    print("Unknown bucket error")

filename = d.strftime("%Y/%m-%d-%H.csv")
s3.put_object(Bucket='sensor-hourly', Key=filename,
Body=csv_data)
print(f"Added object {filename} to bucket sensor-hourly")
```

Apply the ConfigMap:

```
$ kubectl apply -f 01-configmap-hrdump.yml
```

The Python script in the ConfigMap requires a container with Python preinstalled with required libraries. Before creating a custom container, start with adding the required Python packages[29] and versions into a file named requirements.txt as shown in Listing 11-6.

Listing 11-6. Python data dump script requirements.txt

```
boto3==1.13.18
botocore==1.16.18
certifi==2020.4.5.1
chardet==3.0.4
docutils==0.15.2
idna==2.9
jmespath==0.10.0
numpy==1.18.4
pandas==1.0.3
python-dateutil==2.8.1
pytz==2020.1
requests==2.23.0
s3transfer==0.3.3
six==1.15.0
urllib3==1.25.9
```

Next, create a Dockerfile (see Listing 11-7) based on python:slim-buster, copy requirements.txt into the container image, and use pip to install the needed Python libraries. Build and push the new container to a public or private container registry (or use the public image apk8s/pyreqobj:0.0.1 built for this example).

---

[29]https://pip.pypa.io/en/stable/reference/pip_freeze/

Listing 11-7. Python Dockerfile with requirements

```
FROM python:slim-buster

COPY requirements.txt .
RUN pip install -r requirements.txt
```

Finally, create Kubernetes CronJob[30] in a file named 01-cronjob-hrdump.yml from Listing 11-8. The CronJob creates a Pod with the custom Python container (developed earlier), mounts the ConfigMap into the /scripts directory, and populates ACCESS_KEY_ID and ACCESS_KEY with credentials for MinIO. The CronJob runs one minute after every hour.

Listing 11-8. Python data dump hourly CronJob

```
apiVersion: batch/v1beta1
kind: CronJob
metadata:
  name: hrdump
  namespace: data
spec:
  schedule: "1 * * * *"
  jobTemplate:
    spec:
      template:
        spec:
          restartPolicy: OnFailure
          containers:
            - name: hrdump
              image: apk8s/pyreqobj:0.0.1
```

---

[30]https://kubernetes.io/docs/concepts/workloads/controllers/cron-jobs/

```
            command: [
                "/usr/local/bin/python",
                "/scripts/hrdump.py"
            ]
            env:
              - name: ACCESS_KEY_ID
                valueFrom:
                  secretKeyRef:
                    name: minio-creds-secret
                    key: accesskey
              - name: ACCESS_KEY
                valueFrom:
                  secretKeyRef:
                    name: minio-creds-secret
                    key: secretkey
            volumeMounts:
              - name: scripts
                mountPath: /scripts
        volumes:
          - name: scripts
            configMap:
              name: hrdump
```

Apply the CronJob:

```
$ kubectl apply -f 01-cronjob-hrdump.yml
```

Leveraging CronJobs in Kubernetes for scheduled execution brings all the advantages of Kubernetes container orchestration, including resource scheduling, network, and service abstraction, self-healing, monitoring, and more. CronJobs, although simplistic in their implementation, can fill an essential role for even complex ETL operations within any Kubernetes-based data management platform.

The majority of this chapter and book focus on Kubernetes as a platform capable of interconnecting a wide range of data applications and reducing the conceptual distance between raw data collection, ETL operations, data access, and data science activities.

The remainder of this chapter focuses on Machine Learning tools for constructing, training, tracking, storing, and serving Machine Learning–based artificial intelligence models with Kubernetes.

Machine Learning Automation

Machine Learning Automation, also known as AutoML,[31] is a rapidly evolving field of software engineering, with new projects beginning to leverage Kubernetes specifically. Kubeflow[32] and Pachyderm[33] stand out as specially designed for running their containerized workloads on Kubernetes. Both projects tackle two significant areas of AutoML: the automation of model training (hyperparameter tuning, algorithm selection, and model assessment) and model serving. These projects consist of several components brought together to standardize AutoML workflows.

Kubeflow and Pachyderm support installation into existing Kubernetes clusters, such as those demonstrated in this book, with some limitations on supported versions of Kubernetes. Kubeflow and Pachyderm are both worth researching as candidates for any enterprise-grade AutoML platform.

---

[31]Hwang, Yitaek. "What Is AutoML? Promises vs. Reality." Blog. IoT For All (blog), March 29, 2018. www.iotforall.com/ what-is-automl-promises-vs-realityauto/.

[32]www.kubeflow.org/

[33]www.pachyderm.com/

This section demonstrates a subset of AutoML components through the project MLflow,[34] suitable for a more focused exhibition of model tracking and serving. The chapter ends with an example of Seldon Core[35] (also used in Kubeflow) for production model deployment.

Jupyter Notebook GPU Support

Earlier, this chapter introduced a GPU-equipped workstation as a node in the new hc1 hybrid Kubernetes cluster, installed NVIDIA operating system drivers, and enabled NVIDIA container runtime support. This section covers methods for developing Jupyter Notebook containers with access to NVIDIA's CUDA GPU drivers on the host node.

The Jupyter Docker Stacks[36] project maintains a set of prebuilt containers with Jupyter applications and various assortments of data science, machine learning, statistics libraries, and support for multiple kernels, including Python, Julia, and R.

Docker Stacks's prebuilt containers consist of the essential tools needed for everyday data science activities and suitable base containers for developing more specialized environments.

One approach to creating containers similar to the Jupyter Docker Stacks project begins with NVIDIA's CUDA 10.1 (Ubuntu 18.04) container and adding layers supporting any required libraries and applications. The gpu-jupyter[37] project on GitHub has automated this method and is great for experimenting and exploring the construction of GPU-enabled Jupyter containers. By default, gpu-jupyter starts with NVIDIA's CUDA container, clones the Jupyter Docker Stacks repository, and aggregates the layers of each Dockerfile into one new Dockerfile (just under 500 lines).

---

[34]https://MLflow.org/
[35]www.seldon.io/
[36]https://github.com/jupyter/docker-stacks
[37]https://github.com/iot-salzburg/gpu-jupyter

The generated Dockerfile is an excellent template for adding and removing functionality; however, be aware that building it as is will result in a >14 gigabyte container image.

CUDA Data Science Container

Create a new CUDA Jupyter data science container. First, clone the GitHub project gpu-jupyter:

```
$ git clone \
https://github.com/iot-salzburg/gpu-jupyter.git
$ cd gpu-jupyter
```

Next, generate a Dockerfile based on NVIDIA's CUDA 10.1 running Ubuntu 18.04 and aggregating Dockerfile configs from Jupyter Docker Stacks:

```
$ ./generate-Dockerfile.sh
$ cd .build
```

Finally, edit the generated Dockerfile or leave as is. Build with a tag, in this case apk8s/jupyter-ds:cuda-10.1, and push:

```
$ docker build -t apk8s/jupyter-ds:cuda-10.1 .
$ docker push apk8s/jupyter-ds:cuda-10.1
```

Building this enormous container may take from several minutes to hours, depending on the speed and resources allocated to the Docker daemon on the local workstation.

The following section uses this container as an option provided by JupyterHub.

JupyterHub Spawner Options

Chapter 6 introduced JupyterHub as a means to provision Jupyter containers for users. Install JupyterHub into the new hc1 cluster (set up earlier in this chapter) with an updated singleuser section for the values. yml (used to configure the Helm chart). Replace the singleuser section with the contents of Listing 11-9.

Listing 11-9. Updated singleuser configuration for JupyterHub

```
singleuser:
  image:
    name: apk8s/datalab
    tag: v0.0.5
  defaultUrl: "/lab"
  storage:
    dynamic:
      storageClass: rook-ceph-block
      capacity: 10Gi
  extraEnv:
    MLFLOW_TRACKING_URI: "http://mlflow.data:5000"
    MLFLOW_S3_ENDPOINT_URL: "http://minio-internal-service.
    data:9000"
  profileList:
    - display_name: "DataLab Environment"
      description: "Python, Julia, Octave and R."
      default: true
    - display_name: "GPU Data Science Environment."
      description: "Data science applications and libraries
with cuda-10.1 support."
      kubespawner_override:
        image: apk8s/jupyter-ds:cuda-10.1
```

```
extra_resource_guarantees:
  nvidia.com/gpu: "1"
extra_resource_limits:
  nvidia.com/gpu: "1"
```

The new `singleuser` configuration creates a `profileList`, providing the user with options for selecting a Jupyter environment.[38] The first entry is the default data science container used in Chapter 6; the second option is the new `apk8s/jupyter-ds:cuda-10.1` GPU-enabled container built in the previous section. The key `extra_resource_guarantees` informs the Kubernetes scheduler to place the container on a node with at least one GPU available. The key `extra_resource_limits` ensures that users do not get access to more than one GPU. The environment variables `MLFLOW_TRACKING_URI` and `MLFLOW_S3_ENDPOINT_URL` are used later in this chapter.

The following section uses this new GPU data science container to develop machine learning models. It introduces MLflow to track their learning progress and submit the models to a registry.

Model Development

Machine Learning model development is similar to any software development—a desire by an organization or individual to solve a problem, increase productivity, or create new value. In data science, the raw material is data and the potential value that may exist in it. This book demonstrates the ability to offer a large stack of data management applications alongside data science environments.

Machine Learning is a diverse field with a vast ecosystem of technology, terminology, and practices. This book does not cover the development of Machine Learning models, as this is a fast-moving field

---

[38]`https://zero-to-jupyterhub.readthedocs.io/en/latest/customizing/user-environment.html`

with new frameworks and techniques introduced continuously. However, a few patterns have arisen over the years that lend themselves to automation and, along with containerization, make an excellent fit for Kubernetes. The remaining sections cover the four components of Machine Learning automation: tracking models, versioning and storing models, serving models, and deploying inference workloads (APIs) that use them.

MLflow

MLflow[39] is an open source machine learning platform initially developed by Databricks[40] and donated (in 2020) to the Linux Foundation. MLflow, with over two million downloads a month,[41] has been quickly advancing in adoption by the machine learning community.

The remainder of this section installs MLflow into the new hc1 Kubernetes cluster built earlier in this chapter. The following examples use MinIO (see Chapter 7) as S3-compatible object storage used by MLflow for models and artifact storage,[42] and a Jupyter environment (see the previous section of this chapter) for developing models and interacting with MLflow.

Installation

MLflow supports local and cloud-based operation. Sharing an MLflow instance on Kubernetes requires a containerized version. Create a new MLflow container by first creating a requirements.txt file with the contents of Listing 11-10.

---

[39]https://MLflow.org/

[40]https://databricks.com/

[41]MSV, Janakiram. "Databricks Donates MLflow Project To Linux Foundation." Forbes. June 25, 2020. www.forbes.com/sites/janakirammsv/2020/06/25/databricks-donates-MLflow-project-to-linux-foundation/.

[42]https://docs.paperspace.com/machine-learning/wiki/artifacts

Listing 11-10. MLflow container requirements.txt

```
mlflow==1.8.0
awscli==1.18.65
boto3==1.13.15
```

Next, in the same directory as the requirements.txt, create a Dockerfile with contents of Listing 11-11.

Listing 11-11. MLflow Dockerfile

```
FROM python:slim-buster

COPY requirements.txt /requirements.txt
RUN pip install -r /requirements.txt
ENV PORT 5000

ENTRYPOINT ["mlflow"]
```

Next, build and push the MLflow container:

```
$ docker build -t apk8s/mlflow:1.8.0-v0 .
$ docker push apk8s/mlflow:1.8.0-v0
```

Next, configure Kubernetes with MLflow. Create the directory cluster-apk8s-hc1/020-data/800-mlflow. Within the new 800-MLflow directory, create a file named 10-service.yml from Listing 11-12.

Listing 11-12. MLflow Service

```
apiVersion: v1
kind: Service
metadata:
  name: mlflow
  namespace: data
  labels:
    app: mlflow
```

```
spec:
  selector:
    app: mlflow
  ports:
    - protocol: "TCP"
      port: 5000
      targetPort: 5000
  type: ClusterIP
```

Apply the Service:

```
$ kubectl apply -f 10-service.yml
```

Next, create a StatefulSet for MLflow in a file named 40-statefulset. yml from Listing 11-13. The StatefulSet configuration uses the new MLflow container created earlier. It sets the environment variables MLFLOW_S3_ ENDPOINT_URL to the service endpoint of the MinIO cluster running on hc1 (in the data namespace), AWS_ACCESS_KEY_ID, and AWS_SECRET_ACCESS_ KEY mounted from a Kubernetes secret containing MinIO credentials. MLflow uses these environment variables to access object storage for models and artifacts.

Listing 11-13. MLflow StatefulSet

```
apiVersion: apps/v1
kind: StatefulSet
metadata:
  name: mlflow
  namespace: data
  labels:
    app: mlflow
spec:
  serviceName: mlflow
  replicas: 1
```

```
revisionHistoryLimit: 1
selector:
  matchLabels:
    app: mlflow
template:
  metadata:
    labels:
      app: mlflow
  spec:
    containers:
      - name: mlflow
        image: apk8s/mlflow:1.8.0-v0
        imagePullPolicy: IfNotPresent
        args: [
          "server",
          "--backend-store-uri=sqlite:///MLflow/data.db",
          "--default-artifact-root=s3://MLflow/artifacts",
          "--expose-prometheus=/metrics",
          "--host=0.0.0.0",
          "--port=5000"
        ]
        env:
          - name: MLFLOW_S3_ENDPOINT_URL
            value: http://minio-internal-service.data:9000
          - name: AWS_ACCESS_KEY_ID
            valueFrom:
              secretKeyRef:
                name: minio-creds-secret
                key: accesskey
          - name: AWS_SECRET_ACCESS_KEY
            valueFrom:
```

```
            secretKeyRef:
                name: minio-creds-secret
                key: secretkey
        volumeMounts:
          - name: mlflow-data-volume
            mountPath: /mlflow
        ports:
          - name: http
            containerPort: 5000
  volumeClaimTemplates:
    - metadata:
        name: mlflow-data-volume
      spec:
        storageClassName: rook-ceph-block
        accessModes: [ ReadWriteOnce ]
        resources:
          requests:
            storage: 10Gi
```

Apply the StatefulSet:

```
$ kubectl apply -f 10-service.yml
```

Next, create an Ingress for MLflow in a file named 50-ingress.
yml from Listing 11-14. This demonstration uses Basic Auth[43] for simple
password protection of the public ingress. However, for advanced
authentication support, consider writing a plug-in.[44]

---

[43]https://imti.co/kubernetes-ingress-basic-auth/
[44]www.mlflow.org/docs/latest/plugins.html#writing-your-own-mlflow-
  plugins

Listing 11-14. MLflow Ingress

```
apiVersion: extensions/v1beta1
kind: Ingress
metadata:
  name: mlflow
  namespace: data
  annotations:
    cert-manager.io/cluster-issuer: letsencrypt-production
    kubernetes.io/ingress.class: traefik
    ingress.kubernetes.io/auth-type: "basic"
    ingress.kubernetes.io/auth-secret: "sysop-basic-auth"
spec:
  rules:
    - host: mlflow.hc1.apk8s.dev
      http:
        paths:
          - backend:
              serviceName: mlflow
              servicePort: 5000
            path: /
  tls:
    - hosts:
      - mlflow.hc1.apk8s.dev
      secretName: mlflow-production-tls
```

Apply the Ingress:

```
$ kubectl apply -f 50-ingress.yml
```

MLflow is now available on the hc1 cluster at the service endpoint
mlflow.data:5000 and the publicly accessible web-based user interface
https://mlflow.hc1.apk8s.dev. The next sections demonstrate the use
of MLflow for tracking, storing, and versioning models.

481

Tracking Models

Machine Learning model development involves detailed record-keeping throughout the process. Data scientists modify source code, hyperparameters, and training data, all to achieve higher-quality models. Tracking the parameters, code versions, output metrics, and artifacts associated with a resulting model is key to efficient and stable Machine Learning development. MLflow, installed in the previous section, exposes an API endpoint for tracking model development at `http://mlflow. data:5000`.

Open a Jupyter environment from JupyterHub running in the new `hc1` cluster (`https://hub.hc1.apk8s.dev/`).

Note   For brevity, the following examples do not use GPU; however, using the new GPU-enabled environment (configured in this chapter), more advanced readers may adapt the following examples to TensorFlow or PyTorch. Additionally, more advanced users may want to experiment with the Raspberry Pi sensor data collected and stored (earlier in this chapter) in Elasticsearch and MinIO.

The following exercise is an adaptation of an official MLflow tutorial[45,46] using the scikit-learn ElasticNet[47] linear regression model using the Wine Quality Data Set.[48]

---

[45]https://github.com/mlflow/mlflow/blob/master/examples/sklearn_
elasticnet_wine/train.ipynb

[46]www.mlflow.org/docs/latest/tutorials-and-examples/tutorial.html

[47]https://scikit-learn.org/stable/modules/generated/sklearn.linear_
model.ElasticNet.html

[48]P. Cortez, A. Cerdeira, F. Almeida, T. Matos and J. Reis. Modeling wine preferences by data mining from physicochemical properties. In Decision Support Systems, Elsevier, 47(4):547-553, 2009.

Add each of the following code blocks as individual cells in a new Python 3 Jupyter Notebook.

First, install the following packages:

```
!pip install mlflow==1.8.0
!pip install scikit-learn==0.23.1
!pip install boto3==1.10.35
```

Next, MLflow requires the following environment variables: MLFLOW_ TRACKING_URI to access the API server; MLFLOW_S3_ENDPOINT_URL to upload models and artifacts; and AWS_ACCESS_KEY_ID and AWS_SECRET_ ACCESS_KEY containing credentials to the MLFLOW_S3_ENDPOINT_URL. There are various ways to set environment variables accessible by Jupyter Notebooks through JupyterHub (see JupyterHub singleuser configuration in the previous section). These values may also be set directly in the Jupyter Notebook for testing and debugging purposes only; do not set S3 credentials within source code for production work:

```
import os

# api and object access
os.environ['MLFLOW_TRACKING_URI'] = "http://mlflow.data:5000"
os.environ['MLFLOW_S3_ENDPOINT_URL'] = "http://minio-hl-svc.
data:9000"

# minio credentials
os.environ['AWS_ACCESS_KEY_ID'] = "REDACTED"
os.environ['AWS_SECRET_ACCESS_KEY'] = "REDACTED"
```

Next, import required packages and set a seed for NumPy random to aid in reproducing results:

```
import pandas as pd
import numpy as np
```

```
from sklearn.metrics import mean_squared_error, mean_absolute_
error, r2_score
from sklearn.model_selection import train_test_split
from sklearn.linear_model import ElasticNet
from urllib.parse import urlparse
import mlflow
import mlflow.sklearn

np.random.seed(70)
```

Next, create a function for evaluating model performance:

```
def eval_metrics(actual, pred):
    rmse = np.sqrt(mean_squared_error(actual, pred))
    mae = mean_absolute_error(actual, pred)
    r2 = r2_score(actual, pred)
    return rmse, mae, r2
```

Next, download and split data into training and test sets:

```
csv_url =\
    'http://archive.ics.uci.edu/ml/machine-learning-databases/
wine-quality/winequality-red.csv'

data = pd.read_csv(csv_url, sep=';')
train, test = train_test_split(data)
```

Next, prepare test and training sets by separating the quality column:

```
train_x = train.drop(["quality"], axis=1)
test_x = test.drop(["quality"], axis=1)
train_y = train[["quality"]]
test_y = test[["quality"]]
```

Next, create a new MLflow experiment if one does not exist:

```
experiment_name = 'SkLearnWineQuality'
experiment = mlflow.get_experiment_by_name(experiment_name)

if experiment == None:
    mlflow.create_experiment(experiment_name)
    experiment = mlflow.get_experiment_by_name(experiment_name)

mlflow.set_experiment(experiment.name)
```

Next, train the model, logging metrics, and parameters to MLflow, along with trained model and source code:

```
alpha = 1
l1_ratio = 2.5

with mlflow.start_run() as run:

    mlflow.set_tags({
        "mlflow.user": "apk8s",
        "mlflow.source.type": "NOTEBOOK",
        "mlflow.source.name": "SkLearnWineQuality",
    })

    lr = ElasticNet(
        alpha=alpha,
        l1_ratio=l1_ratio,
        random_state=42
    )
    lr.fit(train_x, train_y)

    predicted_qualities = lr.predict(test_x)

    (rmse, mae, r2) = eval_metrics(
        test_y, predicted_qualities)
```

```
print("Elasticnet model (alpha=%f, l1_ratio=%f):"
      % (alpha, l1_ratio))
print("  RMSE: %s" % rmse)
print("  MAE: %s" % mae)
print("  R2: %s" % r2)

mlflow.log_param("alpha", alpha)
mlflow.log_param("l1_ratio", l1_ratio)

mlflow.log_metric("rmse", rmse)
mlflow.log_metric("r2", r2)
mlflow.log_metric("mae", mae)

mlflow.log_artifact("SkLearnWineQuality.ipynb")
mlflow.sklearn.log_model(lr, "model",
                         registered_model_
                         name="SkLearnWineModel")

mlflow.end_run()
```

Each run of the previous code results in a new entry into the SkLearnWineQuality experiment. Browse to https://mlflow.hc1.apk8s.dev/ and navigate to the experiment. From there, observe the various runs and their results (see Figure 11-12).

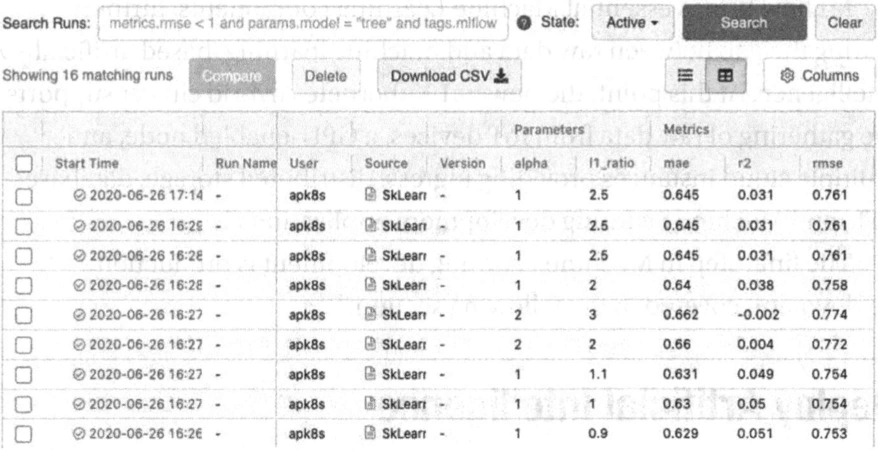
Search Runs: metrics.rmse < 1 and params.model = "tree" and tags.mlflow
State: Active
Search
Clear
Showing 16 matching runs
Compare
Delete
Download CSV
Columns

Start Time	Run Name	User	Source	Version	Parameters: alpha	Parameters: l1_ratio	Metrics: mae	Metrics: r2	Metrics: rmse
2020-06-26 17:14	-	apk8s	SkLearn	-	1	2.5	0.645	0.031	0.761
2020-06-26 16:29	-	apk8s	SkLearn	-	1	2.5	0.645	0.031	0.761
2020-06-26 16:28	-	apk8s	SkLearn	-	1	2.5	0.645	0.031	0.761
2020-06-26 16:28	-	apk8s	SkLearn	-	1	2	0.64	0.038	0.758
2020-06-26 16:27	-	apk8s	SkLearn	-	2	3	0.662	-0.002	0.774
2020-06-26 16:27	-	apk8s	SkLearn	-	2	2	0.66	0.004	0.772
2020-06-26 16:27	-	apk8s	SkLearn	-	1	1.1	0.631	0.049	0.754
2020-06-26 16:27	-	apk8s	SkLearn	-	1	1	0.63	0.05	0.754
2020-06-26 16:26	-	apk8s	SkLearn	-	1	0.9	0.629	0.051	0.753

Figure 11-12. *MLflow logged training/experiments*

Click a run entry to view details along with artifacts associated with the run, including, in this case, a model package[49] and source code (see Figure 11-13).

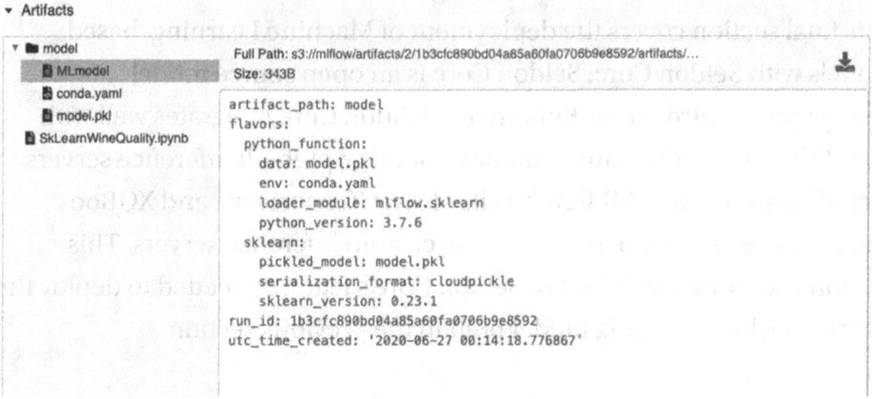
Artifacts
model
MLmodel
conda.yaml
model.pkl
SkLearnWineQuality.ipynb
Full Path: s3://mlflow/artifacts/2/1b3cfc890bd04a85a60fa0706b9e8592/artifacts/...
Size: 343B
artifact_path: model
flavors:
python_function:
data: model.pkl
env: conda.yaml
loader_module: mlflow.sklearn
python_version: 3.7.6
sklearn:
pickled_model: model.pkl
serialization_format: cloudpickle
sklearn_version: 0.23.1
run_id: 1b3cfc890bd04a85a60fa0706b9e8592
utc_time_created: '2020-06-27 00:14:18.776867'

Figure 11-13. *MLflow packaged model*

---

[49] https://mlflow.org/docs/latest/models.html

MLflow brings essential Machine Learning components, further closing the gap between raw data and machine learning–based artificial intelligence. At this point, the new hc1 Kubernetes hybrid cluster supports the gathering of raw data from IoT devices, a GPU-enabled node, and multiple cloud instances providing ingress, distributed storage, databases, ETL, and Machine Learning development applications.

The final step in Machine Learning development is production deployment, covered in the following section.

Deploy Artificial Intelligence

The method of deployment for machine learning models often depends on the problem domain, business requirements, and existing infrastructure. However, a few projects have gained significant traction in moving toward standardization, specifically the open source[50] project Seldon Core.

Seldon Core

This final section covers the deployment of Machine Learning–based models with Seldon Core. Seldon Core is an open source model deployment controller for Kubernetes. Seldon Core integrates well with established model packing standards, offering prebuilt inference servers, including supporting MLflow,[51] scikit-learn, TensorFlow, and XGBoost, and provides an interface for building custom inference servers. This section uses only a small set of Seldon Core's features needed to deploy the simple machine learning model built in the previous section.

---

[50]Housley, Alex. "Our First Year Open-Sourcing Machine Learning." Medium, April 3, 2016. https://medium.com/seldon-open-source-machine-learning/our-first-year-open-sourcing-machine-learning-59241f2f0dd0.

[51]https://docs.seldon.io/projects/seldon-core/en/v1.1.0/servers/MLflow.html

At the time of this writing, Seldon Core does not support the Kubernetes 1.18 used by the hc1 cluster developed in this chapter. However, Seldon Core is an active project, and support for the newest Kubernetes versions is not far behind. However, this minor limitation presents the opportunity to configure an additional cluster called c2, in this case, a single-node k3s cluster on Linode.[52]

Create one Linode instance with 4 CPU, 8 GB RAM, and 160 GB storage, running Ubuntu 18.04, and to keep with the global theme, use the Tokyo 2 region. Name the server tokyo2-1 and create DNS A entries for tokyo2-1.c2.apk8s.dev and *.c2.apk8s.dev pointing to its public IP.

Instruct k3s to install Kubernetes v1.17:

```
$ export INSTALL_K3S_VERSION=v1.17.7+k3s1
```

Create and save a cluster secret, needed for expanding this cluster with additional nodes:

```
$ export K3S_CLUSTER_SECRET=$(head -c48 /dev/urandom | base64)

# copy the echoed secret
$ echo $K3S_CLUSTER_SECRET
```

Install k3s:

```
$ curl -sfL https://get.k3s.io | sh -s - server
```

Download the k3s kubectl config file to a local workstation:

```
$ scp root@tokyo2-1.c2.apk8s.dev:/etc/rancher/k3s/k3s.yaml
~/.kube/apk8s-c2
```

---

[52]www.linode.com/

Edit the new config to point the c2 Kubernetes API along with naming the cluster and contexts:

```
$ sed -i .bk "s/default/apk8s-c2/" ~/.kube/apk8s-c2
$ sed -i .bk "s/127.0.0.1/tokyo2-1.c2.apk8s.dev/" ~/.kube/apk8s-c2
```

Use the new apk8s-c2 config to work with the c2 cluster in a new terminal on a location workstation:

```
$ export KUBECONFIG=~/.kube/apk8s-c2
```

Create a Namespace for Seldon Core:

```
$ kubectl create namespace seldon-system
```

Install Seldon Core Operator[53] with Helm:

```
$ helm install seldon-core seldon-core-operator \
    --repo https://storage.googleapis.com/seldon-charts \
    --set usageMetrics.enabled=true \
    --namespace seldon-system
```

Create the directory cluster-apk8s-c2/. Within the new directory, create a file named 000-sd-s3-secret.yml with the contents from Listing 11-15. Replace redacted values with MinIO credentials needed to access the model, stored with MLflow (refer to the MLflow configuration earlier in this chapter).

Listing 11-15. Secret containing s3 (MinIO) config and credentials

```
apiVersion: v1
kind: Secret
metadata:
  name: seldon-s3-model-secret
```

---

[53]https://docs.seldon.io/projects/seldon-core/en/latest/charts/seldon-core-operator.html

```
type: Opaque
stringData:
  AWS_ENDPOINT_URL: "https://minio.hc1.apk8s.dev"
  AWS_ACCESS_KEY_ID: "REDACTED"
  AWS_SECRET_ACCESS_KEY: "REDACTED"
  USE_SSL: "true"
```

Apply the Secret:

```
$ kubectl apply -f 000-sd-s3-secret.yml
```

Next, create a file named 100-sd-quality.yml with the contents from
Listing 11-16. Change the modelUri: value to the location of the MLflow
model (see Figure 11-13) configuration. The additional componentSpecs:
are optional and configured with more extended wait periods for
the readiness and liveness probes to better account for the resource-
constrained c2 cluster. Install Cert Manager as covered initially in Chapter 2,
for TLS support on the attached Ingress configuration.

Listing 11-16. SeldonDeployment with Ingress

```
apiVersion: machinelearning.seldon.io/v1alpha2
kind: SeldonDeployment
metadata:
  name: quality
spec:
  name: quality
  predictors:
    - graph:
        children: []
        implementation: MLFLOW_SERVER
        modelUri: s3://mlflow/artifacts/2/1b3cfc890bd04a85a60fa
        0706b9e8592/artifacts/model
```

```
      envSecretRefName: seldon-s3-model-secret
      name: quality
    name: default
    replicas: 1
    componentSpecs:
      - spec:
          containers:
            - name: quality
              readinessProbe:
                failureThreshold: 10
                initialDelaySeconds: 120
                periodSeconds: 10
                successThreshold: 1
                tcpSocket:
                  port: http
                timeoutSeconds: 5
              livenessProbe:
                failureThreshold: 10
                initialDelaySeconds: 120
                periodSeconds: 10
                successThreshold: 1
                tcpSocket:
                  port: http
                timeoutSeconds: 5
---
apiVersion: extensions/v1beta1
kind: Ingress
metadata:
  name: quality
  labels:
    app: quality
```

```
annotations:
    cert-manager.io/cluster-issuer: letsencrypt-production
    kubernetes.io/ingress.class: traefik
spec:
  rules:
    - host: quality.c2.apk8s.dev
      http:
        paths:
          - backend:
              serviceName: quality-default
              servicePort: 8000
            path: /
  tls:
    - hosts:
        - quality.c2.apk8s.dev
      secretName: default-quality-production-tls
```

Apply the SeldonDeployment and Ingress:

```
$ kubectl apply -f 100-sd-quality.yml
```

It may take several minutes to deploy the model. Monitor the newly generated Pod in the default namespace for status; once two of two containers report ready, the Pod can accept posted data and serve predictions.

Test the deployment with curl by posting the model's expected input, in this case a two-dimensional array (or an array of arrays), each containing the 11 values required to make a prediction. The model returns one prediction per inner array:

```
$ curl -X POST https://quality.c2.apk8s.dev/api/v1.0/
predictions \
    -H 'Content-Type: application/json' \
    -d '{ "data": { "ndarray": [[ 6.4, 0.57, 0.02, 1.8,
    0.067, 4.0, 11.0, 0.997, 3.46, 0.68, 9.5]] } }'
```

Returned prediction is 5.703684339252623:

```
{"data":{"names":[],"ndarray":[5.703684339252623]},"meta":{}}
```

This section moved quickly, lightly scratching the surface of Seldon Core's capabilities. However, it demonstrated nearly seamless interoperability between a range of diverse components, from building scikit-learn models in Jupyter Notebooks and tracking and serving the models in MLflow to their final deployment with Seldon Core, all integrated atop Kubernetes.

Summary

This chapter installed nine nodes across Raspberry Pi devices, public clouds, and on-premises, communicating across the globe on an encrypted network, utilizing resource-constrained, low-cost infrastructure. The purpose is to demonstrate the creation of a Machine Learning platform with Kubernetes and to cover the entire life cycle of the data that fuels it.

This chapter exhibited the suitability of Kubernetes in providing a wide range of capabilities and abstracting and unifying the underlying infrastructure of IoT deployments, ETL, data science, and artificial intelligence. While some components such as Apache NiFi and Elasticsearch have no direct connection with the Kubernetes API, others like Jupyter's KubeSpawner and Seldon Core use it directly.

While this chapter covered a lot of ground, it only briefly touched on each critical aspect of developing and deploying Machine Learning–based Artificial Intelligence as a platform. However, what makes a platform a platform is the framework for improvement and expansion.

Kubernetes facilitates an advanced concept of platform architecture, standardizing methods of construction through both aggregation and composition. Kubernetes provides the ability to aggregate components with no direct awareness of it, alongside components built to leverage or extend its API directly, with a near-full abstraction of the underlying infrastructure while providing scaling, fault tolerance, and self-healing. Kubernetes facilitates the exploration of innovative problem-solving platforms through the combinatorial effects that arise when connecting the latest innovations in IoT, Machine Learning, Blockchain, Big Data, and the Kubernetes API.

Index

B

H

I

P, Q

Printed in the United States
By Bookmasters